REGULATORY
ASSESSMENT
TOOLKIT

REGULATORY ASSESSMENT TOOLKIT

A Practical Methodology for Assessing Regulation on Trade and Investment in Services

Martín Molinuevo

Sebastián Sáez

THE WORLD BANK
Washington, D.C.

ISBN (paper): 978-1-4648-0057-3
ISBN (electronic): 978-1-4648-0058-0
DOI: 10.1596/978-1-4648-0057-3

Cover design: GSD, World Bank.

Library of Congress Cataloging-in-Publication Data has been requested.

CONTENTS

Boxes

Figures

Tables

FOREWORD

In recent years, services tradability has increased. Services that previously required the physical proximity between the consumer and the producer can now be delivered across borders. As technology opens new channels for international trade in services, laws and regulations become more and more relevant in supporting this economic activity and setting the conditions for its success. Domestic regulations, such as limitations on foreign participation, monopoly rights, and laws that limit the temporary movement of people, directly affect the provision of services.

Economic reforms that have privatized and deregulated industries over the last two decades have allowed for the greater participation of private providers, both national and foreign, in services such as telecommunications, finance, and transport. Other services, such as professional ones, which have traditionally been supplied by the private sector, are increasingly being exposed to international competition, expanding the variety and quality of services offered. But countries' legal and regulatory frameworks have not kept pace with these vast market (and policy) transformations. Now is an opportune time for countries to modernize their regulatory regimes and reap the economic and social benefits of increasing trade in services.

Most administrations, especially in developing and least developed countries, face a number of constraints in adopting this agenda of modernization. First, reviewing a regulatory framework is a time- and resource-consuming task that requires highly technical knowledge. Second, most developing countries have limited skills and human resources to put in place new, independent, regulatory agencies, and at the same time maintain capacity to define broad policies in ministries that are often sector based. Finally, assessing the impact of existing regulations and designing suitable alternatives requires a careful balance between technical feasibility, trade impact, and policy goals. Achieving this balance is challenging for countries at all levels of development.

The question is not whether to regulate, but how to do so in a way that maximizes policy objectives and economic benefits. Not only can a well-designed regulatory framework for services trade help prevent market failures and achieve legitimate policy goals, it can also promote access to low-cost and high-quality services to benefit the poor, increase competitiveness, and foster growth. Moreover, with rapidly changing technology—in particular, information and communication technology innovations—there is an ongoing need to reassess the existing regulatory environment to take full advantage of the new opportunities opened by services trade, to diversify the economy, and to participate in global value chains.

Services trade costs are still significant, despite technology and reforms. Regulations that affect trade—including those that aim to achieve legitimate policy objectives such as safety, health, and consumer protection—can also create unnecessary barriers to trade, reducing welfare and potential growth opportunities. By some estimates, the trade costs caused by regulatory measures can be two to three times higher in services than for trade in goods.

One objective of this toolkit is to help countries mitigate these costs. The toolkit is designed to assist policy makers, regulators, and experts in assessing their countries' regulatory environments. It proposes a three-step approach to the reform of services regulations. The first step is to map all regulations that affect a wide range of activities; this might include, for example, cataloguing the laws and regulations that affect investment, labor, and migration. The focus is not only on formal regulations but also on the administrative practices that determine how the regulations are applied. Many countries have state-of-the-art regulations on the books, but allow wide discretion in their application. This creates uncertainty, instability, and regulatory risks. In other cases, the institutional setting is weak, which undermines enforcement. In that situation, the regulations and their administration might be adequate, but the capacity to enforce those regulations may not exist.

Because this is a *de facto* barrier to trade, the methodology includes an assessment of countries' regulatory institutional settings.

The toolkit's second step helps policy makers understand how significant their country's services regulations are and the impacts of those regulations on the economy and business environment. While acknowledging the constraints of often-inadequate data, the toolkit reviews the empirical literature on the impact of services regulations. This analysis helps users provide information on prices and costs, levels of competition, and market structure. It also enables them to benchmark their countries' service performance. Quantifying the benefits and costs of maintaining or implementing services regulations is crucial to well-informed decision making and reform.

The ultimate goal of the regulatory assessment is to encourage countries to adopt better regulations. The third and final step of the toolkit helps countries identify alternatives to the existing regulations. Using the information gathered and the analysis performed, the toolkit steers users—without being prescriptive—toward viable regulatory alternatives that reduce unnecessary restrictions to services trade. It does so by considering the policy goals of the existing measures, the impact they have on the domestic services sector and foreign services suppliers, and the institutional and market context in which the measures operate. Because the regulatory alternatives are largely context-specific, the toolkit discusses options adopted by other countries, including the adoption of internationally recognized best regulatory practices. Policy makers, regulators, and experts should be mindful of a country's capacities when assessing which regulatory options are viable.

Assessing the services trade regulatory environment can be burdensome. The toolkit acknowledges the information- and time-intensive nature of applying the proposed methodology. In order to partially overcome this hurdle, the methodology can be used in a modular way. The user can focus on specific, priority issues by mapping related regulations, assessing their impact, or assessing possible regulatory alternatives.

The careful balance between policy goal and economic impact, and the strong focus on a data- and information-driven approach make this toolkit a valuable contribution to the modern regulation of services trade. Its guidance can help policy makers design regulatory frameworks that support competitiveness and shared growth and help their economies harvest the gains from international trade in services.

Jeffrey D. Lewis
Director
Economic Policy, Debt, and Trade
Poverty Reduction and Economic Management Network
The World Bank

ACKNOWLEDGMENTS

The Regulatory Assessment Toolkit is the result of the work undertaken at the World Bank's International Trade Unit, Poverty Reduction and Economic Management Network of the World Bank (PRMTR). The toolkit was prepared by Sebastián Sáez (Task Team Leader) and Martín Molinuevo, with contributions from Carolina Lennon (module 2) and Ben Shepherd (module 3).

Appendix A on professional services is based on the work carried out by Nora Dihel. The team is particularly indebted to Nora Dihel whose constant support and intellectual generosity was invaluable. Appendix B on information technology–enabled services is based on input provided by Michael Engman and Randeep Sudan, and appendix C on trade in financial services benefited from input from Pierre Sauvé.

The team would like to thank other colleagues who contributed their input and expertise in the development of this toolkit, including Ian Gillson, Charles Kunaka, Mariem Malouche, José Guilherme Reis, Daniel Reyes, and Daria Taglioni. Carolina Lennon and Ben Shepherd provided extensive and useful comments that improved the toolkit. The team is also indebted to Verena Fritz for her guidance and references on the political economy of reforms.

The authors would like to thank the peer reviewers for their valuable input, including Nora Dihel (Africa PREM, WB), Massimo Geloso-Grosso (OECD), and Martin Roy (WTO). The team also benefited from discussions with Hoe Lim and Aaditya Mattoo, and from inputs from Gonzalo Varela. The team acknowledges the support of Julian Clarke, Frederico Gil Sander, and Ekaterine Vashakmadze in the partial implementation of pilot assessments.

Additionally, thanks to the many others who provided comments and input during the concept and final review meetings and throughout the development process, including to the participants at the internal workshop at the International Trade Unit.

We are grateful to Shienny S. Lie and Marinella Yadao for their assistance on administrative issues, and to Amir Fouad who supported the publication process. We also thank Susan Graham, Stephen McGroarty, and Andres Meneses of the World Bank's Publishing and Knowledge Division in the External and Corporate Relations Vice Presidency for the valuable advice and guidance during the publication. Finally, the toolkit benefited from the professional editorial work of Barbara Karni.

This toolkit was prepared under the direction of Mona Haddad (Sector Manager), Bernard Hoekman (former Director), and Jeff Lewis (Director) of the International Trade Unit.

ABOUT THE AUTHORS

Martín Molinuevo is an expert in international economic law with a specialty in trade and investment. He is currently a consultant at the International Trade Unit of the World Bank, where he assists governments of developing countries on trade policy and trade-related regulatory matters and investment. His areas of expertise include World Trade Organization (WTO) Law, international trade and investment agreements, and services trade policies. He has worked for several international organizations, including the WTO, the United Nations Economic and Social Commission for Asia and the Pacific (UNESCAP), the Inter-American Development Bank, and the World Trade Institute. He holds a PhD in international economic law with honors from the University of Bern, a master's degree from the University of Bologna, and a law degree from the University of Buenos Aires. He is the author of the book *Protecting Investment in Services: Investor-State Arbitration versus WTO Dispute Settlement* (2012), and has published numerous articles and reports on trade policy.

Sebastian Saez is a Senior Trade Economist in the International Trade Unit of the Poverty Reduction and Economic Management Network at the World Bank. He has extensive experience in trade policies. He served as advisor to Chile's Minister of Finance (1990–94) and was involved in the Uruguay Round negotiations of the General Agreement on Tariffs and Trade (GATT). Subsequently, he was Deputy Permanent Representative of Chile to the World Trade Organization, coordinator of the Free Trade Agreement of the Americas negotiations, and participated in talks with the European Union, the Republic of Korea, and the United States. Prior to joining the World Bank he worked at the International Trade and Integration Division of the United Nations Economic Commission for Latin America and the Caribbean (UNECLAC). He has published numerous articles and books on international economic relations and trade policies.

ABBREVIATIONS

APEC	Asia-Pacific Economic Cooperation
BPO	business processing outsourcing
CGE	computable general equilibrium
CIF	cost insurance freight
FDI	foreign direct investment
FOB	freight on board
GATS	General Agreement on Trade in Services
GTAP	Global Trade Analysis Project
IAASB	International Auditing and Assurance Standards Board
ICAO	International Civil Aviation Organization
ICT	information and communications technology
IFRS	International Financial Reporting Standards
IT	information technology
ITES	information technology–enabled services
ITU	International Telecommunications Union
OECD	Organisation for Economic Co-operation and Development
PCA	principal component analysis
PEZA	Philippine Economic Zone Authority
PMR	product market regulation
RASTI	Regulatory Assessment of Services Trade and Investment
RIA	regulatory impact assessment
ROSC	Reports on the Observance of Standards and Codes
SOX	Sarbanes-Oxley Act
STRI	Services Trade Restrictiveness Index
UNCTAD	United Nations Conference on Trade and Development
VoIP	Voice over Internet Protocol
WTO	World Trade Organization

Terms explained in the glossary at the back of the book are bolded the first time they are used in the text.

OVERVIEW

What Is Trade in Services and How Is It Regulated?

There is no commonly agreed-on definition of "trade in services"; government officials and experts tend to rely on the ordinary meaning of the term. International trade in services is likely to encompass any international transaction beyond merchandise trade and, arguably, intellectual property rights.

The services sector includes a diverse array of sectors, such as telecommunications, banking, and business processing outsourcing (box O.1). It is a crucial part of any trade strategy, both as a source of export diversification and as a key component of a country's competitiveness.

Over the last two decades, trade in services expanded rapidly to reach more than a fifth of global trade flows. The participation of developing countries in world services exports increased from 11 percent in 1990 to 20 percent in 2011 (World Development Indicators). Technological changes are bringing about new services and new ways to trade them, making services a relevant option for export diversification.

The trade costs of services are two to three times as high (in ad valorem terms) as the trade costs of goods (Miroudot, Sauvage, and Shepherd 2010). The trade costs of goods fell about 15 percent over the last decade, whereas the trade costs of services remained relatively stable. Governments can reduce these costs by adopting less-restrictive regulations, strengthening governance, and establishing the right incentives to adopt new technologies that would facilitate trade in services (see Francois and Hoekman 2010; Goswami and others 2012).

Trade in services takes place through four modes of supply:

- Mode 1, cross-border trade, which is analogous to goods trade and involves producing services in one country to be consumed in another. Examples include activities such as distance education, call centers, and telemedicine.

- Mode 2, consumption abroad, which occurs when consumers (for example, tourists, students, or patients) travel across borders to consume services
- Mode 3, commercial presence, in which the producer of a service establishes a local presence (for example, a subsidiary) in the country where the consumer is located
- Mode 4, temporary movement of labor, in which the producer (for example, a mining engineer) travels across borders to provide a service

Unlike trade in goods, which is traditionally governed by border measures that regulate the entry of foreign merchandise, international trade in services is governed entirely by domestic regulation.[1] Services are typically subject to a variety of regulations that govern access and operations in the sector, for both domestic and foreign firms.

Many services sectors, especially sectors with significant network characteristics (such as telecommunications and transport services), are characterized by imperfect and asymmetric information, lack of competition, and natural barriers to entry. Regulations are necessary to provide safeguards in sectors where market failures or externalities are prevalent and to ensure that noneconomic policy objectives are met. It is often difficult to differentiate between legitimate policy objectives and protectionist measures that introduce market distortions and inefficiency. The key question is how to identify the best regulatory approach for services while reaching legitimate policy objectives.

Regulations often fail to respect the basic principles of transparency and nondiscrimination—by imposing restrictions on foreign ownership, market access, and the operation of services providers, for example. Regulatory measures can be discriminatory or nondiscriminatory; they can affect entry and market access or the operation of the business. They can be considered trade restrictions when other regulatory alternatives exist that are equally effective in achieving the desired policy objective but less restrictive of trade in services.

Box 0.1. What Are Services?

The Services Sectoral Classification List of the World Trade Organization (WTO)—known as W120—lists 154 services, divided into 12 categories. WTO rules apply to all services, including services that are not listed. The major sectors on the list include the following:

1. Business services
   a. Professional services
   b. Computer and related services
   c. Research and development services
   d. Real estate services
   e. Rental/leasing services without operators

2. Communication services
   a. Postal services
   b. Courier services
   c. Telecommunication services
   d. Audiovisual services

3. Construction and related engineering services
   a. General construction work for buildings
   b. General construction work for civil engineering
   c. Installation and assembly work
   d. Building completion and finishing work

4. Distribution services
   a. Commission agents' services
   b. Wholesale trade services
   c. Retailing services
   d. Franchising

5. Educational services
   a. Primary education services
   b. Secondary education services
   c. Higher education services
   d. Adult education

6. Environmental services
   a. Sewage services
   b. Refuse disposal services
   c. Sanitation and similar services

7. Financial services
   a. All insurance and insurance-related services
   b. Banking and other financial services (excluding insurance)

8. Health-related and social services
   a. Hospital services
   b. Other human health services
   c. Social services

9. Tourism and travel-related services
   a. Hotels and restaurants (including catering)
   b. Travel agencies and tour operators services
   c. Tourist guides services

10. Recreational, cultural, and sporting services
    a. Entertainment services (including theater, live bands, and circus services)
    b. News agency services
    c. Libraries, archives, museums, and other cultural services
    d. Sporting and other recreational services

11. Transport services
    a. Maritime transport services
    b. Internal waterways transport
    c. Air transport services
    d. Space transport
    e. Rail transport services
    f. Road transport services
    g. Pipeline transport
    h. Services auxiliary to all modes of transport

12. Other services not included elsewhere

The W120 list is based on the United Nations' Central Product Classification (CPC). The CPC offers greater disaggregation for a total of more than 5,000 services, classified at the six-digit level, as well as a brief summary of what is covered in each service.

Source: WTO 1991.

Regulatory quality depends not only on the regulation-making process but also on regulatory institutions. In developing countries, especially least developed countries, these institutions are typically weak. Reform proposals may be unrealistic if they do not include an assessment of whether a country should also reform, strengthen, or create the regulatory institutions responsible for issuing and enforcing laws and regulations. It is necessary to address both regulations and the framework in which they are designed, adopted, and applied.

Why Is Trade in Services Important for Developing Countries?

Services have a direct impact on developing countries' competitiveness. Low-cost, high-quality, reliable services are key to developing countries' connectivity to the global economy because they are inputs in the production of many goods and services (Cattaneo and others 2010). Reducing trade costs for services trade increases productivity because openness in services helps attract foreign investment and strengthens competition between foreign and domestic providers. One would expect this competitive dynamic to deliver better and more reliable provision of existing services, new varieties of services, and competitive pricing in the services sector (Duggan, Rahardja, and Varela 2013).

Openness in services matters crucially for labor productivity and total factor productivity (TFP) growth because input services facilitate transactions through space (information and communications technologies and logistics services) or time (financial services) (Hoekman and

Mattoo 2009; Francois and Hoekman 2010). The quality of logistics services can influence firms' decisions on where to locate, which suppliers to buy from, and which consumer markets to enter. Efficient logistics systems are therefore a critical determinant of a country's connectivity to the world and an important tool for development (Kunaka, Mustra, and Sáez 2013).

Given the deep linkages the services sector has with the rest of the economy, efficiency in services is closely linked to efficiency in other sectors. For a panel of countries in the Organisation for Economic Co-operation and Development (OECD), Francois and Woerz (2008) find that increased import penetration of services has a positive effect on the skill and technology mix of exports, although countries with greater openness in producer services sectors witnessed greater improvement in export performance for skill- and technology-intensive industries. Their results suggest that protecting intermediate services sectors places manufacturing sectors (especially high-wage sectors) at a competitive disadvantage. In sum, there is strong evidence that the openness of the services sector is potentially beneficial in the evolution of efficiency in the most technology-intensive manufacturing industries.

Other evidence at the firm level reinforces the significant positive correlation between the performance of services sectors and manufacturing productivity. Arnold, Mattoo, and Narciso (2008) find a significant positive relationship between firm productivity and the performance of the services sector. Their finding confirms that inadequate access to essential producer services hurts African firms by undermining their productivity.

A vital element of India's rapid economic growth since the early 1990s has been the improved performance of its manufacturing sector. According to Arnold and others (2012), policy reforms in the services sectors played a major role in the transformation of the manufacturing sector in India, allowing greater foreign and domestic competition with greatly improved regulation.

Van der Marel (2012) finds that the main determinants of comparative advantage in services are skills, institutions, and regulatory and governance frameworks. Services trade is associated with increased levels of trust on the part of importers. Behind-the-border measures (that is, internal laws and regulations not necessarily related to foreign trade) have a higher impact on services than on goods.

Amin and Mattoo (2006) find that countries with better institutions have larger and more dynamic services sectors. They suggest that regulatory and contract-enforcing institutions play a key role in the development of services

sectors because of the complex web of transactions with the rest of the economy. Lejour and Verheijden (2004) find that regulatory barriers to services trade in a country and its trading partners, as measured by the OECD's Product Market Regulation (PMR) Indicators, negatively affect trade within the European Union. Kox and Lejour (2005) find that heterogeneity in regulatory opacity significantly reduces bilateral service exports.

What Is a Regulatory Assessment of Services Trade and Investment (RASTI)?

A Regulatory Assessment of Services Trade and Investment (RASTI) can help policy makers assess regulations consistently, streamline the regulatory framework in services to improve efficiency, and set up a process for introducing new regulations. It complements a similar toolkit developed for regulations governing nontariff measures, which has been successfully implemented in development policy loans granted by the World Bank and in policy dialogue across regions (Cadot, Malouche, and Sáez 2012).

Regulatory assessments in services are information intensive and require exhaustive field work. Trade in services is affected by domestic regulations, which may have differentiated impacts depending on the sector, the regulation's relevance for a mode of supply, and the importance of the modes of supply for the sector. In the retail sector, for example, commercial presence is the main mode of supply; specific measures, such as zoning regulations or restrictions on land ownership, may be important determinants for access and operations. A RASTI of the sector would thus have to consider measures that affect commercial presence as well as measures affecting cross-border trade that may affect that mode of supply.

This toolkit is structured as follows:

- A Policy framework provides the basic concepts and defines the analytical approach to conducting a RASTI.
- Module 1 reviews the goals and challenges of regulation and the main regulatory instruments that apply to services markets.
- Module 2 discusses the quantitative literature on the impact of services regulation. Evaluating the economic impact of services regulation is a key step toward developing economically sound services policies and assessing how economic and noneconomic policy objectives support (or fail to support) the development of an efficient services market.
- Module 3 presents regulatory alternatives to regulatory approaches, instruments, or institutions to achieve

policy objectives and regulate effectively the service markets. The outcome of implementing alternatives is to remove unwarranted restrictions to services trade and investment in order to create a regulatory framework that facilitates the development and expansion of services trade while ensuring the fulfillment of social and development goals.

- The appendixes provide analysis and methodological guidance on conducting a RASTI of selected services sectors (professionals and professional services, information technology–enabled services, and financial services).

Objectives of the Regulatory Assessment

This toolkit can help policy makers evaluate whether the regulatory framework is promoting the development of an efficient domestic services market and whether services regulation is addressing market failures and achieving public interest goals in an appropriate manner. The performance of the RASTI can be tailored to serve different purposes, depending on the circumstances and the needs of the authorities.

Filling Information Gaps

A first objective of a RASTI is to fill information gaps on the regulatory framework for services trade. Many countries, especially countries in the process of economic reform, have only recently embarked on the regulation of the services sector. In some cases, economic opening has predated regulatory reform, posing serious sequencing problems and adding to the challenge of regulating the domestic and international services market. A horizontal RASTI provides comprehensive information on the features of the regulatory framework for all services industries, highlighting institutional weaknesses and regulatory deficiencies that impair services trade and the development of an enabling services sector.

Supporting Regulatory Reform

Identifying laws and regulations that restrict services trade and investment is a key first step in the process of regulatory reform (Sáez 2010). Where the required data are available, a quantitative analysis presents additional information on how regulatory restrictions affect the services sectors. This information can identify the measures and sectors that are most restrictive. Policy makers can then consider regulatory alternatives that can promote a better regulatory framework for services trade. A RASTI can be conducted as part of a broader policy to attract foreign investment, as the streamlining of the services regulatory framework can identify and eliminate unnecessary hurdles.

Supporting Trade Negotiations

Countries engaged in international trade negotiations can use a RASTI to identify potential inconsistencies with international disciplines that may affect the negotiation process or compliance with the agreed commitments. A RASTI can also help identify regulations that serve legitimate policy objectives and should not be affected by international trade agreements.

A detailed mapping of the regulatory framework gives trade negotiators an accurate picture of the sectors and measures that require attention. It can, for instance, inform trade negotiators of sensitive sectors and measures that may conflict with a proposed agreement and provide a comprehensive view of the services markets necessary to define the negotiating strategy. Once the agreement enters into force, a RASTI can help regulators implement the agreement by identifying inconsistent laws and regulations or sectors that may need to be reregulated in accordance with new international obligations.

Assessing Regulatory Performance

Analysis of the governance framework assesses regulatory institutions' ability to develop a regulatory framework that stimulates the services sector while achieving policy goals. It also identifies administrative practices that impair the services sector, such as excessively burdensome registration requirements, nontransparent allocation mechanisms, and weak regulation monitoring and enforcement procedures.

Promoting Better Regulatory Practices

The goal of a RASTI is to promote better regulatory practices and governance. Achieving this goal can help developing countries expand their services sector, which would both increase economic competitiveness and export diversification and promote services exports. Using a RASTI for a horizontal or sectoral analysis—including a quantitative analysis and assessment of alternative regulations—can contribute to the incorporation of concepts and means of more complex regulatory impact analysis (RIA) procedures. A full RIA may be adopted later, once sufficient capacity has been developed.

Levels of Analysis

Analysis of the entire regulatory framework on services trade would be a colossal endeavor. A RASTI is therefore best performed in modules at different levels of regulation. A horizontal assessment sheds light on the general policies that affect trade in services, as well as on the main laws and regulations affecting some key services sector. A sectoral analysis focuses on a specific sector, such as professional services, tourism, or financial services. A RASTI can also conducted on a specific service, such as accounting, road transport services, or insurance.

All RASTIs need to consider both regulation and the governance framework. Laws and regulation are the main barriers to services trade; they affect both the ability to supply a service and the way in which services are provided. But the ways in which laws and regulations are developed, administered, and implemented can be as big an obstacle to services trade as the rules themselves. A RASTI therefore takes into account the main institutional aspects and regulatory procedures of services regulatory bodies (governance).

The assessment must also analyze the effect of the regulatory framework on all modes of services supply. Figure O.1 summarizes the levels of analysis and provides examples of regulations at the horizontal level.

Figure O.1. Horizontal, Sectoral, and Service-Level Analysis of a Regulatory Assessment of Services Trade and Investment (RASTI)

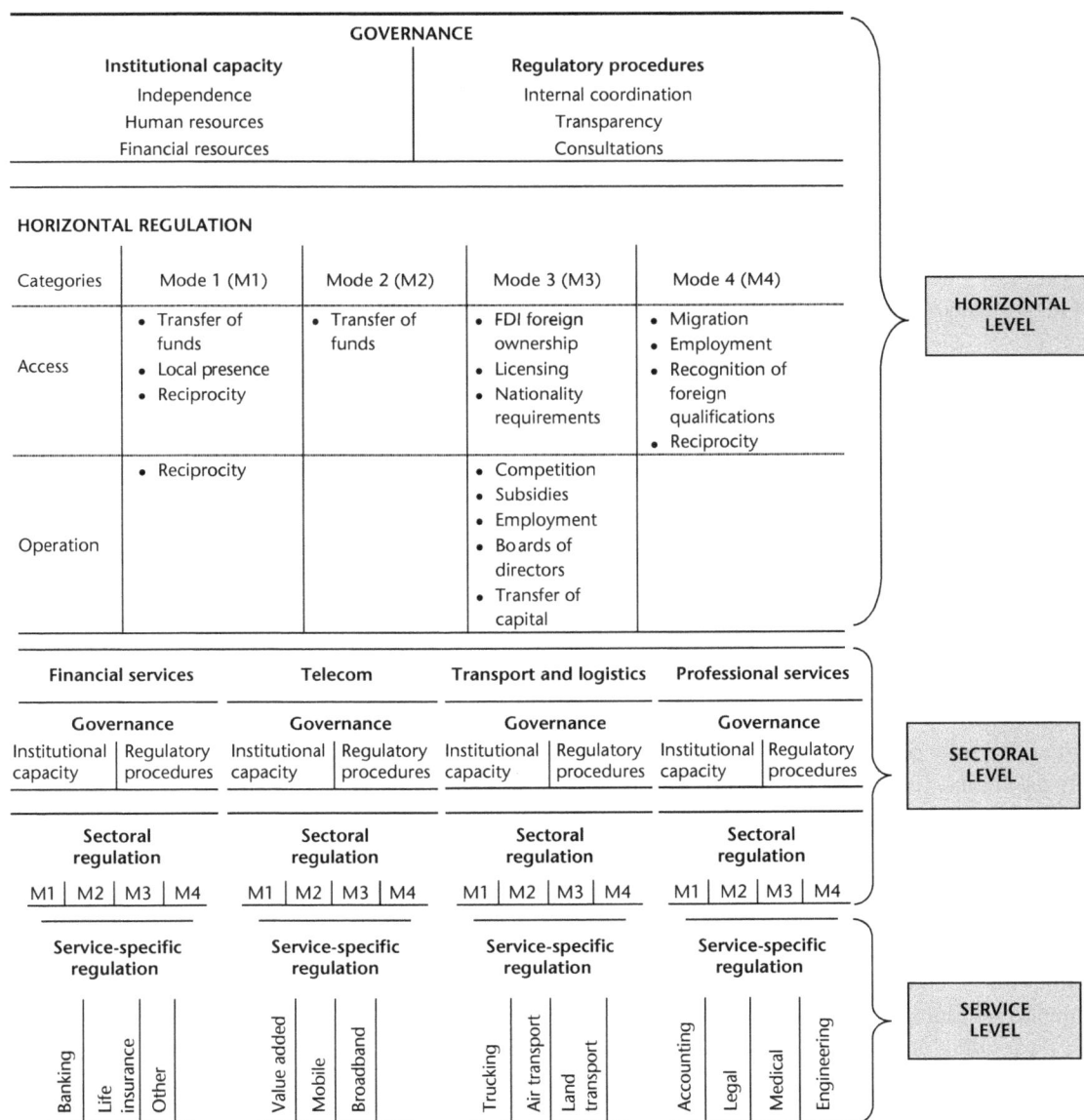

Note: FDI = foreign direct investment; M1 = cross-border trade; M2 = consumption abroad; M3 = commercial presence; and M4 = presence of natural persons to provide services.

Coverage of the Assessment

The ultimate purpose of the regulatory assessment will determine its coverage. For instance, a RASTI performed as background for trade negotiations will typically be broad, covering laws, regulations, and institutions that govern a wide range of services. This horizontal assessment could be complemented by sectoral or service-level assessments in the most sensitive areas. A similar approach could be used when designing a national strategy for trade and investment in services. In contrast, if the goal is to improve conditions in a specific sector, a sectoral or service-level analysis would be appropriate.

Regardless of the level of analysis, the main aspects of the assessment are identical. They include identifying a comprehensive set of laws and regulations that restrict services trade and investment and examining the institutions that regulate them.

A RASTI also covers the institutional setting and institutional arrangements for reform, because the way governments administer and implement the laws and regulations may affect trade. Processing licensing applications in an untimely fashion or enforcing measures selectively can hurt trade in services, for example, as can the lack of institutional capacity and resources to enforce regulations.

Coordination of the Assessment

Services span a large number of sectors, some of them connected. Services play many roles—supporting other economic activities, with logistics and transportation, and spurring development policies, through education, health, and social protection, for example. Unlike in manufacturing, agriculture, or mining, no single entity is responsible for services oversight. Given the wide range of services, how can countries conduct a regulatory assessment aimed at reforming the sector?

If reform affects only one sector, the ministry or other public entity responsible for policies and regulations should lead the process, including consultations with stakeholders. If the reform process affects a wide range of service activities, coordination across public entities, including ministries and regulatory agencies, and stakeholders is required. Determining which public entity is best suited to coordinate reform depends on the country context: different countries will find different solutions. Certain key conditions must be met, however, including the following:

1. The entity coordinating policy must be politically strong. The political economy of services reforms is complex, involving politically sensitive issues that affect powerful interests and a wide range of stakeholders. Therefore, the entity responsible for coordination must be relatively high up the political echelon. It must be capable of conducting an assessment and monitoring progress of the works performed by various parties and instructing other entities on how to improve implementation.

2. A strong political entity must be supported by a strong secretariat. Both must have good technical capabilities and adequate resources, including sufficient staff to execute the secretariat's mandate. Where the government's capacity is weak, it may make sense to allow an international organization, donor, or other expert to perform the assessment, under the guidance and oversight of the coordination entity. This secretariat would be responsible for, among other things, overseeing the regulatory assessment.

3. Coordination should include relevant stakeholders who may be interested in the results of the regulatory assessments and recommendations or affected by proposed reform.

Modules

The toolkit proposes that the RASTI be conducted in three steps, or modules (figure O.2):

- Module 1: Map horizontal and sectoral regulations, and assess the regulatory process and institutional arrangements.
- Module 2: Where possible, provide a quantitative assessment of the impact of regulations on performance and market structure, including prices, quality, and access.
- Module 3: Recommend alternative regulations and institutional arrangements.

Module 1: Mapping Regulations and Assessing the Regulatory Process

Measures affecting the services sectors can be enshrined in general laws and regulations or specific ministerial measures governing a specific services sector. Three levels of regulation can be distinguished:

- The horizontal level includes measures affecting all services industries, such as restrictions on the transfer of funds, limitations on the movement of people, caps on foreign equity participation, and legislation granting preferential treatment to some minorities.
- The sectoral level encompasses broader regulation governing certain services. Laws on tourism

Figure O.2. Three Steps of a Regulatory Assessment of Services Trade and Investment (RASTI)

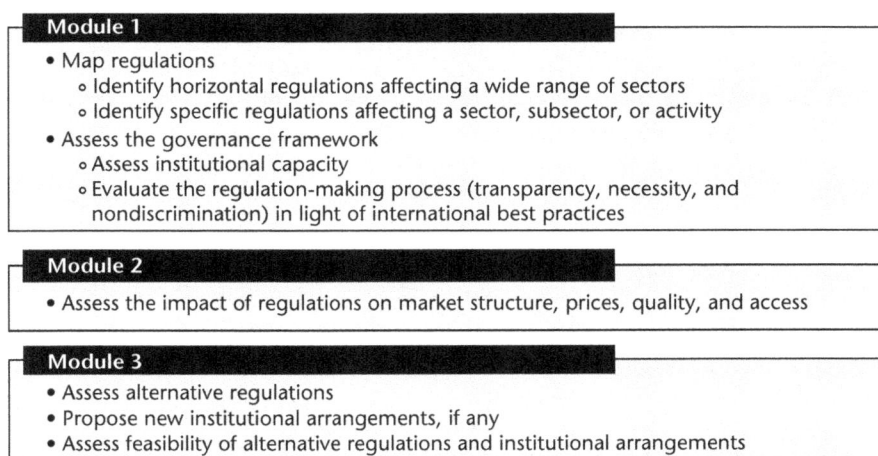

Module 1
- Map regulations
  - Identify horizontal regulations affecting a wide range of sectors
  - Identify specific regulations affecting a sector, subsector, or activity
- Assess the governance framework
  - Assess institutional capacity
  - Evaluate the regulation-making process (transparency, necessity, and nondiscrimination) in light of international best practices

Module 2
- Assess the impact of regulations on market structure, prices, quality, and access

Module 3
- Assess alternative regulations
- Propose new institutional arrangements, if any
- Assess feasibility of alternative regulations and institutional arrangements

or telecommunications or a general framework on professional services correspond to this level.
- The service level covers measures that regulate specific activities. This level of regulation is common in professional services, where each service is normally governed by a specific body, such as a national bar for legal services or an accounting association. Service-specific regulation can also stem from general laws. Laws on cultural heritage protection, for instance, restrict trade in audiovisual services or entertainment services by setting limits on foreign films or productions.

The mapping identifies measures that affect trade in services at each regulatory level. It evaluates their practical effects on services by examining the following:

- Restrictions on access to and operation in a market
- Quantitative and qualitative measures, which may or may not be discriminatory in intention or effect
- Laws and regulations as well as restrictions imposed by informal administrative practices

In addition, aspects of governance and regulation are considered at each level of analysis. These considerations are particularly relevant at the horizontal level, where the institutional and legal linkages are broader and more complex and affect more industries.

Module 2: Assessing the Impact of Regulations
The quantitative analysis is the most challenging step of a RASTI. It provides prices and costs, levels of competition, and market structure while outlining benchmarks of performance. It estimates the expected benefits of

liberalization or reform and gives an indication of potential winners and losers from reforms, as well as possible mitigation or transitional arrangements.

Policy makers need to be aware of two limitations of a RASTI. First, some aspects of the regulatory process cannot be measured, because basic data are often lacking. Second, resource limitations mean that policy makers must decide which dimensions to assess—the quality of the regulatory process, the standard of performance represented by the implementation and enforcement of the regulations, or the performance of regulation. Some of these aspects, such as regulatory quality or enforcement capacity, are hard to quantify. Policy makers should consider the impact of regulations on both their direct objectives and broader policy objectives (Baldwin 2012).

Quantitative tools help policy makers prioritize. By quantifying the impact of regulations, a RASTI can help guide regulatory reform. It can identify groups of interests that may oppose or favor particular policy directions, allowing public opinion and alliances to be formed to overcome political resistance to reform. Quantification may also contribute to a reform's design. By identifying the worst inefficiencies, a RASTI can help policy makers focus reforms on areas that may have the biggest impact.

Collecting data on regulatory information is a challenge. Moreover, that information must be complemented by data on actual trade and investment in services, ideally disaggregated at least at the sectoral level. In many developing countries, such data may not be available. Where data are not available, quantitative analysis cannot be conducted. The lack of sufficient data does not render a regulatory assessment impracticable, however. If necessary, the assessment can omit this module.

Module 2 reviews and explains tools that can help policy makers quantify the effect of regulations. Quantifying the benefits and the costs of maintaining or implementing regulations is a valuable part of a well-informed decision-making process and reform. Module 2 classifies quantitative tools according to three taxonomies: whether they employ direct or indirect methods for measuring the impact of regulation, whether they focus on sectoral or economy-wide outcomes, and whether they use a retrospective or prospective approach.

The link between services regulation and services outcome is more straightforward in studies employing direct methods. The viability and reliability of studies using direct methods depend on the quality and availability of the data (that is, whether countries periodically collect and update data on policy measures in the services sector).

Retrospective analyses quantify the impact of service restrictions using econometric estimations and information about past episodes of liberalization and deregulation. Prospective analyses try to project the impact of further liberalization of services trade, usually based on estimations of tariff equivalents.

Module 2 focuses on retrospective methods, which are carried out through econometric analyses, and sectoral studies. The analysis is complemented by detailed descriptions of the data requirements for applying these quantitative techniques; the source of the data; and, if the data are not available, suggested methods for collecting them, such as using firms' surveys and standard questionnaires.

Module 3: Identifying Alternative Regulations and Institutional Arrangements

Module 3 is based on the findings of the regulatory mapping (module 1) and, where available, the quantitative impact assessment of services trade (module 2). It describes options available to policy makers wishing to reform services regulations, identifying the pros and cons, the requirements, and the means of implementing each alternative (table O.1). A RASTI helps policy makers identify which strategies are suitable for a particular country and services sector depending on the desired policy goals.

Linkages with Other Initiatives

Trade Restrictiveness Indexes

In 2012, the World Bank made public a comprehensive database on restrictions to trade and investment in services. Building on methodologies originally proposed by

Hoekman (1995) and the Australian Productivity Commission, the Services Trade Restrictions Database contains information on discriminatory policies that affect international trade in services in 103 countries. The data, collected in 2007 and 2008, cover 79 developing countries and 24 countries from the OECD, broadly representing all regions and income groups. Through surveys, the database collected information on 19 services in the financial services (banking and insurance), telecommunications, retail, transportation, and professional services (legal and accounting) sectors.

The broad scope of the data allows the creation of a Services Trade Restrictiveness Index (STRI) for each service and mode of supply. The STRI enables users to easily compare levels of restrictiveness across countries, regions, and sectors. This ambitious global exercise provides a first approximation to policies in services. It provides extensive data, facilitates comparative analysis of services policies, and makes information on policies publicly available (Borchert, Gootiiz, and Mattoo 2012).[2]

A RASTI provides in-depth understanding of current services regulation, the regulatory environment, and existing regulatory capacity in a specific country or services sector. It proposes (a) collecting information through intensive field work on laws and regulations on services and the governance framework and (b) helping countries identify alternative means to regulate services trade. This detailed analysis of regulations and their application generates a more precise picture of countries' regulatory conditions. A RASTI helps identify alternative measures for reform, including from a political economy point of view. It thus builds on the STRI's foundations by revealing how domestic regulations are implemented. It provides country-specific regulatory advice based on qualitative and, where possible, quantitative analysis. It can also complement the STRI by potentially including additional sectors, subsectors, and activities and by covering a broader set of measures (discriminatory and non-discriminatory) and countries in a manner comparable with the STRI database. It can help update and enhance the information provided by the global database for the analyzed country.

Regulatory Impact Analyses

A regulatory impact analysis (RIA) is a systematic appraisal of how legislation affects certain categories of stakeholders, economic sectors, or the natural environment. It is used to scrutinize proposed laws and regulations and examine the effects of current regulatory measures (Radaelli and de Francesco 2010).

Table O.1. Advantages and Disadvantages of Selected Regulatory Strategies

Regulatory strategy	Main characteristic	Main advantages	Main disadvantages
Direct action by the state	State is responsible for providing services for consumers or facilities for businesses	Ensures a particular level of investment in goods or services with a strong public good component	Government failure can be as big a problem as market failure
Command and control	Regulation usually involves imposition of binding standards and their enforcement by legal sanctions	Bans particular types of conduct, ensuring relatively certain and immediate effect	Regulated businesses can capture process; introduces rigidity into the system; may create barrier to entry; difficult and costly to enforce
Incentive-based regimes	Uses taxes or subsidies to encourage services providers to act in accordance with the public interest	Reduces the danger of regulatory capture; encourages firms to limit harmful conduct as much as possible	Requires information to set tax or subsidy at correct level
Competition law	Can ensure level of competition in individual markets that results in supply at socially optimal levels	Can be applied across the board to multiple sectors, thus creating economies of scale in regulation; does not unduly intrude into firms' private decision-making processes	Flexibility may create uncertainty
Franchising (concessions)	Replaces competition within the market with competition for the market	Effective regulatory tool for activities that display strong natural monopoly characteristics; includes payment of a license fee or negotiation of a minimum subsidy, which can have fiscal benefits for the government	Requires high level of governance capacity
Disclosure regulation	Requires firms to make public information regarding the quantity, quality, and price of their outputs, as well as in some cases the processes followed during production	Relatively light-handed government strategy; once information is publicly available, consumers can make informed choices that conform to their individual levels of risk perception and tolerance	Costs of disclosing and processing information may be significant; must be combined with additional measures
Self-regulation	Group of firms or individuals determines its own membership and behavior	Less intrusive than other state-based mechanisms	Provides incentive to use standards of conduct or licensing requirements as barriers to entry

A RASTI is a one-time analysis of the regulations affecting services trade. It has a narrower scope than an RIA, as it is limited to the regulation of trade in services. It seeks to identify the set of policies and measures that affect trade in services regardless of the policy area from which they emanate. It goes further than an RIA in that it also evaluates the governance framework related to services trade regulation.

Services Competitiveness Analysis

Policy makers increasingly recognize the unexploited potential of services trade. More governments want to improve their understanding of the size, scope, and potential of services exports and of the obstacles that need to be removed to unlock the competitiveness of the domestic services sector. Analysis of the determinants of competitiveness in trade in services is more complex than it is for goods, because it involves analysis of international movement of factors, including foreign direct investment and temporary labor mobility. Barriers to trade in services involve domestic policy and regulations that affect foreign firms, and trade in services can take various forms other than cross-border trade. A regulatory assessment is a natural complement to a service competitiveness analysis.

Notes

1. This study defines *domestic regulation* broadly to include both discriminatory and nondiscriminatory regulations. Under the General Agreement on Trade in Services (GATS), domestic regulations refer only to nondiscriminatory regulations. Other regulations that affect trade in services are considered either market access restrictions or discriminatory (national treatment) regulations (Mattoo, Stern, and Zanini 2007). Following Black (2001), as quoted by Baldwin, Cave, and Lodge (2010), *regulations* means "the intentional use of authority to affect behavior of a different party according to set standards, involving instruments of information-gathering and behaviour modification."

2. The OECD is developing a similar restrictiveness index covering more services sectors for its members and some observer countries.

References

Amin, Mohammad, and Aaditya Mattoo. 2006. "Do Institutions Matter More for Services?" Policy Research Working Paper 4032, World Bank, Washington, DC.

Arnold, Jens M., Beata S. Javorcik, Molly Lipscomb, and Aaditya Mattoo. 2012. "Services Reform and Manufacturing Performance: Evidence from India." Policy Research Working Paper 5948, World Bank, Washington, DC.

Arnold, Jens, Aaditya Mattoo, and Gaia Narciso. 2008. "Services Inputs and Firm Productivity in Sub-Saharan Africa: Evidence from Firm-Level Data." *Journal of African Economies* 17 (4): 578–99.

Australian Productivity Commission. Database. Measures of Restrictions on Trade in Services. http://www.pc.gov.au/research/memorandum/servicesrestriction.

Baldwin, Robert, Martin Cave, and Martin Lodge, eds. 2010. *The Oxford Handbook of Regulation*. Oxford: Oxford University Press.

———. 2012. *Understanding Regulation: Theory, Strategy and Practice.* Oxford: Oxford University Press.

Black, Julia. 2001. "Decentring Regulation: Understanding the Role of Regulation and Self-Regulation in a 'Post-Regulatory' World." *Current Legal Problems* 54: 103–47.

Borchert, Ingo, Batshur Gootiiz, and Aaditya Mattoo. 2012. "Policy Barriers to International Trade in Services: Evidence from a New Database." Policy Research Working Paper 6109, World Bank, Washington, DC.

Cadot, Olivier, Mariem Malouche, and Sebastián Sáez. 2012. *Streamlining Non-Tariff Measures: A Toolkit for Policy Makers.* Washington, DC: World Bank.

Cattaneo, Olivier, Michael Engman, Sebastián Sáez, and Robert M. Stern. 2010. "Assessing the Potential of Services Trade in Developing Countries: An Overview." In *International Trade in Services: New Trends and Opportunities for Developing Countries*, ed. Olivier Cattaneo, Michael Engman, Sebastián Sáez, and Robert M. Stern, 1–28. Washington, DC: World Bank.

Duggan, Victor, Sjamsu Rahardja, and Gonzalo Varela. 2013. "Service Sector Reform and Manufacturing Productivity: Evidence from Indonesia." Policy Research Working Paper 6349, World Bank, Washington, DC.

Findlay, Christopher, and Tony Warren, eds. 2000. *Impediments to Trade in Services: Measurement and Policy Implications.* London: Routledge.

Francois, Joseph, and Bernard Hoekman. 2010. "Services Trade and Policy." *Journal of Economic Literature* 48 (3): 642–92.

Francois, Joseph, Miriam Manchin, and Patrick Tomberger. 2013. "Services Linkages and the Value Added Content of Trade." Policy Research Working Paper 6432, World Bank, Washington, DC.

Francois, Joseph, and Julia Woerz. 2008. "Producer Services, Manufacturing Linkages, and Trade." *Journal of Industry, Competition and Trade* 8: 199–229.

Goswami, Arti Grover, Poonam Gupta, Aaditya Mattoo, and Sebastián Sáez. 2012. "Service Exports: Are the Drivers Different for Developing Countries?" In *Exporting Services: A Developing Country Perspective*, ed. Arti Grover Goswami, Aaditya Mattoo, and Sebastián Sáez, 1–24. Washington, DC: World Bank.

Hoekman, Bernard. 1995. "Tentative First Steps: An Assessment of the Uruguay Round Agreement on Services." Policy Research Working Paper 1455, World Bank, Washington, DC.

Hoekman, Bernard, and Aaditya Mattoo. 2008. "Services Trade and Growth." In *Opening Markets for Trade in Services,* edited by Juan Marchetii and Martin Roy, 21–58, Cambridge, UK: Cambridge University Press.

Kox, Henk, and Arjan Lejour. 2005. "Regulatory Heterogeneity as Obstacle for International Services Trade." CPB Discussion Paper 49, CPB Netherlands Bureau for Economic Policy Analysis, The Hague, the Netherlands.

Kunaka, Charles, Monica Alina Antoci, and Sebastián Sáez. 2013. "Trade Dimensions of Logistics Services: A Proposal for Trade Agreements." *Journal of World Trade* 47(4): 925–50.

Lejour, Arjan, and Jan-Willem de Paiva Verheijden. 2004. "Services Trade within Canada and the European Union: What Do They Have in Common?" CPB Discussion Paper 42, CPB Netherlands Bureau for Economic Policy Analysis, The Hague, the Netherlands.

Marconini, Mario, and Pierre Sauvé. 2010. "Negotiating Trade in Services: A Practical Guide for Developing Countries." In *Trade in Services Negotiations: A Guide for Developing Countries,* ed. Sebastián Sáez, 19–86. Washington, DC: World Bank.

Mattoo, Aaditya, Robert M. Stern, and Gianni Zanini, eds. 2007. *A Handbook of International Trade in Services.* Oxford: Oxford University Press.

Miroudot, Sébastien, Jehan Sauvage, and Ben Shepherd. 2010. "Measuring the Cost of International Trade in Services." MPRA Paper 27655, University Library of Munich, Munich.

Radaelli, Claudio M., and Fabrizio de Francesco. 2010. "Regulatory Impact Assessment." In *The Oxford Handbook of Regulation*, ed. Robert Baldwin, Martin Cave, and Martin Lodge, 279–300. Oxford: Oxford University Press.

Sáez, Sebastián, ed. 2010. *Trade in Services Negotiations: A Guide for Developing Countries.* Washington, DC: World Bank.

van der Marel, Erik. 2012. "Trade in Services and TFP: The Role of Regulation." *World Economy* 35 (11): 1530–58.

WTO (World Trade Organization). 1991. "Services Sectoral Classification List." WTO Document MTN.GNS/W/120, Note by the Secretariat, Geneva.

POLICY FRAMEWORK FOR REGULATING TRADE AND INVESTMENT IN SERVICES

Objectives

The policy framework reviews the main rationales for regulating services. It identifies the objectives of regulation, provides examples of measures adopted to achieve particular regulatory objectives, and discusses the main challenges developing countries face in regulating trade and investment in services. Upon completing this section, readers will be able to:

- *Identify the economic rationales for regulation and how they apply to trade and investment in services*
- *Identify the noneconomic goals of regulating trade and investment in services*
- *Evaluate the regulatory goals pursued by various regulatory measures and determine whether regulatory failure may prevent the goals from being met*
- *Assess the governance framework for services based on principles of good regulatory practices*

An assessment of laws and regulations must take into account the policy goals that inspire them and their impact on trade in services. Understanding the objectives of services regulation is therefore a central component of any regulatory assessment. The regulatory objectives of policy areas outside the services sector must also be kept in mind, because these laws and regulations often affect trade in services. Migration law, for example, regulates the movement of individual services providers.

The underlying economic and social rationale for regulation of services sectors rests on three pillars (Mattoo and Sauvé 2003):

- Preventing monopolies in network-based services (for example, telecommunications, transportation, and energy)
- Addressing externalities and **asymmetric information** in knowledge- and intermediation-based services (for example, financial and professional services)

- Striving for universal access in essential services (for example, health and education)

Regulatory objectives come in all shapes and sizes; they can be related to social issues, economic development, improvements in health, and protection of the environment. By and large, however, the objectives of economic regulation fall into two broad categories: addressing market failures and serving the public interest. These two categories provide a valuable framework for assessing a regulation's effectiveness.

Regulators may choose among several instruments to encourage individuals to behave in ways that yield socially desirable outcomes. Regulation can ban or mandate a behavior outright (for example, prohibiting an establishment from operating in certain areas), or it can set desirable goals and let the concerned actors determine how best to achieve them (for example, requiring shops in residential areas to limit noise). The state may also provide a service (such as public health or public security) in ways private individuals would not. The various regulatory options afford more or less freedom to agents to operate in the market. This level of freedom determines the economic impact of regulation.

The choice of regulatory instrument is also important because different instruments require different levels of capacity and resources to develop, implement, and monitor. The economic, regulatory, and institutional context will condition which instrument is most appropriate for achieving the desired regulatory goals. It is useful to put on the table alternative regulatory strategies and instruments specific to a country's needs. Table PF.1 outlines some key regulatory issues in selected services sectors.

In a perfect world, in which all consumers knew every detail about the services they wished to purchase and suppliers competed with one another, regulatory intervention

Table PF.1. Key Regulatory Issues and Modes of Supply in Selected Services Sectors

Type of service	Key regulatory issues	Modes of supply
Business	• Human capital and skills; telecommunications infrastructure • Institutions that affect contract enforcement • Labor mobility and foreign direct investment regulations; outward policies • Trading partners' policies	• Cross-border, commercial presence, and presence of natural persons
Financial	• Prudential regulations and regulations affecting board members and management • Electronic infrastructure and regulations on personal data protection and transfer • Innovation of new products, access to payment system • Effect on social security through links to health insurance and pension assets management • Regulations that limit scope of services (for example firewalls between banking, securities, and insurance)	• Cross-border, consumption abroad, commercial presence, and temporary movement of labor
Professional	• Nationality and residency requirements that limit access to market • Labor laws and regulations affecting professionals • Differential treatment of applications from foreign and domestic suppliers, including criteria relating to education, experience, examinations, and ethics; competence of applicants; and the need for in-country experience examinations	• Presence of natural persons was traditional mode of delivery, but cross-border professional services are increasingly becoming a substitute or complement to this mode
Telecommunications	• Electronic (virtual) delivery of services, especially on a cross-border basis • Terms, conditions, quality, and reliability of physical infrastructure, absence of which limits electronic delivery of services • Barriers to new entrants by incumbents and other limitations to competition	• Cross-border and commercial presence
Transportation	• Intensive use of physical infrastructure • Customs and border management • Regulations dealing with international cargo and passengers, sabotage, and nondiscriminatory access to and use of basic infrastructure • Regulations on drivers, pilots, and crew	• Cross-border and commercial presence
Travel	• Physical infrastructure and natural endowments • Customs and border management (for example, entry requirements) • Other services, such as transportation and health and security standards	• Consumption abroad and commercial presence

would not be necessary. Consumers could choose the best possible service at the price they were willing to pay, and welfare gains would be optimal. Unfortunately, such **Pareto-efficient** conditions are not in place in many services markets. Regulation is therefore necessary to bring about optimal results.

Economic Rationales for Regulation

Many services markets are prone to **market failures**, primarily as a result of **monopolies, externalities**, and information and coordination deficits. Left unattended, market failures lead to a loss of social welfare, driving the market to produce too much of some services (high-risk financial assets) and too little of others (telecommunications services in isolated areas,

environmental services). Market failures also limit consumer options and raise prices. Regulatory oversight helps prevent market failure.

Preventing Monopolies or Reducing Their Impact

Economic theory assumes that consumers have options in the quality and price of the goods they buy. No or too little competition allows monopolists to extract "**rent**" from higher prices, restrict supplies, and prevent the market from delivering the best outcomes. As a result, consumers lose, and economic welfare is reduced. Competition is hence central to a market economy.

A **monopoly** can restrict supply and keep prices unduly high. **Oligopolies** (markets dominated by a few sellers) can produce similar effects, through **price-fixing** or **collusion**.

Both setups have negative dynamic effects on the economy, reducing the incentive to innovate and thus lowering long-term growth prospects.

To address problems caused by monopolies and oligopolies, regulators focus on competition policy. This regulatory tool aims at correcting the negative impact of anticompetitive practices, including price-fixing, **cross-subsidization** of goods or services, **predatory pricing**, and collusion. Competition rules are particularly relevant in services sectors such as transport and distribution, in which economies of scale are large, favoring the development of large suppliers that may engage in anticompetitive practices. In some industries, such as network industries with high fixed costs, market structures with limited competition emerge. Industries such as public utilities (water and electricity) and telecommunications entail such immense sunk investments that costs are lowest when only one firm is responsible for setting up the network (Baldwin, Cave, and Lodge 2012; Ogus 1994). This situation is referred to as a **"natural" monopoly**. Natural monopolies also exist in sectors—including railroad transport, telecommunications, energy distribution, and water and sanitation—that require network infrastructure. Table PF.2 provides examples of regulatory measures used to promote competition in services.

Regulation of natural monopolies is necessary for two main reasons (Krajewski 2003). The first is that natural monopolies charge monopolistic prices, reducing social welfare. Because competition is not possible in these markets, the regulatory goal is to control the consequences of monopolization. Regulating prices often creates tension, however, because the monopolist needs high prices to recoup its initial network investment. Moreover, governments have imperfect information on incumbents' cost structures, making it difficult for them to set prices.

Although the goal of regulation is to ensure competitive prices, in practice, prices in natural monopolies are higher than in more competitive environments.

A second reason for regulating natural monopolies is that the government may wish to promote a sector in which some state-owned enterprises and private companies have natural monopoly characteristics (Krajewski 2003). In this case, regulation attempts to establish a legal monopoly while preventing monopolist abuses. This situation exists in public services, including telecommunications, energy distribution, and transport (Sidorenko and Findlay 2003).

Regulation of monopolies commonly includes obligations on **universal access**. Universal access seeks to ensure that services are offered throughout society, not just in profitable areas. These obligations are particularly important to essential services that are often provided by natural or legal monopolies, such as water distribution, sewerage, other environmental services, and telecommunications.

Internalizing Externalities

Another form of market failure is third-party effects, or externalities. Production of some goods and services imposes costs on parties other than the producer that are not reflected in the price paid by users. Because purchasers pay less than the social cost of the product, they consume more of the good or service than is socially optimal (Ogus 1994). Table PF.3 provides examples of regulatory interventions relating to externalities in services sectors.

Pollution is a traditional example. Left unregulated, producers would not internalize the costs they impose on third parties. Regulatory intervention introduces mechanisms that mandate or encourage the producer to internalize those costs—by, for instance, requiring firms to use filters or adopt less-polluting technologies or forcing

Table PF.2. Policy Goals and Approaches to Ensuring Competition in Services by Regulating Monopolies

Type of monopoly	Policy instrument	Policy goal	Regulatory measures		Main services sectors affected
			Market access	Operations	
Market power	Competition law	Maintaining and restoring a competitive market	Prior approval of mergers and acquisitions	Standards: prohibition of collusion, cross-subsidization, price-fixing, predatory pricing, and other anticompetitive practices	• Air transport • Retail distribution • Road transport • Telecommunications
Natural	Regulation	Preventing abuse of monopolistic position	Mitigating entry barriers (compulsory licensing)	Standards: price controls, mandatory cross-subsidization (universal access requirements)	• Rail transport • Sanitation • Telecommunications

Table PF.3. Examples of Regulatory Interventions for Dealing with Market Failures

Type of market failure	Type of regulatory intervention		Sectors affected and measures
	Market access	**Operation**	
Externalities	Direct provision of services by the state		National and internal security services Firefighting Central banking Education
	Entry control: licensing (public concessions)		Construction of infrastructure
	Entry control: geographical restrictions		Distribution services (retail stores, gas stations)
		Behavior control: standards (target)	Air transport: noise limitations Road transport: limits on emissions
		Behavior control: standards (specification)	
		Economic incentives: subsidies	Research and development: tax benefits and direct incentives
Information deficits	Entry control: prior approval (licensing)		Financial services: assessment of technical and financial capacity during licensing procedures
	Entry control: prior approval (certification)		Professional services: certification (title) requirements
		Information requirements: disclosure	Sporting and recreational services: risk information
Coordination problems		Behavior control: standards (specifications)	Telecommunications services: technological standards
		Self-regulation	Road transport services: cargo standards

polluters to compensate communities for the costs they impose on them ("polluter pays" policies).

Externalities in the services sector abound. They include environmental damage by maritime transport, traffic congestion and possible effects on housing markets by large retail outlets, interference by telecommunications equipment, and market instability by expansion of certain financial services. Regulatory intervention attempts to prevent or remedy these problems based on market conditions and the risks posed by each sector.

Promoting Public Goods

Not all externalities result in negative effects on third parties: externalities can also be positive. **Public goods** exist when one party's consumption of a good does not affect the consumption of other parties and the supplier of the good cannot exclude nonpaying parties from consuming it. The price of a public good does not reflect the benefits enjoyed by nonpaying consumers (Krajewski 2003).

Although few services are pure public goods, many have strong public good characteristics. Education, for instance, promotes knowledge that is beneficial not only to the person being educated but also to society at large.

Pure or partial public goods require regulation because of two problems. One is that the difference between private and social costs and benefits can result in underproduction. The second is the **free-rider problem**: the difficulty of excluding others from enjoying a good once it is produced means that people who do not pay for the good (free riders) can still consume it, removing the incentive to produce it. Regulation helps ensure that public goods are produced in socially optimal quantities.

Encouraging Technology Transfer

Foreign investment can generate positive spillovers (externalities) in production technology for other firms in the sector, particularly by upgrading technology and developing workforce capacities.[1] Developing countries often support technology transfer by multinationals to increase these positive externalities.

Technology transfer also influences services policies. For example, requiring that a foreign investor enter a joint venture or similar arrangement with a local firm might help ensure that the foreign investment results in spillovers for local firms. The next section discusses whether restrictions on the legal form are the most efficient way of achieving this goal.

Dealing with Information Asymmetries

Economic theory assumes that actors have perfect information when buying and selling. This is not the case for many markets, leading to inefficient outcomes and choices. In an unregulated market, information is often underprovided (in much the same way as a public good) (Stiglitz 2010; Ogus 1994). Regulation can help ensure that consumers have access to "optimal" levels of information about the price and quality of all goods and services. (For examples of regulatory interventions relating to information asymmetries in services sectors, see table PF.3.)

Disclosure requirements may demand that suppliers reveal information about their product, including production processes, use of certain inputs, and potential risks. Disclosure requirements abound in the regulation of food and chemical products. They exist in services sectors, too, especially to address potential liability issues (examples include regulation of the securities market and adventure tourism). Box PF.1 describes regulatory solutions to information problems in four markets.

In many services sectors, mandatory disclosure is not sufficient because the information is too technical for consumers to understand and assess. Consumers cannot fully assess a bank's financial position, for example, and they may not be able to evaluate or compare the quality of service in other sectors. What information should, say, architects be required to disclose to vouch for their competency and quality?

Regulation can address some of these consumer protection issues through licensing. In most countries, only providers who meet certain standards of education and training are authorized to practice law or medicine. Most countries require commercial drivers to pass licensing procedures.

Information asymmetries provide a strong economic rationale for requiring licenses in some services. Policy makers need to determine what the appropriate licensing requirements are (in order to prevent them from becoming unnecessarily restrictive). Licensing requirements may include holding a degree or certification from certain schools or institutions, demonstrating certain technical capacity, having experience, or passing an examination. For example, aspiring lawyers in New York State must first demonstrate that they have completed a period of study at a U.S. or foreign law school and then pass an exam to demonstrate competency. In selecting the requirements for licensing, policy makers should seek to reduce information asymmetries in a way that is economically efficient.

Box PF.1. Regulatory Solutions to Information Problems in Selected Markets

In many sectors, it is difficult for consumers to know how much they are actually paying for a service. Governments sometimes regulate practices in order to make prices more transparent.

Loans
Most loan contracts contain pages of fine print, and many of the items in the contract may not be readily understood by individuals or small businesses. Individual borrowers typically focus on the loan rate, paying little or no attention to commissions, service fees, and penalties for late payments.

Government intervention to make the true costs of a loan clearer can help consumers find better loans. One policy response would be to demand price transparency for key terms by requiring lenders to provide a one-page "loan contract fact sheet" to all borrowers that contains information on the loan rate (expressed in a standardized form, such as the annual percentage rate); commissions; fees and surcharges; penalties for default; penalties for late payment; and any other costs.

Foreign Exchange
Tourists changing money often look only at the exchange rate. But service fees and commissions can significantly add to the cost of the transaction. Consumers often see these charges only after they exchange their money, when they receive a printout of the effective cost. Requiring foreign exchange dealers to indicate the true cost beforehand would allow consumers to get the best effective rate.

Automobile Insurance
Cost is only one factor in assessing the value of an insurance policy. There is also an important quality dimension to automobile insurance: consumers need to know how likely and quickly the company is to pay claims. This dimension is opaque unless the insured has access to additional information: consumers who buy based only on price could be in for a shock when they find that the company drags its heels when processing claims. Requiring insurance companies to reveal their average rejection rates for claims and average length of time to resolve claims could help consumers to make better decisions.

Funerals
Lack of transparent price information practices in the funeral industry motivated the U.S. Federal Trade Commission to require all funeral homes in the United States to provide itemized estimates of the costs of a funeral before it is held.

Source: Based on OECD 2011.

Addressing Coordination Problems

High transaction costs may justify regulating certain markets. Private law provides mechanisms to reduce transaction costs, mainly through contracts, corporate law, and tort law (Ogus 1994), but in some situations, regulatory intervention may be less expensive than private coordination. The classic example is regulation of road traffic: the market would not provide an efficient solution for determining which side of the road people drive on. A much more efficient solution is for the regulator to require drivers to drive on a particular side of the road, thereby eliminating the coordination problem. In the services sector, a regulatory response to coordination problems concerns the setting of technical standards, such as the selection of appropriate technology for digital television broadcasting. (Table PF.3 provides examples of regulatory interventions relating to coordination problems.)

Noneconomic Rationales for Regulation

Correction of market failures motivates most market regulation, but governments also regulate to achieve noneconomic goals. Ogus (1994) identifies three main noneconomic grounds for regulation: **distributional justice**, community values, and individual well-being (or "paternalism").[2] Table PF.4 below provides an overview

of noneconomic regulatory objectives and examples of related measures in the services sector while box PF.2 discusses how these objectives are addressed in international agreements.

Achieving Distributional Justice

A true market economy can lead to efficient outcomes, but it does not necessarily produce socially just outcomes. Governments can use regulatory tools to promote not only the well-being of the market but also the market dynamics that produce equitable outcomes.

Distributional justice policies encompass several elements. The basic approach involves redistributing wealth and income usually through fiscal policies, direct payments or social benefits, compulsory social security systems, or national health and pension schemes. These policies go well beyond regulation to the direct supply of certain services, such as education, health care, and pensions.

In services regulation, governments strive toward distributional justice by ensuring consumer rights and setting minimum conditions for services that, left unregulated, would not be accessible to consumers with little bargaining power. Distributional considerations often impose **universal service** requirements on monopolistic suppliers, for example. Distributional justice considerations may also

Table PF.4. Noneconomic Regulatory Objectives and Common Interventions

| Goal | Types of regulatory intervention | | Sectors affected and measures |
	Market access	Operation	
Achieve distributional justice	Direct provision of services by the state		Financial services (national pension scheme)
			Public services: health (publicly funded hospitals)
		Behavioral control: standards (performance: universal services requirement) and price control	Public services (telecom, water distribution, energy distribution)
		Behavioral control: standards (specifications): limitations on private contracting	All services sectors
			Consumer protection measures
		Behavioral control: price control	Leasing of real estate
Reflect community values	Entry control: prohibitions, licensing		Entertainment services (bars, nightclubs, casinos)
		Economic incentives: subsidies	Cultural services (libraries, theaters)
		Behavioral control: standards (specification): national treatment requirements	Screen and stage quotas
Support individual well-being		Information requirements	Distribution services: disclosure of risks in tobacco and alcohol products
		Economic incentives: specific taxes	Distribution services: additional taxes for tobacco and alcohol products
		Information requirements and behavioral control: standards (specification)	Entertainment services: rating of films and video games

---

Box PF.2. Regulation for "Public Interest" under International Trade Agreements

International agreements on trade and investment in services strive to promote reciprocal liberalization of services. These agreements, which include obligations on market access and national treatment in a broad swath of sectors, call for the removal of restrictions to trade in services. However, measures that pursue legitimate policy objectives, including the correction of market failures and noneconomic goals, trump liberalization obligations—under certain conditions.

Such agreements do not force countries to forfeit their ability to regulate services sectors or introduce measures to pursue public policy goals, even if such measures restrict trade and investment in services. The General Agreement on Trade in Services (GATS) provides a standard example of a "general exceptions" provision, which has been replicated in multiple bilateral, plurilateral, and regional agreements. GATS Articles XIV and XIV bis provide that members of the World Trade Organization (WTO) remain free to maintain or introduce such measures necessary to protect public morals or maintain public order; protect human, animal, or plant life or health; or protect their essential security interest. The appendix on trade in financial services entitles members to take measures for prudential reasons, including for the protection of investors, depositors, policyholders, or persons to whom a fiduciary duty is owed by a financial services supplier or to ensure the integrity and stability of the financial system, regardless of other GATS provisions.

These provisions embody the legitimate public interest considerations that justify restrictions to international trade in services even in sectors subject to liberalization obligations. They go beyond the "traditional" exceptions adopted in the General Agreement on Tariffs and Trade (GATT). The language of these exceptions is purposely broad. As a result, WTO dispute settlement bodies have been able to confer a high degree of deference to national authorities in determining what policy objectives can be covered. The United States, for instance, argued successfully that restrictions on online (and cross-border) gambling, maintained to prevent minors from gambling, are covered by such provisions. In the context of trade in goods, governments have argued in favor of certain restrictions to benefit health goals (for example, restrictions on beef with hormones or products with asbestos) or environmental objectives (such as limitations on gasoline additives or imported tuna and shrimp caught in ways that harm other species).

It is not sufficient for governments to invoke the public interest of a measure to exclude it from international trade obligations—if it were, international agreements would be little more than fancy declarations of intent. Instead, if any WTO member challenges a measure as a restriction to services trade, a country has to show that such measures are "necessary" to achieve public interest goals, that they are not arbitrary or discriminatory, and that they are not disguised restrictions on trade in services. In addition, trade restrictions must be proportionate to the interests pursued. Decision makers must consider and evaluate possibly less restrictive alternatives when introducing measures and adopt, to the extent possible, the measure least disruptive to trade and investment in services. (For more detail, see Cottier, Delimatsis, and Diebold 2008.)

---

result in differential pricing for public services, particularly essential services such as gas and electricity distribution.

Often, distributive measures do not transfer resources to a disadvantaged group directly. Instead, they deal with coordination or collective action problems faced by large groups (Sunstein 1990). In these cases, regulation may set out certain conditions for contracts between parties with unequal bargaining power. Labor laws, for instance, may define minimum wages and benefits and maximum employment hours or rental contracts (Baldwin, Cave, and Lodge 2010).

Reflecting Community Values

The market and prices reflect consumers' personal preferences for products and services. But people's community preferences may differ from their personal preferences (Krajewski 2003). People who are not frequent visitors of, say, public libraries, museums, or national parks may still consider them worth maintaining; people who do not attend or even listen to the opera might be upset to learn that La Scala or the Unter den Linden Staatsoper were to close. From a market perspective, individual unwillingness to pay would suggest that there is no demand for such supply, thus driving it to extinction.

Policy makers may choose to reflect community values and regulate in a manner that preserves certain goods and services that embody them. These values are usually promoted through subsidies, but regulatory measures can also be used. Some of these measures—such as quotas for audiovisual and broadcasting services and local employment requirements—affect international trade in services.

Supporting Individual Well-Being

Public policies can at times restrict some individual liberties in the benefit of that very same person. Typical regulatory measures to support individual well-being include the obligation to wear a seat belt or helmet. The support of individual well-being may also lead to regulations on trade in services. Many countries ban minors from purchasing certain goods and services (such as alcohol and tobacco, movies, or gambling) and limit the sale of other goods (requiring prescriptions for some medications, for example). These regulations translate into specific restrictions on retail services. In a similar manner, regulations may limit some financial companies to trade to licensed agents only, since individual consumers may not be familiar with the system or understand the risks involved in some complex financial products.

Challenges to and Principles of Regulation

Government intervention is necessary to prevent market failure and to support the public good. It can help create an efficient services market, increase distributional justice, and promote social values (Stiglitz 2010).

But government intervention can also have the opposite effects. Laws and regulations can curtail competition, increasing the welfare of selected providers at the expense of consumers. Regulation can introduce unnecessary and burdensome procedures on business, raising costs, discouraging innovation, and weakening the country's competitiveness. Nontransparent regulatory mechanisms may deter new suppliers from entering the market, limiting the options of consumers and reducing social welfare.

Regulatory Failure

Regulatory failure occurs when regulation is motivated by illegitimate rationales or its outcomes are welfare reducing. Like market failure, it reduces social welfare and creates distortions that hurt society at large. The challenge for regulators is to prevent or correct market failures and pursue the public interest while avoiding regulatory failure.

Identifying why regulatory failure has occurred is a central step in improving the regulatory framework, as policy makers can use the analysis to develop remedies. For instance, they can address cases of **regulatory "capture"**—the taking over of decision-making processes by the sector subject to regulation—by setting up firewalls between the regulatory agency and providers, strengthening mandatory information requirements, increasing transparency in the regulatory procedures, or promoting the involvement of more stakeholders in a regulatory consultation process. These measures may also improve institutional capacity.

Capture

Regulatory capture is a common cause of regulatory failure. Groups may use pressure, influence, or bribery to protect their interests and subvert the regulators' objectives. One way to prevent capture is to align the interests of regulatory bodies with desired policy objectives (Baldwin, Cave, and Lodge 2012).

Capture is most frequent in the regulation of services industries dominated by monopolies or oligopolies, especially when one of the suppliers is or was a state-owned enterprise. Other groups that may benefit from close links to the policy-making levels of government, such as lawyers, may also benefit from capture. Regulators of industries typically dominated by a few big companies, such as telecommunications or energy distribution, are particularly vulnerable.

Regulators often try to disguise regulatory capture, claiming that measures that actually benefit special interests serve the public good. This type of declaration not only hides the benefits received by the small group, it also bestows greater legitimacy to the laws and regulations. For instance, a rule requiring domestic recertification of, say, medical doctors might not gain wide public support if the stated purpose were to protect domestic doctors. If, however, the measure is portrayed as ensuring quality against an influx of poorly trained foreign professionals, it is more likely to garner support.

Bounded Rationality and Institutional Capacity

Like market agents, regulators lack perfect information. Because knowledge is costly and incomplete and institutional capacity inherently limited, regulation rarely completely achieves its intended effect. Furthermore, information deficits can lead to capture, because the information needed by the regulator is normally controlled by the private sector, which can use it to its advantage.

Institutional capacity affects the ability to plan, develop, and implement regulation efficiently. Estache and Lewis (2009) identify four broad types of limitations of regulation in developing countries: capacity, accountability, commitment, and fiscal efficiency (box PF.3).

Assessing the regulation of monopolies in developing countries, Laffont (2005) points to aspects that often result in institutional limitations:

- The high cost of public funds
- Insufficient capacity to monitor compliance with regulation
- Institutional hierarchies
- Corruption
- Lack of long-term commitment
- Weak rule of law
- Financial constraints

Because trade in services encompasses a broad range of heavily regulated industries, it is particularly sensitive to regulatory capacity and information asymmetries. Furthermore, many services sectors, such as telecommunications and finance, can experience radical changes with technological developments. As these changes create opportunities or new services or expansion of services through new modes of supply, there is an increased risk of regulatory failure linked to the lack of adequate information in the regulatory decision-making process.

Box PF.3. Institutional Limitations Affecting Regulator Capacity in Developing Countries

Institutional problems often constrain the ability of regulators in developed countries. It is in developing countries, however, that these problems are most acute.

Limited Regulatory Capacity
Regulators generally lack resources, usually because government revenues are low, sometimes because funds are withheld to undermine the agency. The lack of resources prevents regulators from employing skilled staff—an already difficult task in countries with few highly educated professionals and inadequate civil service pay scales. A weak auditing system and inexperienced judiciary place further limits on implementation.

Limited Accountability
Institutions in developing countries are often less accountable than their counterparts in the developed world. Where accountability is lax, collusion between the government and various interest groups, including regulated firms, is more likely to occur. Indeed, in least developed countries, there is abundant evidence of corruption in both the privatization process and regulation.

Limited Commitment
The institutional framework in many developing countries makes it impossible to rely on contracts. In Latin America, for example, between 1985 and 2000, more than 40 percent of concessions (excluding the telecommunications sector) were renegotiated, most of them at the request of governments. Fear of future renegotiation is a serious impediment to attracting private sector participation. The private sector's inability to rely on contracts is particularly damaging in least developed countries, where uncertainties about cost, demand, and macroeconomic stability are significant.

Limited Fiscal Efficiency
When consumers have a limited ability to pay for services, public institutions are unable to collect adequate revenue to allow them to subsidize them. In infrastructure, this limitation is apparent in the slow progress state-owned enterprises have made in increasing access to networks. The scale of network expansion required to widen access to services and the inability of many citizens to pay tariffs at a level that will ensure cost recovery mean that private or public enterprises are unlikely to be financially autonomous, but the poorest countries' limited fiscal efficiency means their governments cannot provide high levels of subsidies.

Source: Estache and Lewis 2009; see also Eberhard 2007.

Principles of Good Regulation

Evaluation of regulation should be done on a case-by-case basis and account not only for a measure's intended purpose but also for the context in which it is conceived and implemented. Certain general principles of good regulation should guide the process.

International organizations and countries including the Australia, New Zealand, and the United Kingdom have launched government-wide initiatives to promote better regulatory practices. The principles of good regulation enunciated by the Council of Australian Governments and endorsed by the government in 1998 include the following (Coghlan 2003):

1. Regulation must yield a net benefit to the community, not just to a particular group or sector.
2. Regulation must be set to the minimum level necessary to achieve the objectives and to avoid unnecessary restrictions. It should be targeted at the problem.
3. Regulation should be integrated and consistent with other laws, agreements, and international obligations. Any restrictions on competition should be retained only if they provide a net benefit to the community and government objectives cannot be achieved by other means.

4. Regulation should not be unduly prescriptive; preferably, it should be specified in relation to performance or outcomes. It should be flexible enough to allow businesses some freedom to find the best way to comply and to allow the regulation to adapt to changed circumstances.
5. Regulation should be accessible, transparent, and accountable. The public should be able to readily find out what regulations they must comply with, and the regulations must be reasonably easy to understand and fairly and consistently administered and enforced.
6. Regulation must be clear, concise, and communicated effectively.
7. Regulation should be mindful of the compliance burden imposed, proportionate to the problem being addressed, and set at a level that lessens compliance costs while still achieving the set objective.
8. Regulation must be enforceable and embody the minimum incentives needed for reasonable compliance. Adequate resources must be provided for monitoring and to ensure reasonable compliance.

The Organisation for Economic Co-operation and Development (OECD) has long been promoting discussions on common principles of good regulatory practices. Box PF.4 reproduces the key points of the Asia-Pacific Economic Cooperation (APEC)–OECD Integrated Checklist on Regulatory Reform of 2005.[3]

Baldwin, Cave, and Lodge (2010) describe regulatory principles as responding to the following key questions:[4]

- Is there an appropriate scheme of accountability?
- Are procedures fair, accessible, and open?
- Is the regulator acting with sufficient expertise?
- Is the action of the regime efficient?

Accountability

Regulators can usually perform their technical duties better if their agency benefits from a degree of independence from the political branches. The flip side of independence, however, is that regulators often have vague mandates and are seen as lacking popular legitimacy. Agencies may overcome this legitimacy deficit by being accountable to, and controlled by, other government institutions that enjoy greater legitimacy, particularly institutions that have been democratically elected.

Regulatory bodies must also be independent from the influence of the firms they govern. Although fluid contact between government and the private sector results in more effective regulatory solutions, adequate firewalls are needed to help ensure that regulatory bodies can regulate for public interest and not be captured by their regulatees.

Certain procedural steps in the regulatory decision-making process may enhance accountability. They include offering adequate reasoning for decisions, disclosing information on the procedures leading to decisions, and incorporating public hearings or other mechanisms for public participation into the decision making (Baldwin, Cave, and Lodge 2010).

Due Process

Whether regulation is deemed legitimate by the general public often depends on fair, accessible, and open regulatory procedures. Regulators should thus pay attention to equality, fairness, consistency of treatment, and public participation, including by consumers and relevant services providers (Baldwin, Cave, and Lodge 2010).

Box PF.4. Good Regulatory Principles: Excerpts from the APEC–OECD Integrated Checklist on Regulatory Reform

Regulatory reform refers to changes that improve regulatory quality to enhance the economic performance, cost-effectiveness, or legal quality of regulations and related government formalities.

A. Horizontal Dimension
A1. To what extent is there an integrated policy for regulatory reform that sets out principles dealing with regulatory, competition and market openness policies?
A5. To what extent has regulatory reform, including policies dealing with regulatory quality, competition and market openness been encouraged and coordinated at all levels of government (for example, federal, state, local, supranational)?
A6. Are the policies, laws, regulations, practices, procedures and decision making transparent, consistent, comprehensible and accessible to users both inside and outside government and to domestic as well as foreign parties? And is effectiveness regularly assessed?
A8. To what extent are there effective interministerial mechanisms for managing and coordinating regulatory reform and integrating competition and market openness considerations into regulatory management systems?

B. Regulatory Policy
B2. Are the legal basis and the economic and social impacts of drafts of new regulations reviewed? What performance measurements are being envisaged for reviewing the economic and social impacts of new regulations?
B4. To what extent are rules, regulatory institutions and the regulatory management process itself transparent, clear and predictable to users both inside and outside the government?
B5. Are there effective public consultation mechanisms and procedures, including prior notification open to regulated parties and other stakeholders, nongovernmental organizations, the private sector, advisory bodies, accreditation bodies, standards-development organizations and other governments?
B8. To what extent have measures been taken to assure compliance with and enforcement of regulations?

C. Competition Policy
C9. To what extent does the competition law apply broadly to all activities in the economy, including both goods and services, as well as to both public and private activities, except for those excluded?
C12. In the absence of a competition law, to what extent is there an effective framework or mechanism for deterring and addressing private anticompetitive conduct?

D. Market Openness Policies
D2. To what extent does the government promote approaches to regulation and its implementation that are trade friendly and avoid unnecessary burdens on economic actors?
D8. To what extent are measures implemented in the countries accepted as being equivalent to domestic measures?

Source: OECD 2005.

Government-wide standard rules governing the regulatory process can enhance due process. Following such rules-on-rules can limit the regulator's discretion and promote transparency and accountability.

Expertise

Regulatory functions, particularly in the complex, dynamic services sector, require expert knowledge. Technical proficiency is not only a necessity for tackling the sector's problems and assessing alternatives, it is also a source of legitimacy for the regulator (Baldwin, Cave, and Lodge 2010).

Efficiency and Proportionality

An important source of legitimacy is the belief that a regulation is aimed at achieving efficiency (Baldwin, Cave, and Lodge 2010). An efficiency goal is particularly relevant when adopting regulation to prevent or correct market failure.

Efficiency considerations can also play a role in regulation for noneconomic goals. An efficient regulation seeks to achieve public interest goals and avoid introducing unnecessary burdens in the market. The ideal result imposes the lowest possible (additional) costs on the services providers while achieving its desired policy goal.

Efficient regulation also entails proportionality between the desired policy goals and the regulatory requirements. The regulatory principles adopted in the United Kingdom, for instance, require that policy solutions be proportionate to the perceived problem or risk, justify the imposed compliance costs, and not create unnecessary burdens (BIS 2011).

Regulation in Practice

The principles of good regulation are not always observed, as box PF.5 indicates.

Conclusion

Government regulation is a powerful instrument for preventing or correcting market failures and attaining social goals. It is particularly important in the services sector, because information asymmetries and limited competition often cause market failures and because the sector

---

Box PF.5. Regulatory Failures in Infrastructure Services in Selected Countries

Argentina
A 1996 review of Argentina's gas sector revealed investor concerns about the transparency and predictability of the National Gas Regulatory Authority. In one case, the agency did not permit wholesale prices charged to distribution companies to be passed on to consumers. In addition, it used its authority over transportation and distribution activities to regulate field prices, changing the rules of the game after they were deregulated as part of privatization. The agency did not provide coherent or predictable principles for determining acceptable gas prices. It also reportedly imposed capricious penalties for violations of gas quality standards.

Latvia
In 1999, Latvia's Telecommunications Rate Council approved large increases in telephone rates. The sector ministry called the increases unfair and annulled the council's decision, a move not clearly allowed by the law. The Ministry of Justice evaluated the legality of the annulment and declared it legal. Its decision was backed by Latvia's parliament, which argued that the council had failed to safeguard the interests of consumers. The government then removed the original members and announced that a new council would be formed.

Romania
In Romania, responsibilities for overseeing telecommunications prices were splintered among the National Agency for Communications and Informatics, the Office of Competition, the Cabinet, and the Competition Council. Unclear guidelines for determining which prices should be regulated produced anomalies, such as the lack of regulation of interconnections not involving Rom Telecom, the dominant carrier. In addition, regulators were not required to justify their policies, and they could not request cost information from services providers. As a result pricing decisions were uncoordinated, and inconsistencies—such as different prices for local services, interconnections between Rom Telecom and mobile carriers, and interconnections between mobile carriers—were not explained.

Ukraine
Ukraine's National Electricity Regulatory Commission, established in 1994, was one of the first independent regulators in a transition economy. In 1997, its specialists included about 70 percent engineers, 20 percent economists, and 10 percent lawyers. All but one of the economists had graduated from a Soviet university between 1965 and 1981. The commission had no specialists in regulatory economics, and Ukraine offered no training in energy regulation. Moreover, key employees left the electricity commission to join private companies regulated by it—increasing pro-industry bias and the potential for capture.

Source: World Bank 2004.

plays a vital social role by providing critical services in key sectors, such as health, education, communication, and finance.

Regulation can also become a tool of protectionism and a safeguard of local interest groups. Through inadequate planning and weak administration, it can introduce distortions. There is a high risk of regulatory failure related to capture when regulation is adopted for noneconomic purposes, because these objectives often garner political and public support even if there is no analytical or empirical justification for their adoption. If the government lacks the means to regulate effectively, regulation may create market distortions and welfare losses even when legitimately introduced to correct market failures.

To overcome these regulatory failures, policy makers must establish a process for adopting and enforcing regulation that reflects the main principles of good governance. Public consultations and other procedures that increase transparency enhance the regulators' accountability. They also inform regulated entities of the relevant regulatory process, safeguarding against regulatory capture. Adequate expert advice and interagency coordination mechanisms increase efficiency and enhance analytical support for regulation, reducing the scope for failures related to bounded rationality.

Notes

1. Production technology comprises all means by which a firm produces its services, including methods, management competence, and organizational structures.

2. Prosser (2010) distinguishes three noneconomic rationales for regulation: protection of human rights, promotion of social solidarity, and resolution of problems. Sunstein (1990) offers six motivations: redistribution, collective desires and aspirations, diverse experiences and preference formation, social subordination, endogenous preferences, and irreversibility (regarding the environment and human and nonhuman life). Feintuck (2004) does not propose categories, focusing instead on the specific content of "public interest" in different regulatory instruments and sectors. Stiglitz (2010) adds "market irrationality" as another source of policy concern.

3. See also the OECD Recommendation of the Council on Improving the Quality of Government Regulation of 1995, the 2005 Guiding Principles for Regulatory Quality and Performance, and the OECD Recommendation of the Council on Regulatory Policy and Governance of 2012.

4. Baldwin, Cave, and Lodge (2010) include a fifth principle, which they call "legislative mandate." There is no doubt that the regulator's mandate, particularly when it comes from a democratically elected institution, is an important source of legitimacy. Whether such mandate amounts to a principle is less clear, as suggested by the fact that regulatory handbooks and guidelines do not usually include a similar principle.

References

Baldwin, Robert, Martin Cave, and Martin Lodge, eds. 2010. *The Oxford Handbook of Regulation*. Oxford: Oxford University Press.

———. 2012. *Understanding Regulation: Theory, Strategy and Practice*. Oxford: Oxford University Press.

BIS (Department for Business, Innovation, and Skills). 2011. *Principles of Economic Regulation*. London: BIS. https://www.gov.uk/government/uploads/system/uploads/attachment_data/file/31623/11-795-principles-for-economic-regulation.pdf.

Coghlan, Paul. 2003. "The Principles of Good Regulation." In *Regulation and Market Access*, ed. Alexandra Sidorenko and Christopher Findlay, 17–39. Canberra: Asian Pacific Press and Australian National University.

Cottier, Thomas, Panagiotis Delimatsis, and Nicolas Diebold. 2008. "Article XIV GATS." In *WTO: Trade in Services*, ed. Rüdiger Wolfrum, Peter-Tobias Stoll, and Clemens Feinäugle, 287–328. Leiden: Martinus Nijhoff.

Eberhard, Anton. 2007. *Infrastructure Regulation in Developing Countries: An Exploration of Hybrid and Transitional Models*. Washington, DC: Public-Private Infrastructure Advisory Facility (PPIAF).

Estache, Antonia, and Liam Wren Lewis. 2009. "Toward a Theory of Regulation for Developing Countries." *Journal of Economic Literature* 47 (3): 729–70.

Feintuck, Mike. 2004. *"The Public Interest" in Regulation*. Oxford: Oxford University Press.

Krajewski, Markus. 2003. *National Regulation and Trade Liberalization in Services*. The Hague: Kluwer Law International.

Laffont, Jean-Jacques. 2005. *Regulation and Development*. Cambridge: Cambridge University Press.

Mattoo, Aaditya, and Pierre Sauvé. 2003. "Domestic Regulation and Trade in Services: Key Issues." In *Domestic Regulation and Service Trade Liberalization*, ed. Aaditya Mattoo and Pierre Sauvé, 1–7. Washington, DC: World Bank.

OECD (Organisation for Economic Co-operation and Development). 2005. *APEC–OECD Integrated Checklist on Regulatory Reform*. Paris: OECD.

———. 2011. *Competition Assessment Toolkit*. Vol. 2: *Guidance*. Paris: OECD.

Ogus, Anthony I. 1994. *Regulation: Legal Form and Economic Theory*. Oxford: Hart Publishing.

Prosser, Tony. 2010. *The Regulatory Enterprise: Government, Regulation, and Legitimacy*. Oxford: Oxford University Press.

Sidorenko, Alexandra, and Christopher Findlay. 2003. "Domestic Regulatory Reform and Trade Liberalization." In *Regulation and Market Access*, ed. Alexandra Sidorenko and Christopher Findlay, 1–16. Canberra: Asian Pacific Press and Australian National University.

Stiglitz, Joseph. 2010. "Government Failure vs. Market Failure: Principles of Regulation." In *Government and Markets: Toward a New Theory of Regulation*, ed. Edward Balleisen and David Moss, 13–51. Cambridge: Cambridge University Press.

Sunstein, Cass. 1990. "The Function of Regulatory Statutes." In *After the Rights Revolution: Reconceiving the Regulatory State*. Cambridge, MA: Harvard University Press.

Veljanovski, Cento. 2010. "Economic Approaches to Regulation." In *The Oxford Handbook of Regulation*, ed. Robert Baldwin, Martin Cave, and Martin Lodge, 17–38. Oxford: Oxford University Press.

World Bank. 2004. *Reforming Infrastructure: Privatization, Regulation, and Competition*. Washington, DC: World Bank.

MAPPING REGULATIONS AND EVALUATING GOVERNANCE

Objectives

This module explains how to map the laws and regulations affecting services as well as the governance framework for adopting and implementing those laws and regulations. Upon completing it, readers will be able to:

- *Identify the parameters of regulatory measures relevant for a regulatory assessment*
- *Map the regulatory restrictions that affect services trade and investment by identifying their parameters and the sectors and modes they affect*
- *Assess whether a law or regulation constitutes a restriction to trade and investment in services and identify the category of restrictions into which it falls*
- *Assess the governance framework for adopting and implementing laws and regulations*
- *Distinguish between formal limitations to trade and investment in services and restrictions originating in administrative practices*

The first module of a Regulatory Assessment of Services Trade and Investment (RASTI) involves two main steps (figure 1.1). The first is a comprehensive review—or "mapping"—of all laws and regulations affecting trade and investment in services. These measures include not only laws and regulations governing a particular sector but also measures that affect a wide range of sectors (**"horizontal" measures**). Regulations on tourism, for example, obviously affect services providers in the sector. But so, too, do other laws and regulations, such as regulations on buying and selling foreign currency, laws on entry and stay of foreigners, and procedures related to the establishment of firms.

The second step of a regulatory mapping is the assessment of the governance framework. Governance determines the way rules affecting services are prepared, adopted, and applied. The regulation-making process requires an adequate institutional setting capable of assessing the challenges posed by the services sector. Regulators must evaluate the impact of regulation on services and other economic sectors and identify and implement viable regulatory decisions. These procedures require the cooperation of various entities from the government and the private sector.

Mapping Laws and Regulations Affecting Services Trade and Investment

In principle, a regulatory mapping should include all levels of regulation and institutions that affect services trade. Full analysis of all services sectors at all levels of regulation is rarely efficient or practical, however. It is therefore recommended that the mapping focuses mainly on a horizontal, sectoral, or services level, depending on the information needed.

Relevant laws and regulation include all measures affecting the access of services suppliers to the market or the conditions under which they may operate. In many cases, however, restrictions stem from administrative practices that are not spelled out in formal instruments. Assessment of the governance framework can identify such practices and propose ways to avoid them.

Mapping laws and regulations identifies how they affect services sectors and contribute to achieving policy goals. Policy makers must consider various parameters when assessing how regulation affects trade in services and whether more trade- and investment-friendly alternatives are available. These parameters include the purpose of the measure, the modes of supply, the level of regulation, the nature of the measure, the stage the measure governs, the origin of the measure, the type of impact, and whether the measure discriminates against foreign providers. This information should be summarized in a table, as table 1.1 does for an imaginary country.

Figure 1.1. Module 1 of a Regulatory Assessment of Services Trade and Investment

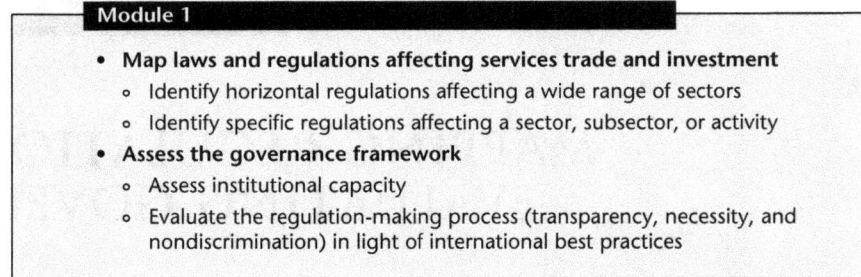

Module 1

- **Map laws and regulations affecting services trade and investment**
  - Identify horizontal regulations affecting a wide range of sectors
  - Identify specific regulations affecting a sector, subsector, or activity
- **Assess the governance framework**
  - Assess institutional capacity
  - Evaluate the regulation-making process (transparency, necessity, and nondiscrimination) in light of international best practices

The mapping should also identify desirable laws and regulations that are not in place. In many sectors, regulation is necessary to prevent or correct market failures and create an efficient services market. Lack of regulation may result in anticompetitive behaviors or translate into inefficient de facto measures.

Parameters

The regulatory mapping should take into account all parameters relevant to identifying regulatory measures and assessing their impact (table 1.2). These parameters help policy makers evaluate possible alternatives.

Sectoral Scope

Three levels of regulation of services can be distinguished:

- Horizontal laws and regulations include measures affecting all services industries, such as restrictions on the transfer of funds, limitations on the movement of people, caps on foreign equity participation, and legislation granting preferential treatment to some minorities.
- Sectoral measures cover regulations that govern a particular industry, such as tourism or telecommunications, or that create a framework for professional services.
- Service-specific regulations refer to measures that regulate specific activities, such as the practice of law, medicine, or accounting.

Mode of Supply

"Modal" regulation (regulation that affects cross-border trade, the movement of people, or the establishment of foreign companies) is usually related to policy objectives other than the regulation of trade in services. Examples of horizontal measures not directly aimed at regulating international trade, but that imply horizontal restrictions on a mode of services supply include the following:

- Cross-border trade: measures on transfer of funds, restrictions on access to foreign currency
- Consumption abroad: exit visas for nationals, restrictions on access to foreign currency
- Commercial presence: limitations on land ownership, restrictions on establishment of juridical persons, and domestic employment requirements for foreign companies
- Presence of individual services suppliers: visa requirements for foreigners, limitations on periods of stay

Stage of Supply Affected

Some regulations limit the entry of services suppliers to the market. They include licensing and registration requirements. Other measures establish conditions that affect business operation. They include taxes, employment conditions, information requirements, and price regulation.

Legitimate policy objectives may justify both types of measures. Licensing may be required to ensure that providers are able to supply a service and have sufficient capital to operate in the industry and cover any damages caused by hazardous activities. Measures regarding operations may be necessary to provide information about key industries, limit the price effects of the lack of competition in natural monopolies, and ensure competition in network industries.

Measures affecting market access tend to restrict trade and investment more than measures affecting operations, because they limit the entry of new market actors, favoring existing providers and limiting competition, which usually raises prices. Measures affecting operations may increase costs, causing prices to rise, but in general they favor a more competitive market (module 2 offers more detail on the economic implications of measures on market access

Table 1.1. Measures Affecting Trade and Investment in Services in Kingdom of Uqbar

Measure	Sectors covered	Mode of supply	Stage affected	Nature of measure	Origin	Impact	Policy goal		Possible alternative
							Market failure addressed by restriction	Noneconomic policy achieved by restriction	
Access to and use of land of indigenous people are restricted	Horizontal	Modes 3 and 4	Entry/market access	Qualitative	Legal	Nondiscriminatory		Protection of minorities	
Subsidies and state support are granted only to Uqbar nationals	Horizontal	All modes	Operation	Qualitative	Legal	Discriminatory		Support of nationals	
Acquisition of Uqbarian businesses of Uq$5 million or more by foreigners is subject to review by National Board of Investment	Horizontal	Mode 3	Entry/market access	Qualitative (economic needs test)	Legal (law or foreign investment)	Discriminatory		Maintenance of national security	
Only individuals residing in Uqbar and enterprises with head offices in Uqbar can apply for import permits	Horizontal/ distribution services	Modes 1 and 3	Market access/ operation	Qualitative	Legal (law on export and import permits)	De facto discriminatory		Prevention of crime (contraband)	Require additional information from foreign companies
Accountants must have been continuously domiciled in Uqbar for at least three years and have at least one year of accounting experience in Uqbar	Accounting	All modes	Market access	Qualitative	Legal (law on accountants)	De facto discriminatory	Information asymmetry		Require all accountants to pass examination
Foreign lawyers are not allowed to become members of the national bar	Legal services	Modes 2 and 4	Market access	Qualitative	Regulatory (Uqbar national bar directive)	Discriminatory	Information asymmetry	Protection of domestic providers	Allow registration for international law only
Sanitary regulations are selectively enforced	Tourism	Mode 3	Operation	Qualitative	Practice (Ministry of Tourism)	Discriminatory			
Licenses to foreign banks are limited	Banking	Mode 3	Market access	Quantitative	Practice (Central Bank)	Discriminatory		Protection of small domestic banks	Provide subsidies to small financial institutions

Note: FDI = foreign direct investment; Mode 1 = cross-border trade; Mode 2 = consumption abroad; Mode 3 = commercial presence; and Mode 4 = presence of natural persons to provide services.

Table 1.2. Parameters for Evaluating Services Regulation

Parameter	Options
Sectoral scope of the measure	• Horizontal • Sectoral • Service
Mode of supply affected	• Mode 1 (cross-border trade) • Mode 2 (consumption abroad) • Mode 3 (establishment) • Mode 4 (presence of individual services supplier)
Stage of supply affected	• Access/establishment • Operation
Nature of measures	• Quantitative • Qualitative
Origin of measures	• Legal or regulatory instrument • Administrative practice
Impact of measures	• Formally discriminatory • De facto discriminatory • Discriminatory application • Nondiscriminatory

Policy goals	• Address market failure
	  ○ Monopoly
	  ○ Public goods
	  ○ Externalities
	  ○ Asymmetric information
	  ○ Coordination problems
	• Achieve noneconomic goal
	  ○ Distributional justice
	  ○ Regulatory failure
	  ○ Public interest

and operations). Where restrictions on services are necessary to achieve public policy goals, it is thus preferable that they focus on the operations stage.

Nature of Measures

Laws and regulations can restrict the number of suppliers (quantitative) or impose obligations on market actors (qualitative) (table 1.3).

Origin and Impact of Measures

Both laws and regulations and the ways in which those laws and regulations are applied (or not applied) can restrict trade and investment in services. Administrative practices that restrict the sector include the following:

- Failure to grant licenses or permits
- Failure to publicly disclose requirements
- Ambiguous/unclear requirements
- Imposition of unofficial fees
- Inconsistent/unpredictable application of regulation
- Discriminatory application of regulation
- Deficient monitoring and enforcement procedures

The impact of laws, regulations, and administrative measures on foreign suppliers is another important parameter in the regulatory mapping exercise. Regulations may affect foreign and domestic services suppliers alike, or they may discriminate against foreign suppliers. The correction of market failures and the achievement of noneconomic goals rarely require discriminatory measures.

The most clearly discriminatory measures set different requirements for foreign and domestic providers. This type of open, de jure discriminatory measure is evident from a superficial review of laws and regulations. For many countries, this type of discriminatory measures appears in the schedules of commitments or lists of reservations to agreements in trade in services. An example of a de jure discriminatory measure is access to certain subsidies and government contracts, which tend to be limited to domestic suppliers.

Laws and regulations may contain nondiscriminatory wording but have different implications for nationals and foreign services providers in practice. Residency requirements for managers and directors are typical de facto discriminatory measures. Language requirements can also be discriminatory.

The impact of these measures needs to be assessed on a case-by-case basis to determine whether they address legitimate concerns or serve only to limit trade in services. For example, language proficiency may help ensure the quality of services provided by health care professionals, thus the requirement. In contrast, such a requirement may not be necessary for other professionals, such as engineers and computer technicians.

The services market may be distorted by measures that are nondiscriminatory in their terms and intent but are applied only to certain services suppliers. Sanitary regulations and controls, for example, may be applied only to foreign-owned hotels; foreign suppliers may be required to abide by harsher competition rules than are domestic providers. These practices not only protect domestic providers from outside competition, they also affect the general governance and regulatory framework.

Policy Goals

Identifying and recording the policy goals of a regulation help officials assess whether the regulations contribute to stated objectives. Mapping the regulatory framework pinpoints the main regulatory obstacles to trade in services and illuminates the context. It helps policy makers determine whether alternatives could help achieve the same objective while introducing fewer restrictions on trade and investment in services.

The purpose of a policy is often difficult to identify. It may be stated in the preamble of a law or regulation. Whenever possible, such goals should be taken into account.

Table 1.3. Measures Affecting Trade and Investment in Services, by Stage of Supply

Stage of supply affected	Quantitative	Qualitative
Market access/establishment	• Establishment of monopoly • Numerical restrictions • Zoning/geographical restrictions • Foreign equity ceilings • Economic needs tests • Authorization/permit requirements (subject to unspecified requirements)	• Licensing, based on qualifications, education, experience, technical capacity • Nationality/residency requirements for services providers • Track record requirements • Requirement to belong to association (syndication requirements) • Approval of mergers and acquisitions • Restrictions on form of establishment • Prohibition of certain services • Minimum capital requirements

Operations	• Numerical restrictions on
	  ○ Transactions
	  ○ Operations/output
	  ○ Employees
	  ○ Repatriation of funds
	  ○ Duration of license/divestment
	  ○ Hours of operation
	• Screen and stage quotas
	• Performance requirements
		• Nationality/residency requirements of managers and directors
		• Restrictions on land ownership
		• Discriminatory taxation
		• Discriminatory access to subsidies
		• Knowledge transfer requirements
		• Advertising restrictions
		• Rules on anticompetitive behavior
		• Restrictions on distribution channels
		• Restrictions on pricing
		• Restrictions on transfer of funds
		• Restrictions on type of shares foreigners can own
		• Performance requirements
		• Need for import permit
		• Discriminatory access to government contracts

These statements are usually general, however; they rarely offer details about individual measures or restrictions. Field work often sheds additional light on regulatory goals, at times suggesting motivations that differ substantially from those stated in the actual regulation.

To a large extent, the nature of a regulatory measure indicates its motivation. Certification requirements, for instance, generally aim at overcoming information asymmetries. Price caps on monopolistic suppliers are usually intended to prevent abuse of a dominant position.

In other cases, the objective may be less clear. Geographical restrictions on the construction of large discount stores, for instance, may be based on the need to limit vehicular traffic in certain areas, or they may be a response to pressure from domestic retailers who wish to avoid competition. Discriminatory licensing is often used to protect domestic providers.

The issuing process of the regulation can also reveal policy objectives. A transparent and participatory process can help officials assess whether regulations are necessary and how stakeholders are affected. The assessment of the governance framework can thus help uncover the goals behind certain trade restrictions, especially when the assessment focuses on a specific sector.

Methodology

A comprehensive review of the laws and regulations affecting trade in services requires extensive field work. Evaluators must also review documents. Examples of laws or regulations that should normally be examined include the following:

• Laws on foreign investment set out the general requirements foreign suppliers must meet to do business in a country. Such laws usually feature the main horizontal conditions for market access and guidelines on the conditions of operation.

• Laws on commercial enterprises set forth the procedural conditions for establishment of firms and the types of juridical persons that may be admitted, including branches and representation agencies of foreign suppliers. Regulations implementing the law should clarify the principles and procedures governing the issuance of operating licenses.

• Regimes on international transfers of funds set out the conditions for movement of funds across borders. Measures on the transfer of funds may affect all modes of supply, including the ability to make cross-border payments, invest and repatriate funds, or receive payments.

• Land laws establish the conditions for access to real estate, including for juridical persons and foreigners.
• Laws governing access to foreign currency may limit trade in services by introducing barriers to international payments and the transfer of funds.
• The legal and regulatory framework on migration affect the provision of services through the movement of natural persons and the establishment of a company.

Other horizontal regimes relevant to the regulatory mapping include the following:

• Access to courts and dispute resolutions, including national and international commercial arbitration
• Government procurement regimes establishing the condition under which foreign services suppliers may access government contracts and concessions
• Subsidies regimes
• Competition policies
• Performance requirements

International trade and investment agreements identify general laws that affect services trade. Further information can be found in the protocols of accession of countries that recently joined the World Trade Organization (WTO). This information generally relates only to formal laws, however; it says little about secondary regulations or the conditions under which such measures are applied. Such sources should therefore be used as initial guidance that is complemented with reviews of laws and regulations on the ground.

Regulatory information can also be obtained from public databases of laws and regulatory measures. The World Bank's Investing across Borders and Services Trade Restrictions databases, the Product Market Regulation Database of the Organisation of Economic Co-operation and Development (OECD), and the WTO's Integrated Trade Intelligence Portal provide basic information on restrictions to trade and investment across the board as well as on selected sectors. These initiatives have also developed indexes on restrictiveness, which facilitate comparison across countries (see the list of references at the end of this module).

These sources can help officials gain a broad idea of the regulatory framework, but an accurate and comprehensive regulatory mapping can result only from research in the field. The main sources normally come from discussions with government officials from regulatory agencies and domestic and foreign services providers. These interviews should be informed by background research and should lead to further, more detailed fact-finding and checking. Table 1.4 provides excerpts from the World Bank questionnaires that can be used in interviews. The full questionnaires can be found at http://www.worldbank.org/trade/RASTI.

The recording should include specific reference to the parameters identified in table 1.2. Explicitly setting out these parameters helps evaluators assess the impact of a measure and analyze it based on the General Agreement on Trade in Services (GATS) and other international free trade agreements. Although trade agreements do not always feature disciplines with identical scope, trade officials can easily associate the parameters with the relevant obligations of most trade and investment agreements. Box 1.1 provides examples of the types of restrictions to trade a horizontal regulatory mapping identifies.

Where possible, it is also important to link the regulatory measure with a particular type of restriction. Table 1.3 identifies 36 types of regulatory restrictions plus 7 administrative practices that impinge on services trade and investment. To keep the task manageable, evaluators should record measures that appear to restrict trade and investment in services, ignoring measures that do not.

Categorizing the measures is also necessary, in order to be able to conduct a quantitative analysis later (see module 2) or to compare the measures with existing restrictiveness indexes. The quantitative record will allow officials to compare regulatory policies across sectors. It provides the background data required in module 2, in which the impact of restrictions is estimated. The RASTI website (http://www.worldbank.org/trade/RASTI) provides a sample form for recording and eventually quantifying the regulatory restrictions.

Assessing the Governance Framework

Many barriers to trade and investment in services stem from opaque and discretionary administration of laws and regulations rather than from outright restrictions. The assessment of the governance framework aims to identify shortcomings in the regulatory process and institutional setting that may undermine the functioning of the services market. This section describes two aspects of the governance framework relevant to a regulatory assessment and offers methodological guidelines for developing and implementing regulation.

Institutional Setting

A weak regulatory environment may arise from an inadequate institutional setting. In such a setting, the government bodies charged with regulating services lack a mandate to regulate, the ability to resist pressures from other government bodies or private interests, and adequate resources to understand and evaluate the complexity of a market and the impact of regulation.

Table 1.4. Sample Questions for Collecting Information for a Regulatory Mapping

Measure	Sample questions
Legal and regulatory measures	
Market access and establishment	
General	• Is private ownership of services companies allowed?
	• Are any sectors monopolies or served by exclusive providers?
	• Does the state own all or part of such monopolies?
Land ownership	• Are there restrictions on private ownership of land?
	• Are there restrictions on ownership of land by foreign individuals and companies that are not applied to nationals? If so, can foreigners lease land? For how long?
Economic needs test	• Is private investment subject to an economic needs tests?
	• Do economic needs tests apply to all private investments or only to foreign investments? Is the restriction set out in a law or regulation, or is it the result of usual practice?
	• What are the requirements of the economic needs test? Are they spelled out in a legal instrument?
Operations	
Regulatory restrictions	• Are there restrictions on advertising? If so, do the same rules apply to foreign and domestic providers?
	• Does a performance requirement apply to services providers? If so, are the requirements the same for foreign and domestic services providers?
Measures regarding movement of people	• Are there quotas for foreign employees?
	• Are there economic needs tests on the employment of foreign personnel?
	• Are labor certification tests required for intracorporate transferees or professionals?
	• Has the country concluded and implemented mutual recognition agreements with other countries?
Administrative practices	
Transparency and application of measures	• How accessible are laws and regulations to the public?
	• How are laws and regulations made publicly available?
	• Do licensing and authorization procedures correspond to the publicly available rules?
	• Are there unofficial fees in licensing procedures?
	• How strong is the monitoring and enforcement of regulations?
	• Are enforcement and monitoring procedures applied evenhandedly?

Ideally, a comprehensive regulatory mapping would analyze all agencies that enact laws or regulations that affect trade in services—that is, virtually all agencies. Depending on the scope of the intended mapping, a more efficient approach focuses on government bodies directly involved with the measure.

A horizontal assessment should map ministries and agencies with broad regulatory mandates that span all sectors of the economy. They include bodies that regulate industry and commerce, handle trade policy and diplomacy, and regulate investment and the establishment of juridical persons. Not every aspect of each government body needs to be analyzed. The focus should be on departments that are closely linked to the regulation, administration, and monitoring of market regulation.

A sectoral analysis should focus on bodies with regulatory mandates over the relevant services sector. In some cases, the mapping may include bodies outside the formal executive branch structure, such as central banks for the regulation of financial services; independent agencies that regulate sectors such as telecommunications and energy sectors; and private regulatory bodies, such as professional associations.

Mandate

An adequate mandate provides the government body with the ability to seek information from other agencies and regulated entities, initiate the lawmaking process where necessary, pass regulation, monitor the services market and services providers, and enforce compliance with regulation.

In sectors that require significant technical expertise, such as financial services, telecommunications, or energy distribution, the regulator needs independence from policy-making bodies to regulate the market. This independence is particularly important when the government also provides the service (through a state-owned enterprise or equity participation in a private company). Requisites for regulatory independence include the following (Wu 2008):

• An independent leader
• Exclusive licensing authority
• Independent funding
• Private sector regulatees
• Minimal staff crossover between industry and regulator
• Consumer offices
• Universal system offices

Box 1.1. Barriers to Trade in Services in Cambodia

Cambodia has experienced extraordinary economic growth in recent years and become one of Asia's most open economies. This impressive growth has been driven largely by a boom in services trade, led by a rapid expansion in tourism. Despite this boom, the services sector remains relatively small. Because its main services industry is export oriented, Cambodia has a high level of services exports but a low level of domestic services relative to GDP. There is therefore still considerable scope to develop the services sector, both domestically and for export.

To maintain growth momentum in the sector, Cambodia needs to move beyond the pillars of tourism and textiles, diversifying into exports of more sophisticated high value-added modern services. To make this transition successfully, Cambodia needs to address several major challenges.

Weak governance and regulation represent main hurdles to the development of an efficient services sector. Lack of transparency in the transport sector is leading to significantly higher transport costs, by creating an environment in which informal payments are ubiquitous. In the tourism sector, establishing a more developed regulatory environment, setting up adequate safety and quality standards, and ensuring equitable legal enforcement would help create a better environment for the expansion of more high-end tourism services, reversing the current emphasis on low-end backpacker tourism. In professional services, deficiencies in the regulatory framework appear to run counter to Cambodia's WTO commitments.

Better infrastructure, particularly in broadband telecommunications, is required for the expansion of Cambodia's services trade. Although mobile telephony has expanded rapidly, broadband communications are available only in a few locations, and the cost is prohibitive for most of the population. As a result, Cambodia has the lowest broadband connectivity in the region after the Republic of the Union of Myanmar. The reason for this disappointing expansion of broadband is that Cambodia has a deficient institutional and regulatory framework in the telecommunications sector—one that is not conducive to attracting foreign direct investment. Consequently, telecommunications services have grown at a meager 3 percent a year in the past seven years, compared with 18 percent for tourism. Cambodia's regulatory framework on telecommunications is patchy, opaque, and inconsistent, with many administrative decisions not made public. The Ministry of Posts and Telecommunications acts as the policy maker as well as the regulator and the supervisory authority in the sector. Therefore, developing an enabling environment through policies and regulations that promote investment and market entry—including the passage of a law on telecommunications in line with internationally accepted principles of telecom regulation and Cambodia's WTO commitments—remains a key priority Among other issues, new regulations should clarify the legal framework for providers, institutionalize a system for spectrum allocation, and establish an independent regulator to monitor the system.

In addition to sector-specific initiatives, the authorities should consider three horizontal measures:

- Ensure that the official legal gazette/journal publishes all laws, subdecrees, *prakas*, and ministerial directives affecting trade and investment in services. The gazette should be published weekly in both electronic and hard-copy form after allowing for early dissemination of drafts and consultation with the private sector.
- Establish annual ministry-specific regulatory programs that outline issues to be tackled through regulation and the desired objectives of the proposed regulations. Public disclosure of the regulatory program (through the gazette) would allow other ministries and regulatory agencies, as well as the private sector, to issue comments and feedback on planned regulations.
- Adopt policy guidelines that set out procedures to be followed in the law- and regulation-making process. These guidelines should be aligned with principles of good regulation, including transparency, public consultations, interagency coordination, and regulatory efficiency.

Source: World Bank 2012a, 2012b.

- Public notice and comment during decision making
- Rules against gifts
- Rules against conflicts of interest
- Rules on postemployment

This does not mean that such a regulatory structure may be feasible for all countries. Particularly in small low-income countries, the optimal institutional setting may require adopting some of these principles in institutional structures that are not necessarily independent.

Capacity and Resources

To regulate efficiently, regulators need solid expertise. Many countries, especially small and developing economies, may not have access to the technical expertise necessary to tackle the most complex regulatory issues

of services. The assessment of the institutional setting must take these limitations into account.

In general, the resources of regular government agencies (ministries and other bodies that report to the executive) should come from the regular government budget (which, ideally, has been approved by the legislature). Allowing policy-making entities, such as the ministry of tourism, to generate revenue (through the collection of fees for approval of licenses for hotels and restaurants, for example) creates incentives that can cause it to deviate from its goal of regulating the market. Revenue from fees and other services should instead feed the regular budget, which should be distributed based on needs and policy objectives. Independent regulatory agencies may collect part of their funding from the services providers under their authority, which helps shield the agency from pressures from other sectors of the government (Brown and others 2006). Adequate transparency and checks should be in place to limit possible abuses of such authority.

Ideally, regulators would conduct a regulatory impact assessment for a proposed regulation, based on the economic and social costs of current and prospective regulation. Many countries lack both the data and the skills to do so, however. However, a number of small developing economies have incorporated key concepts of a regulatory impact assessment in their procedures without engaging in the more demanding and data-intensive steps of the assessment (World Bank 2009).

Regulatory Procedures

Regulatory procedures that ensure transparency, adequate coordination with other government bodies, and consultations with the private sector can strengthen capacity. Indeed, a well-designed and coordinated regulatory process that ensures the smooth and transparent flow of information may help overcome resource limitations in small economies, especially low-income countries.

The mapping of the regulatory procedures identifies deficiencies that affect the preparation, adoption, and application of current regulations. Understanding the procedures regulatory bodies follow in developing and implementing helps policy makers improve the quality of the regulation and avoid or modify administrative practices that may introduce de facto barriers to trade in services. Officials can assess the governance framework based on internationally recognized good regulatory practices.

Except in rare circumstances, the more open the information flow between the concerned regulatory agency and third parties, the better and more legitimate is the resulting regulation. Adequate information flow should include coordination with other government agencies and consultations with stakeholders and the general public.

Interagency Coordination

Coordination with other ministries and agencies ensures that regulation reflects broader public policy objectives and that regulation by one regulator does not obstruct the goals of another. For instance, opening the road transport market to suppliers from neighboring countries requires the regulator—typically, an agency from the ministry of transport—to coordinate with the environmental protection agency and with regulatory agencies from neighboring countries. Regulation from other bodies may affect transport services by introducing unnecessarily burdensome restrictions, such as restrictions on **licensing** for truck drivers.

Most administrations—including many low-income countries at the bottom of governance rankings—engage in internal coordination. However, coordination procedures often remain informal and lack transparency, leaving officials plenty of room to enact regulation with little input from other agencies and no effective policy coordination. To avoid such a situation, all regulatory agencies should adopt standard government-wide coordination procedures. Box 1.2 describes some of the policy-making benefits of effective intragovernmental coordination.

Many countries have adopted a "law on laws" or similar instrument that outlines the steps in the regulation-making

---

Box 1.2. Policy-Making Benefits of Effective Intragovernmental Coordination

Given the regulatory intensity of many services activities and the range of sectors involved, coordination across government agencies is critical. Promoting an effective process of intragovernmental coordination is likely to generate positive policy-making externalities, including the following:

- *Crafting unified government positions.* Coordination is essential to develop negotiating positions based on complete assessment of key national priorities and to ensure that negotiators are informed of the full range of factors influencing the domestic services market.
- *Generating information based on measures affecting trade in services.* Policy makers need accurate information on the domestic regulatory environment affecting trade in services. Trading partners require this information during trade negotiations. Creating and updating a central inventory or focal point (such as a database) of regulatory measures can help meet such transparency obligations.
- *Identifying and analyzing the effects of measures on achieving economic or social policy objectives.* Governments at all levels need to periodically review the effectiveness of domestic policies and regulations in achieving economic and social policy objectives. Doing so may involve analyzing the trade or investment effects of regulatory measures.
- *Avoiding duplicating consultations with other agencies and domestic stakeholders.* Given the multitude of subsectors and measures arising from services trade, officials must achieve a balance between engaging intragovernmental partners on issues of mutual concern and avoiding inundating key departments and agencies with too much information or requests for input. Good regular lines of communication between individuals can assist in quickly addressing issues without creating unnecessary processes.
- *Contributing to an ongoing assessment of the impact of liberalizing services trade.* In most countries, data for impact analysis are the responsibility of the national statistical agency. However, collecting such data is challenging for several reasons. Recourse to anecdotal information can be useful.

Sources: Adapted from Marconini and Sauvé 2009; OECD 2002.

Figure 1.2. Information Flow for Policy on and Regulation of Trade and Investment in Services

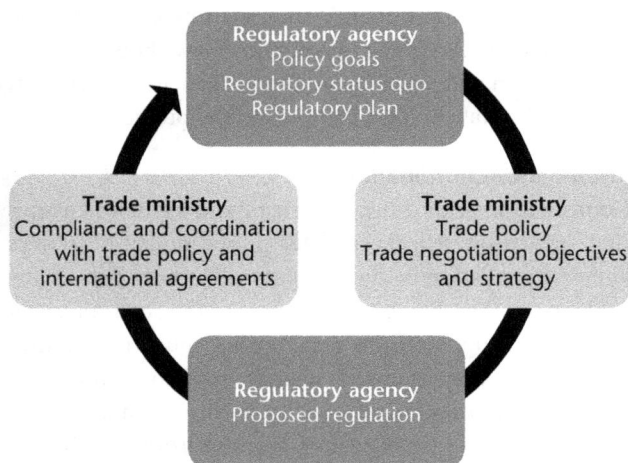

procedure and the information that must be disclosed at each stage. Such steps often include giving public notice of the intention to regulate; identifying the agencies that should be informed of the intended regulation; sharing a proposed draft with other agencies; announcing the proposed rule in order to receive public comments; and publishing an approved regulation before its entry into force.

Standardized and transparent procedures improve the flow of information among agencies, thus increasing cooperation and enhancing knowledge in the regulatory process. Excessive formal requirements on the exchange of information may tax an administration's capacity, especially in small and low-income economies.

For an effective trade policy, information should flow back and forth between the trade ministry and the regulatory agency (figure 1.2). The regulatory agencies should first provide the trade ministry with a clear picture of the regulatory status quo on their specific sector, including current laws and regulations, policy goals, and the regulatory plan. The trade ministry should then articulate a services policy, including guidelines on potential international obligations, as part of a broader national trade policy. The policy can be enacted through the adoption of necessary changes in the regulation under the orbit of each relevant body. The trade ministry and other relevant ministries should have access to proposed new regulations at conception and at the draft stage to assess the impact on trade and its compliance with international trade agreements.

Consultations with Private Stakeholders

To ensure that its decisions are well informed, the regulator should set up an effective consultation mechanism with private stakeholders. Involving stakeholders in the

decision-making process also lends greater legitimacy to the measures, fostering compliance and facilitating implementation.

In low-income countries, consultations help build regulatory capacity, as government officials engage in substantive exchanges with knowledgeable industry representatives. Such exchanges are particularly important for rapidly expanding sectors, because the private sector is often better equipped than the state to attract domestic and international expertise, especially in developing countries.

A number of principles should guide consultations with stakeholders (Better Regulation Office 2009):

- *Continuity*. Consultation should be continuous and start early in the policy development process.
- *Targeting*. Consultation should attempt to capture the diversity of stakeholders affected by the proposed changes.
- *Timeliness*. Consultation should start when policy objectives and options are identified. Throughout the process, stakeholders should be given sufficient time to provide considered responses.
- *Accessibility*. Officials should inform stakeholder groups of consultations and proposals through a range of methods. Agencies should consult jointly with other agencies to reduce the burden on stakeholders.
- *Transparency*. Policy agencies need to clearly explain the objectives of the consultation process and the regulation policy framework. They should provide feedback on how they have considered the responses.
- *Consistency and flexibility*. Arrangements should be consistent but flexible enough to suit the proposal's circumstances.
- *Evaluation and review*. Policy agencies should evaluate consultation processes to make them more effective.

As with interagency coordination, procedures for consultation should be standard and mandatory for all government agencies. Ideally, they should specify the details to be shared at each stage.

A document should reflect stakeholders' comments and explain how the proposal was modified to take account of their views. If the proposal was not modified, the regulation should explain why dissenting views were not reflected.

Methodology

Mapping the institutional setting and the regulatory procedures is an information-intensive exercise. Most low-income countries lack an institutional blueprint that clearly sets out goals, mandates, and competencies of government institutions. Moreover, institutional frameworks are constantly evolving as policies and practice advance and political preferences change. Many developed economies have complex institutional settings, with overlapping mandates based on geographical or thematic areas, often deliberately in an attempt to promote **regulatory competition**.

Unearthing the facts and figures of the governance framework requires extensive field work. The objective of the mapping exercise will determine the desired level of detail and precision of the information sought. In a horizontal mapping, the focus is on regulatory agencies that

tackle across-the-board issues, such as the registration and approval of investment, the movement and stay of natural persons, and the transfer of funds, as well as agencies charged with regulatory coordination and oversight.

A questionnaire to guide the collection of information on the mandate of institutions, their financial and human capacity, and the procedures that govern the regulatory process is available at the World Bank website (http://www.worldbank.org/trade/RASTI). Table 1.5 provides some excerpts from the questionnaire. For additional guidance, see OECD (1995, 2005, 2012) and World Bank (2010).

Table 1.5. Sample Questions for Mapping the Governance Framework

Issue	Sample questions
Institutional setting	
Mandate	• Has the agency the mandate and necessary authority to set tariffs for regulated entities; establish, modify, and monitor market and service quality rules; and investigate, adjudicate, and mediate on consumer complaints?
	• Does the institutional framework provide clear guidelines for the mandates and functions of each governmental unit/agency?
Human resources	• What is the staffing of the agency relative to its mandate?
	• What is the salary difference between agency employees and their counterparts in the private sector?
	• How long do professionals stay at the agency?
Financial resources	• Is the agency's budget sufficient to carry out its regular operations? What percentage of the regulatory agency's budget comes from the regular government budget? What percent comes from payments by regulated entities (for example, license fees) or consumers (for example, specific fees or taxes)?
Regulatory procedures	
General regulatory procedures	• Is there a law or regulation that governs the regulatory process as a whole?
	• Does each governmental unit/agency establish regulatory procedures?
	• Is a "map" of the regulatory process publicly available?
Standards and regulatory impact assessment	• Are agencies required to consider international standards during the regulatory process?
	• How are alternatives to regulation assessed? Are agencies required to formally state the alternatives considered in the proposal for regulation?
Interagency coordination	• Are other governmental units and agencies required to participate in the regulatory process?
	• What information is included in notifications to other agencies?
Public notification	• Are agencies required to make their regulatory activity public?
	• When does the agency make information public?
	• How does it do so?
Stakeholder consultations	• Are there formal public consultation mechanisms and procedures, including prior notification to regulated parties and other stakeholders?
	• Does the agency officially address the submissions received from stakeholders in the regulatory process?
Additional questions for the trade ministry	
Implementation of trade agreements	• Are there specific formal mechanisms in the regulatory decision-making process to promote compliance with international trade agreements?
	• Is there a specific government unit or agency charged with ensuring compliance with and implementation of international trade commitments?
	• How do agencies ensure nondiscrimination in the regulatory process?
Additional questions for independent regulatory agencies	
Institutional context	• How was the agency created?
	• Are appointments subject to approval by the legislature or one of its bodies?
	• Is approval from another institution required?
	• Did appointees who served less than a full term leave voluntarily or involuntarily?

A number of documents can assist in gathering information. Where available, a law on laws or similar decree can inform about the decision-making and regulatory processes. Laws and regulations creating independent agencies provide the mandate of the agency, interagency coordination, and stakeholder consultation. Information from these formal instruments should be compared with and complemented by actual regulatory practices as part of the assessment of the regulatory setting.

Interviews with government officials and stakeholders play a central role in the mapping of the institutional framework, because detailed information on the institutional setting is not usually publicly available in developing countries.

Policy makers can use the regulatory mapping to evaluate the institutional setting and procedures based on principles of good regulatory practices, including transparency, internal and public consultations, and efficiency. Internationally recognized guidelines such as those developed by the *OECD Guiding Principles for Regulatory Quality and Performance* (OECD 2005) or the *APEC–OECD Integrated Checklist on Regulatory Reform* (APEC–OECD 2005) and government manuals on domestic regulation (such as New Zealand's *Best Practice Guidelines* [State Services Commission 2004] and Australia's *Best Practice Regulation Handbook* [2010]) can serve as benchmarks.

Conclusion

Mapping of the regulatory framework on trade and investment in services entails identifying the laws and regulations that affect services and assessing the governance framework. Documents and websites provided in this module may provide relevant material for the mapping. However, obtaining detailed regulatory information requires field work in the country concerned. Substantive discussions with a wide range of government officials, representatives of the private sector, academics, and other domestic experts are essential to understanding how policies work in practice. Information garnered from field work may complement or contradict the information indicated by formal laws and regulations. Indeed, it often indicates that formal measures that appear restrictive are not so in practice, because they are not applied or because easy ways around them exist. Conversely, opaque administrative practices may make legal regimes that look open to services trade and investment restrictive in practice.

The main benefit of field work lies not in providing detailed information on law and regulations, however, but in providing insight into the policies and market conditions on services in the country. These insights reveal the environment in which services regulations must be implemented. Only based on a regulatory mapping that takes account of the country's social and economic background can analysts offer specific guidance on regulatory practices that allow a country to reap the benefits from services trade and investment while achieving other desired policy objectives.

References

APEC–OECD (Asia-Pacific Economic Cooperation and Organisation for Economic Co-operation and Development). 2005. *Integrated Checklist on Regulatory Reform.* Paris: APEC–OECD Co-operative Initiative on Regulatory Reform.

Australian Government. 2010. *Best Practice Regulation Handbook.* Canberra: Commonwealth of Australia.

Better Regulation Office. 2009. *Guide to Better Regulation.* Department of Premier and Cabinet, New South Wales, Australia.

Brown, Ashley, Jon Stern, Bernard Tenenbaum, and Defne Gencer. 2006. *Handbook for Evaluating Infrastructure Regulatory Systems.* Washington, DC: World Bank.

Investing across Borders (database). World Bank, Washington, DC. http://iab.worldbank.org/.

Marconini, Mario, and Pierre Sauvé. 2009. *Negotiating Trade in Services: A Practical Guide for Developing Countries.* Washington, DC: World Bank.

OECD (Organisation for Economic Co-operation and Development). 1995. *Recommendation of the Council on Improving the Quality of Regulation.* Paris: OECD.

———. 2002. *Managing the Request-Offer Process.* Paris: OECD.

———. 2005. *OECD Guiding Principles for Regulatory Quality and Performance.* Paris: OECD.

———. 2012. *Recommendation of the Council on Regulatory Policy and Governance.* Paris: OECD.

OECD Product Market Regulation Database. Organisation for Economic Co-operation and Development, Paris. http://www.oecd.org/economy/pmr.

State Services Commission. 2004. *Best Practice Guidelines for Departments Responsible for Regulatory Processes with Significant Commercial Implications.* Ministry of Economic Development, State Services Commission, Wellington, New Zealand.

World Bank. 2009. *Making It Work: "RIA Light" for Developing Countries.* Investment Climate Advisory Services, Washington, DC.

———. 2010. *Regulatory Quality and Competition Policy.* Investment Climate Advisory Services, Washington, DC.

———. 2012a. *Cambodia Services Trade Performance and Regulatory Framework Assessment.* Washington, DC: World Bank.

———. 2012b. "Trade Development: Helping Cambodia to Become a Sophisticated Services Exporter." Policy Note, Washington, DC.

World Bank Services Trade Restrictiveness Index (STRI). Washington, DC. http://iresearch.worldbank.org/servicetrade/home.htm.

WTO Integrated Trade Intelligence Portal. World Trade Organization, Geneva. https://www.wto.org/english/res_e/statis_e/itip_e.htm.

Wu, Irene. 2008. "Who Regulates Phones, Television, and the Internet? What Makes a Communications Regulator Independent and Why It Matters." *Perspectives on Politics* 6 (4): 769–83.

ASSESSING THE IMPACT OF SERVICES REGULATIONS: A REVIEW OF EMPIRICAL METHODS

Objectives

This module reviews the main empirical methods for assessing the impact of regulations on the provision of services. Upon completing it, readers will be able to:

- *Gather information on restrictions*
- *Score, classify, and construct regulatory indexes*
- *Estimate tariff equivalents of regulatory measures*
- *Estimate the level of restrictiveness when direct measures of regulation are not available*
- *Use econometric models to estimate the level of restrictiveness*

A quantitative assessment calculates the costs and benefits of maintaining or implementing regulations.[1] It is a critical component of a well-informed decision-making process and reform. Quantifying the impact of regulation can help policy makers choose the most efficient regulatory mix. It can help them both prioritize and design reforms.

This module offers practical guidance on sources of statistical data and methods that can be used in quantification exercises. Statistics on services trade and regulation are generally limited, especially in developing countries, sometimes making quantitative analysis impracticable. Quantitative assessment should therefore be considered an optional step that can complement the qualitative assessment described in module 1.

Even where statistics are available, there is no perfect way to conduct a quantitative assessment; every aspect of the process involves trade-offs. Impact estimations should therefore be interpreted as indications of orders of magnitude rather than precise estimates of impact.

With these caveats in mind, countries should attempt to undertake some degree of quantitative analysis when conducting a regulatory assessment. Such an assessment is particularly important in countries that do not have mechanisms such as regulatory impact analyses (RIAs) in place (see box 3.1 in module 3).

Many developing countries lack the resources or capacity to use highly sophisticated methodologies without hiring external experts. For this reason, this module does not describe in detail computable general equilibrium (CGE) models. Therefore, an economy-wide assessment of welfare is outside the scope of this review. The approaches described do provide options for estimating tariff equivalents, which are crucial inputs for assessing welfare gains and losses using CGE models.

Quantitative methods can be classified according to three not mutually exclusive taxonomies: whether they employ direct or indirect measures, whether they focus on sectoral or economy-wide outcomes, and whether they use a retrospective or a prospective approach. Direct methods use information on service restrictions and policy in econometric analyses to assess the impact of restrictions on certain outcomes. Indirect methods are used when direct information on restrictions is not available. In these cases, analysts estimate or infer the level of openness, restrictiveness, or contestability of a market by comparing it with a particular benchmark (normally a country that has no restrictions or is relatively open). The main limitations of indirect methods are that the resulting estimates may capture more than trade barriers and that it is usually difficult to link these estimates to a specific policy measure. For these reasons, this approach is less suitable to guide policy decisions than the direct approach.

Retrospective analyses quantify the impact of services restrictions using econometric estimations and information about past episodes of liberalization and deregulation. Prospective analyses try to project the impact of a further liberalization of services trade (for example, by means of

CGE models). They usually rely on estimations of tariff equivalents provided by retrospective analyses.

This module focuses on retrospective methods carried out through econometric analyses and on sectoral studies. It also presents two indirect methods, **gravity equations** and estimated markups across sectors and countries, and briefly examines CGE modeling.

Direct Methods

Many studies based on direct methods assess the impact of service regulation on a sector-by-sector basis. Researchers first gather information on restrictions and policies in a sector. They then use econometric models to estimate the impact of restrictions and policies on industry-specific measures of performance, such as prices, costs, profits, and quantities. An advantage of this method is that the impact on performance can be directly linked to a particular policy.

In the 2000s, the Australian Productivity Commission and the Australian National University conducted one of the most comprehensive studies of services sector regulation across industries and countries.[2] They collected information on restrictions in the banking (McGuire and Schuele 2000; Kalirajan and others 2000); telecommunications (Warren 2000); maritime transport (Kang 2000; McGuire, Schuele, and Smith 2000); wholesale and retail distribution (Kalirajan 2000); education (Kemp 2000); and professional services (Nguyen-Hong 2000) sectors in selected economies in Europe, Asia, and North and South America.[3]

The Organisation for Economic Co-operation and Development (OECD) has mapped services regulation and assessed the impact of restrictions in the electricity (Steiner 2001), telecommunications (Boylaud and Nicoletti 2001), and air passenger transport (Gönenç and Nicoletti 2001) sectors. Findlay (2011) summarizes a set of studies on the impact of policy and structural reforms in telecommunications, energy, and transport in Asia-Pacific Economic Cooperation (APEC) economies.

Direct methods typically involve some or all of the following steps:

- Gathering information on restrictions affecting the provision of services in a particular sector
- Translating qualitative information into quantitative measures, classifying regulations, and constructing a regulatory index
- Estimating the impact of regulations on the provision of services (price, cost, price-cost margin, quantity, or productivity) while controlling for other factors that may affect performance

- Using the results from the impact estimations to construct price, cost, or productivity impact measures as a proxy for tariff equivalents.

Policy makers can use information gathered from direct methods as an input for calculating tariff equivalents for a set of out-of-the-sample countries or assessing welfare gains and losses using CGE modeling.

Step 1: Gathering Information on Restrictions

Step 1 involves collecting information on both domestic and foreign regulations. Ideally, domestic information is obtained by conducting horizontal and sectoral regulatory mappings (as described in module 1). Analysts should also gather information on measurable indicators of the goals regulations seek to achieve and related implementation and enforcement costs.

To obtain information on regulations for a larger number of economies, some researchers rely on trade policy information. They collect data on countries' commitments under the frameworks of multilateral services trade negotiations at the World Trade Organization (WTO) (that is, the General Agreement on Trade in Services [GATS]) and preferential trade agreements. Secondary information can also be useful. It includes information gathered by international organizations (primarily the OECD, the WTO, the World Bank, the United Nations (UN) Conference on Trade and Development [UNCTAD], and the International Telecommunication Union [ITU]); by intergovernmental associations, such as APEC; and by governmental agencies such as the Office of the U.S. Trade Representative. Country surveys and sector-specific questionnaires can also provide information. Table 2.1 identifies some good sources of services policy information.

Using trade policy measures from countries' commitments and negotiating offers (also referred to as *schedules*) under the GATS has both advantages and disadvantages.[4] An advantage is the extensive country coverage: all 159 WTO members have provided information on commitments and negotiating offers. In addition, under the GATS framework, countries make commitments by services sector and mode of supply, allowing policy makers to construct indicators by sector, country, and mode of supply and to compare trade liberalization across countries.

A disadvantage relates to the **"positive listing"** approach. In a positive list, countries list or mention only the sectors they want to liberalize (*none,* for no limitations, in GATS terminology). If a country does not list a sector, it has not made a commitment to liberalize that sector (in GATS terminology, the sector is ***unbound***). Researchers

Table 2.1. Sources of Information on Regulatory Measures Affecting Trade and Investment in Services

Institution/type of information	Source or example
World Trade Organization (WTO)	
Services trade regulations (joint with the World Bank)	http://i-tip.wto.org/services/
General Agreement on Trade in Services (GATS) schedules	http://tsdb.wto.org/default.aspx
Database on GATS schedules, GATS proposals, and service regional trade agreements	Roy (2011); http://www.wto.org/english/tratop_e/serv_e/dataset_e/dataset_e.htm
GATS negotiating offers	
Regional trade agreements	http://rtais.wto.org/UI/PublicMaintainRTAHome.aspx
Trade policy reviews	http://www.wto.org/english/tratop_e/tpr_e/tpr_e.htm
Air services agreements	http://www.wto.org/asap/index.html
Background documents produced by the WTO Secretariat, for instance	S/C/W/270/ on air transport
World Bank	
Services Trade Restrictions Database and Services Trade Restrictiveness Index (STRI), which cover five key sectors: financial services (banking and insurance), telecommunications, retail distribution, transportation, and professional services	http://iresearch.worldbank.org/servicestrade/ Borchert, Gootiiz, and Mattoo (2012)
Regulation and supervision of banks database	http://econ.worldbank.org/WBSITE/EXTERNAL/EXTDEC/EXTRESEARCH/0,,contentMDK:20345037~pagePK:64214825~piPK:64214943~theSitePK:469382,00.html
Organisation for Economic Co-operation and Development (OECD)	
Product Market Regulation (PMR) survey	http://www.oecd.org/document/1/0,3746,en_2649_37443_2367297_1_1_1_37443,00.html
U.S. Trade Representative (USTR)	
National Trade Estimate (NTE) Report on Foreign Trade Barriers	http://www.ustr.gov/about-us/press-office/reports-and-publications/2013/NTE-FTB
Asia-Pacific Economic Cooperation (APEC)	
Individual Action Plans	http://www.apec-iap.org/

MODULE 2

typically assume that trade is restricted in unlisted sectors, but these sectors may be fully liberalized (see Gootiiz and Mattoo 2009).

When using GATS as a source of information on service regulations, officials should also consider three other limitations:

- GATS schedules of commitments do not necessarily reflect current regulatory regimes.
- Air transport regulations lie largely outside multilateral negotiations.[5]
- Some barriers to trade in services, including barriers associated with domestic regulations, are not explicitly listed in the GATS schedules.

Australia's Productivity Commission noted the last limitation in the studies it reviewed. It recognized that because of its reliance on different modes of supply, trade in services is subject to a wide set of **behind-the-border measures**. Services are subject not only to discriminatory regulations against foreign services suppliers but also to nondiscriminatory regulations—regulations that apply equally to domestic and foreign providers. Consequently, in addition to trade policy information, the Productivity Commission collected information on nondiscriminatory service regulations.

This information is valuable, but relying on different sources of information can undermine comparability across countries. Documentation of services regulation tends to be greater for developed than for developing countries. This difference could lead to the erroneous belief that countries for which data are available have more restrictive regimes.

Country surveys and sector-specific questionnaires can provide data on restrictions that are comparable across countries. The OECD Product Market Regulation (PMR) Indicators are examples. The PMR data come mainly from surveys of member countries (the OECD Regulatory Indicators Questionnaire). They are thereby highly comparable across countries. The 1998, 2003, and 2008 PMRs cover several nonmanufacturing sectors as well as network industries such as energy (electricity and gas); transport (air, rail, and road transport); communications (post and telecommunications); retail trade; and professional services.

The World Bank has compiled the Services Trade Restrictions Database (Borchert, Gootiiz, and Mattoo 2012). It contains information on an unprecedented range of countries and sectors: 103 countries; 5 services sectors (financial services, telecommunications, retail distribution, transportation, and professional services); and 18 subsectors. The database classifies services regulations based on their mode of supply.

The World Bank's Services Trade Restrictiveness Index (STRI) includes information from country surveys conducted between 2008 and 2010 on 79 developing countries. It indicates whether services policies discriminate against foreign services providers. It does not include information on domestic services regulations that apply equally to domestic and foreign suppliers.

Countries can benefit from previous studies and from the efforts of international organizations such as the OECD and the World Bank. Particularly useful are the Regulatory Assessment of Services Trade and Investment (RASTI) questionnaires (available at http://www.worldbank.org /trade/RASTI) and the questionnaire used to construct the World Bank's Services Trade Restrictions Database (http:// iresearch.worldbank.org/servicestrade/).

Based on the mapping conducted in module 1, analysts should also gather information on measurable indicators of the goals of services regulation as well as on implementation and enforcement costs.

Step 2: Scoring, Classifying, and Constructing Regulatory Indexes

Step 2 consists of creating quantitative measures (that is, translating qualitative information into scores); classifying regulations; and constructing regulatory indexes.

Scoring Regulations

Once regulations have been identified, their stringency must be translated into quantitative measures, typically by a system of scores. Table 2.2 shows scores for two banking sector measures. The first measure relates to the duration of stay of foreign executives, senior managers, and specialists. In this example, the scores range from 0 to 1; the more stringent a regulation, the higher the score. The second measure relates to restrictions on foreign ownership. In this case, a country's score is inversely related to the foreign ownership share allowed.

Table 2.2. Scoring Regulations in the Banking Sector

Type of restriction	Score	Regulation
Restrictions on duration of stay of executives, senior managers, and specialists	1.00	No temporary entry of executives, senior managers, or specialists allowed
	0.75	Entry allowed for stays up to 30 days
	0.50	Entry allowed for stays up to 60 days
	0.25	Entry allowed for stays up to 90 days
	0	Entry allowed for stays up to 120 days
Restrictions on foreign equity	1.00	Foreign ownership not permitted
	0.99–0.01	Inversely related to maximum share of foreign ownership allowed
	0	No restrictions on foreign ownership

A note of caution is warranted concerning the scoring process: when adding scores, analysts must consider the interaction between regulations. In some cases, a policy measure may be sufficient to completely close the market to foreign suppliers. In such a context, other regulations— on, for instance, the operation of foreign firms—will have no additional impact on the market under analysis. Treating restrictions as additive would therefore be flawed. When regulations are logically linked, analysts should take this information into account and try to incorporate it into the scoring system.

Classifying Regulations

Depending on the study's purpose, regulations can be classified according to predefined taxonomies. One common classification is shown in table 2.3, which classifies regulations based on (a) their impact on the establishment of a business and its ongoing operations and (b) whether they discriminate against foreign providers. Kalirajan (2000) and Nguyen-Hong (2000) use this type of classification.

Once restrictions on entry and establishment are separated from those on ongoing operations, the results can be used as inputs in a CGE model. In such models, restrictions affecting the entry of service suppliers can be modeled as restrictions on the movement of capital, and restrictions on ongoing operations can be modeled as affecting output.

Crozet, Milet, and Mirza (2011) use a slightly different type of classification, distinguishing restrictions affecting fixed costs (which may be associated with restrictions on entry) from restrictions affecting variable costs (which may affect ongoing operations). Jensen, Rutherford, and Tarr (2008) distinguish between discriminatory and nondiscriminatory policy measures. Their CGE model of the Tanzanian economy finds that the largest gains derive from liberalization of nondiscriminatory regulatory barriers.

Dihel and Shepherd (2007); Bottini, Marouani, and Munro (2011); and Borchert, Gootiiz, and Mattoo (2012) classify regulations based on mode of supply (table 2.4). This classification can help policy officials analyze interdependencies between modes of supply. For instance, restricting cross-border trade (Mode 1) could increase or decrease the effect of restricting commercial presence

(Mode 3). Officials could also use this type of classification to understand how different modes of supply affect performance variables.

In some cases, rather than rely on a predefined classification, it may be preferable to develop a classification system based on data analysis. One type of such analysis is principal component analysis (box 2.1).

Constructing Regulatory Indexes

Many regulations affect the provision of services, making comparison of the contestability of markets across countries difficult. Studies normally deal with this problem by constructing regulatory indexes that summarize in a single indicator a set of policies affecting the provision of services. Once the methodology is applied to several countries, the market contestability of a service category can be compared across economies.

An important issue is determining how regulations can be grouped or added in a single indicator. What weights should be assigned to individual regulations? The simplest method is to give restrictions equal weights (that is, simply averaging the regulation scores). This method has been used to construct regulatory indexes based on GATS commitments and offers (see, for example, Hoekman 1996, Eschenbach and Hoekman 2006, and Roy 2011).

Table 2.3. Assessing Banking Regulations Based on a Two-Dimensional Taxonomy

	Impact on entry/ establishment	Impact on ongoing operations
Nondiscriminatory	Number of banking licenses is restricted.	Banks are restricted in the manner in which they can raise funds.
Discriminatory	Number of foreign banking licenses is restricted.	Foreign banks are restricted in the manner in which they can raise funds.

Source: Adapted from McGuire 2003.

Table 2.4. Assessing Regulations in the Telecommunications, Engineering, and Banking Sectors Based on the Mode of Supply

Mode	Telecommunications	Engineering	Banking
1: Cross-border trade	Restrictions on leased lines or private networks, third-party resale and Internet telephony (VoIP), and connections of leased lines and private networks to the public switched telecommunications network (PSTN)	Restrictions on provision of cross-border engineering services or local presence requirement to provide the service	Limits on cross-border provision of deposits by foreign banks
2: Consumption abroad	Restrictions on provision of call-back services	Restrictions on the purchase of engineering services abroad by country's residents living abroad	Restrictions on the purchase of financial services by country's residents abroad
3: Commercial presence	Restrictions on foreign equity, joint venture arrangements, issuance of new licenses, screening and approval for new entry	Limits on ownership of engineering firms by nonprofessionals; restriction on form of establishment (for example, incorporation prohibited or permitted)	Restrictions on provision of nonbanking services, such as insurance and securities services
4: Movement of natural persons	Limits on duration of stay of executives, senior managers, or specialists; restrictions on nationality of members of company's board of directors; and restrictions on issuance of working permits and visas subject to, for instance, professional qualifications	Burdensome requirements or procedures for licensing and accreditation of foreign professionals; Imposition of economic needs tests for granting of work permits	Limits on duration of stay of executives, senior managers, or specialists; restrictions on nationality of members of company's board of directors; and restrictions on issuance of working permits and visas subject to, for instance, professional qualifications

Source: Adapted from Dihel and Shepherd 2007.

MODULE 2

Another common method is to use a priori judgments about the relative economic importance of different restrictions. Kalirajan (2000), for example, considers commercial presence the most important mode of supply in distribution services and assigns restrictions affecting foreign investments heavier weights.

A third alternative is to use statistical techniques, such as **factor analysis**, in particular principal component analysis, to derive weights based on data characteristics. (Figure B2.1.1 provides an example applied to the energy sector.)

Finally, econometric analysis can be used to estimate the relative impact of regulations on a variable of service

---

Box 2.1. Principal Component Analysis of the Electricity Sector

Principal component analysis (PCA) is a statistical technique that summarizes information from a large set of variables into a reduced number of new variables referred to as *factors* or *latent variables*.

These latent variables can be used not only to classify regulations but also to group them and to construct summary indicators such as regulatory indexes. Using the latent variables, analysts can plot countries visually, to show how countries are clustered.

Steiner (2001) provides an example of PCA applied to services regulations (see also Nicoletti, Scarpetta, and Boylaud 2000; Gönenç and Nicoletti 2001; Boylaud and Nicoletti 2001; Barth, Caprio, and Levine 2004; Fontagné and Mitaritonna 2009; and Bottini, Marouani, and Munro 2008). She assesses the impact of liberalization and privatization on efficiency and price in the electricity industry. As a first step, she collected information on energy regulations for 19 OECD countries over a 10-year time period. She then clustered the 13 original regulatory variables (the rows in table B2.1.1) into 3 factors or latent variables (the columns in table B2.1.1).

The factors are linear combinations of the original variables and are therefore correlated with them. Thus, although the method does not provide an explicit economic interpretation of the factors, they can be interpreted by their correlation with the original variables, in this case the 13 original regulatory variables. The first factor in the table is highly correlated with the first eight regulatory variables, which are related to the degree of liberalization of the energy market. Accordingly, Steiner renamed factor 1 "liberalization." Factor 2 was correlated mainly with regulations related to the degree of privatization of the market (rows 9–11). Steiner therefore relabeled it "privatization."

Subsequently, countries can be rescored and plotted using the liberalization and privatization variables, as shown in figure B2.1.1. The liberalization and privatization variables can be thought of as regulatory indexes, as they combine different regulations in a single indicator that can be used to produce countries' rankings.

Once the countries are plotted, clusters of countries can be identified. Steiner identifies five groups. One is formed by a single country, the United Kingdom (GBR), which scores high on both liberalization and privatization. At the opposite end, in the bottom left-hand corner of figure B2.1.1, is a large cluster of economies with low scores on both liberalization and privatization.

In order to conduct a PCA, the regulatory variables should be correlated. If regulations correlate, then they carry similar information, and the PCA is capable of summarizing the information into a reduced number of variables.

Sometimes it proves difficult to give an interpretation to the factors in economic terms. This problem might prevent researchers from implementing this approach.

The factors are by construction orthogonal (that is, the correlation between factors equals 0). Therefore, it could prove useful to include them rather than the original regulatory variables in the econometric analysis, in order to avoid **multicollinearity** (the correlation of two or more variables) in step 3 (described in the next section).

Table B2.1.1. Identification of Factors through Principal Component Analysis of Regulations in the Energy Sector

Regulation	Factor 1: Liberalization	Factor 2: Privatization	Factor 3: Ancillary regulation
1. Liberalization	0.928	0.052	−0.083
2. Time to liberalization	0.744	−0.166	0.114
3. Third-party access	0.827	0.122	0.152
4. Unbundling of generation and transmission	0.909	0.120	0.121
5. Vertical integration	0.759	0.093	0.38
6. Interaction of integration and ownership	0.615	0.526	0.369
7. Wholesale pool	0.932	0.104	−0.081
8. Choice threshold	−0.711	−0.259	0.497
9. Privatization	0.023	0.930	−0.157
10. Private ownership	0.126	0.900	0.011
11. Time to privatization	0.093	0.836	0.197
12. Price regulation	0.207	−0.254	0.369
13. State preference for renewable technology	0.003	0.233	0.817

Source: Steiner 2001.

(continued on next page)

Box 2.1. *(continued)*

Figure B2.1.1. Identification of Clusters of Countries through Principal Component Analysis of Regulations in the Energy Sector

Electricity supply industry, 1986–96

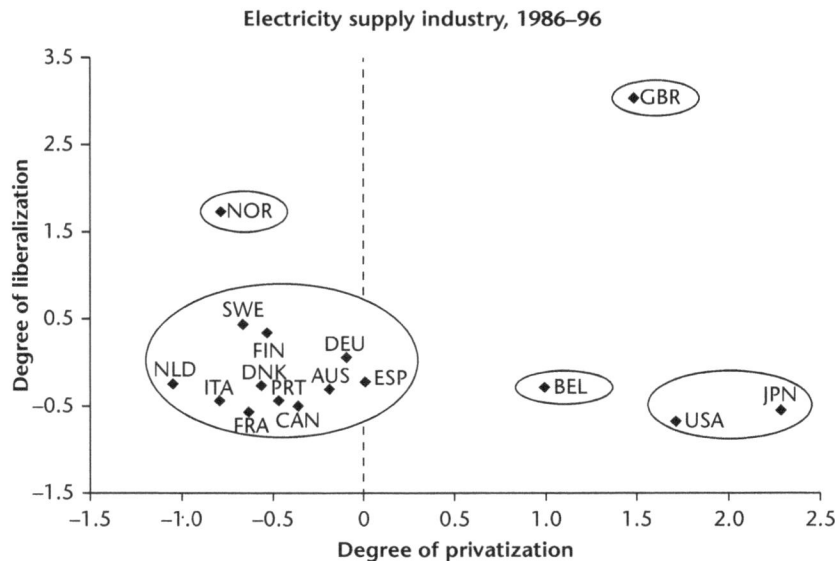

Source: Steiner 2001.

MODULE 2

performance, and the resulting coefficient estimates can be used to construct regulatory indicators.

All of these methods suffer from limitations; the choice of method will depend on the study's purpose. On the one hand, using averages is simple, transparent, and objective. On the other hand, assigning equal weight to regulations fails to account for the varying economic importance of individual restrictions. Therefore, it is not very informative about the level of restrictiveness of different regulatory regimes.

Using a priori judgments—based on expert or industry opinions, for example—might better analyze the restrictiveness of the regulatory regime. But these judgments are contentious and subjective.

PCA weights are strictly data based; regulations with higher in-sample variation receive heavier weights in this method. The PCA is thus objective but not very informative about the level of restrictiveness. Another limitation of PCA is that weights are not stable. Indeed, they are likely to change with the data sample. Thus, applying them to different country and year samples is likely to be inappropriate.[6]

Different weighting methodologies may result in different indicator values, which could affect country rankings. Therefore, it is important to test the sensitivity of the regulatory indexes and the resulting country rankings to different weighting techniques.

In theory, using econometric analysis results in an objective indicator that is meaningful in economic terms.

In practice, the lack of in-sample variation of some regulations and the presence of multicollinearity among them frequently prevent researchers from conducting econometric analysis.

Step 3: Estimating the Impact of Regulation

Step 3 consists of estimating the impact of regulation on measures of economic performance while controlling for other factors that might affect the variables.

Measures of Economic Performance

Because trade barriers in services typically operate behind the border, studies usually quantify the barriers' effects on behind-the-border measures of performance (Dee 2011; see annex table 2A.1). Except for studies on the international transport sector, most studies rely on behind-the-border measures of economic performance (dependent variable). (Measures of economic performance in the transport sector relate mainly to trade rather than behind-the-border measures. For instance, fares and the number of international flights are used as dependent variables in studies on air transport services.)

Many studies investigate how service regulations affect the ability of service suppliers to set prices above marginal costs (that is, monopolistic prices) by using markups as a measure of service performance. Several studies use price-cost margins to assess the effects of service regulations on professional services, telecommunications, distribution, and insurance and net interest margins for the banking sector. Studies of the energy and the telecommunications industries have investigated the impact of regulation on domestic prices; studies on telecommunications have analyzed the impact of regulation on the number of telephone lines and mobile subscribers per inhabitant (penetration rate).

Cost-Creating versus Rent-Creating Regulations

The empirical literature recognizes the need to distinguish cost-creating from rent-creating regulations. The first type prevents firms from operating efficiently, pushing up variable costs. The second type protects existing firms from competition, allowing them to set monopolistic prices and capture rents. This distinction is important because restrictions have different impacts on welfare depending on their type. If services restrictions are cost creating, removing them may yield greater welfare gains than if they are rent creating (Francois and Hoekman 2010). Imposition of a rent-creating restriction may have only a redistributive effect (that is, it transfers rent from the government to the private sector or from domestic to foreign firms). In contrast, imposition of a cost-creating restriction creates inefficiencies, thus affecting the optimal allocation of resources and reducing production to below optimal levels.

To identify whether restrictions are cost creating or rent creating, analysts need data on prices (or markups) and costs.[7] Because these data are not readily available (except for the banking sector), many studies rely on price-cost margins. They interpret regulations as rent creating when regulations increase price-cost margins and as cost creating when they reduce them. This approach may underestimate the real impact of regulations. For instance, a regulation could be cost creating but services suppliers could increase prices and pass on to consumers the higher costs generated by the new regulation. Under such circumstances, the econometric estimation would not identify any regulatory impact.[8]

Individual Restrictions versus a Regulatory Index

Lack of data often limits empirical work on services. Coverage of countries and years is spotty, leaving too little data for estimation models. Moreover, the lack of in-sample variation of some regulations and the presence of multicollinearity frequently prevent researchers from including regulations separately in the same estimation model.

Using a regulatory index can be a good alternative. Regulatory indexes have important limitations, however. First, this approach does not allow users to differentiate between barriers that actually restrict trade (that is, binding restrictions) from those that do not because they are redundant (Whalley 2004). Second, the use of regulatory indexes may overlook the different impacts regulations have on performance variables and the fact that different regulations may cancel out each other's effects.[9] Third, this approach does not allow analysts to investigate the potential interdependence of regulations—that is, whether other regulations augment or diminish the effect of a particular regulation.

In their estimation models, Fink, Mattoo, and Rathindran (2003) investigate the impact of privatization and competition on labor productivity and the number of telephone main lines per inhabitant. They find that privatization and competition independently lead to significant improvements in performance and that they are complementary—that is, larger gains accrue when both are present.

Given the limitations of using individual regulations and regulatory indexes, analysts often seek an intermediate solution, namely, subindicators. To construct subindicators, analysts can use a regulatory taxonomy or factor analysis.

Control Variables and Panel Data

To ensure that the impact of service regulation on the performance variable is not the result of omitted variables, analysts must collect data on nonregulatory restrictions that may also affect the service performance. The set of control variables is sector specific. It may involve collecting information on private sector practices, such as buyer-supplier networks in distribution services and existing agreements in maritime services; variables of market structure; and firm-specific variables, such as size.

Alternatively, depending on the level of data disaggregation, analysts can use panel data techniques, such as fixed effects, to control for sector characteristics. This technique is possible when firm-level data for a number of countries, bilateral data, or data for several years are available. Many studies use firm-level data; bilateral data are frequently used for transport services. In contrast, few studies use data with time variation, mainly because regulatory data were inconsistently collected over time, making it difficult to control for country characteristics to investigate whether the sequencing of policies played a role.[10] For instance, using data that expanded from 1985 to 1999, Fink, Mattoo, and Rathindran (2003) find that the sequence of reform matters. Their results indicate that mainline penetration tends to be lower when competition is introduced after, rather than at the same time, as privatization.

Regulations with Legitimate Objectives

Some regulations guarantee a market's contestability while addressing environmental, equity, and other social objectives. Indeed, as Doove and others (2001) note, "In many service industries, the relevant question is not whether to regulate, but rather what type of regulation is the most appropriate, and at what level."

The absence of regulation can have an adverse effect on the economy, but too much regulation can reduce welfare as well. In a study of maritime transport services, Clark, Dollar, and Micco (2004) find that some level of regulation positively affects port efficiency but excessive regulation reverses these gains.

Ideally, the regulatory assessment should focus not only on the costs but also on the benefits of the imposition of regulations. It should identify whether regulations have brought about desired outcomes in environmental, equity, and social objectives.

Most studies investigate associated costs—whether regulations increase firms' rents (price-cost margins), production costs, and prices or reduce efficiency and the supply of services in a market. Most studies include all regulations—whether they pursue legitimate objectives or not—in the construction of regulatory indexes and econometric estimations. This approach fails to yield a complete picture of the costs and benefits of regulation. Only when policy makers have information on the trade-offs involved in regulation can they identify whether regulations are more burdensome than necessary and whether other regulations may be equally effective but less costly.

Most studies recognize this limitation. Gönenç and Nicoletti (2001, 186), who study airfares to assess the impact of regulation on the air passenger sector, point out that "while price outcomes are studied in detail, limitations on available data made it impossible to consider the implications of liberalization for service quality and consumer convenience." By the same token, by focusing on fares, the authors disregard benefits from regulations, such as reductions in noise, pollution, and accidents.

Among the studies applying direct methods listed in annex table 2A.1, only Barth, Caprio, and Levine (2004) adopt a cost-benefit approach. Using the World Bank's database on bank regulation and supervision, they assess the impact of regulations and supervisory practices in the banking sector in 107 countries. They analyze the impact of a regulatory regime not only on the costs regulations may impose (by, for example, increasing banks' interest margins and the number of nonperforming loans) but also on the potential benefits of the regulatory framework (such as improving banking system stability and bank development).

In the banking sector, regulators may restrict bank activities in order to prevent conflicts of interest and risky behavior that could lead to a crisis. They typically try to do so by restricting banks' involvement in activities such as securities, insurance, and real estate investment.[11] Whether such restrictions are effective is not clear: Barth, Caprio, and Levine (2004) find no clear relationship between nonperforming loans and restrictions on bank activities. Instead, they find that restricting the scope of bank activities has a negative impact on bank development and increases the incidence of banking crises. Their results suggest that some policy measures that seem to have legitimate objectives may not bring about desired outcomes, thus highlighting the need for conducting cost-benefit analyses and a regulatory assessment.

Step 4: Constructing Tariff Equivalents

RASTI can use impact assessments of service regulations (step 3) to construct tariff equivalents.[12] A **tariff equivalent** (also known as an **ad valorem equivalent**) is the tariff that would yield the same effect as a nontariff barrier. Tariff equivalents are used as inputs in assessing the impact of regulation on welfare through a CGE model.

The tariff equivalents in the studies reviewed in this module capture the impact of full liberalization of the services sectors on costs/prices. They are obtained by comparing the service costs/prices that would have existed in the absence of the regulatory restrictions with actual costs/prices given the restrictions.[13]

This approach raises the problem of determining an appropriate benchmark. As Doove and others (2001) point out, using a fully unregulated world as a benchmark fails to recognize that some regulations may have legitimate objectives. Using econometric estimations, they use as a benchmark the regulatory regime that brings about the best estimated economic outcome, which in practice does not necessarily relate to the most liberalized regime.

Another problem—and probably the major criticism of constructing tariff equivalents from price and cost impacts—lies in its economic underpinning. As Deardorff and Stern (2008) describe, there is only one case in which the price change resulting from a restriction equals the import tariff that brings about the same economic effect (that is, in which price changes equal the tariff equivalent measure). This scenario is a world in which markets are highly competitive: a world without **market failures**, in which products are perfect substitutes, and in which no country is big enough to have an impact on world prices. These conditions are not met in the services sector, where market failures are frequent and the level of product differentiation is high.

MODULE 2

In the absence of perfect competition, the price change resulting from an imposed restriction is typically smaller than its tariff equivalent. Therefore, constructing tariff equivalents from price and cost impacts tends to underestimate the level of restriction, resulting in conservative measures of barriers and gains from liberalization in CGE models.

Some studies apply estimates from previous econometric analyses to countries not included in the estimation sample to estimate tariff equivalents. This technique is useful when countries have resource constraints. Analysts must still collect information on regulations, score regulations, and construct regulatory indexes for the out-of-the-sample country. Once analysts construct regulatory indexes, they can estimate tariff equivalents by using coefficients from previous cross-country analyses without conducting another econometric estimation (as shown in the next section).

Doove and others (2001) use OECD results to project tax equivalents for non–OECD countries. Dee (2005) calculates tariff equivalents for several services categories in Vietnam, based mainly on research by the Productivity Commission and Australian National University. Researchers have drawn on the work of the Productivity Commission to calculate tariff equivalents for out-of-the-sample countries in Armenia (Jensen and Tarr 2011); Kazakhstan (Jensen and Tarr 2007); Kenya (Balistreri, Rutherford, and Tarr 2009); the Russian Federation (Jensen and others 2004); and Tanzania (Jensen and others 2008). Whether the econometric sample in the previous analysis is representative enough to be applied to the out-of-the-sample countries is the main concern of this approach.

Steps 1–4 Applied to the Engineering Sector

Two studies construct tax equivalents using the coefficient estimates obtained in their econometric estimations. Nguyen-Hong (2000) constructs regulatory indexes for accounting, architecture, engineering, and law in Asia Pacific, Europe, and the Americas, examining 34 economies for the first three subsectors and 29 for legal services. He also conducts an impact analysis for engineering using firm-level accounting data for 20 economies.

Dihel and Shepherd (2007) construct regulatory indexes for banking, insurance, telecommunications (fixed and mobile), engineering, and distribution services for selected countries in Africa, Asia, Central and Eastern Europe, Latin America, and the Middle East. Their country coverage ranges from 10 to 29, depending on the data available. They conduct impact assessments for each sector under analysis. For engineering services, they estimate the impact of service regulations in 10 economies.

Step 1: Gathering Information on Restrictions

Nguyen-Hong (2000) and Dihel and Shepherd (2007) rely on secondary sources for information on the engineering sector. Nguyen-Hong gathers information on 17 categories of regulations using the OECD Inventory of Measures Affecting Trade in Professional Services (OECD 1996), APEC Individual Action Plans, and WTO Trade Policy Reviews. Dihel and Shepherd draw on OECD projects on trade in services in transition economies carried out by the Trade Directorate, data from the Organization of American States, National Trade Estimates from the *Report on Foreign Trade Barriers* of the U.S. Trade Representative, GATS schedules, and product market regulation.

Step 2: Scoring, Classifying, and Constructing Regulatory Indexes

With the information on the 17 categories of regulations, both research teams classify regulations and estimate their quantitative effect using a system of scores. Dihel and Shepherd (2007) classify regulations by mode of supply (table 2.5). Nguyen-Hong (2000) uses the classification shown in table 2.6. The 17 categories of regulations are first classified based on whether they apply equally to domestic and foreign services providers and whether they treat foreigners in a discriminatory way. They are then classified based on whether they affect entry of new services providers or the operations of service providers that have already entered the market.

Nguyen-Hong and Dihel and Shepherd employ a similar system of scores. Table 2.7 shows the scores Nguyen-Hong applied to the 17 regulations.

Table 2.5. Regulatory Indexes for Engineering Services in Selected Countries, by Mode of Supply

Country	Aggregate	Mode 1	Mode 2	Mode 3	Mode 4
Malaysia	2.01	1.07	1.28	2.72	0.53
China	1.71	2.15	0	1.64	1.53
Indonesia	1.57	2.15	2.57	0.96	1.6
Brazil	1.42	2.15	2.57	1.01	1.21
Thailand	1.39	2.15	0	1.73	0.72
Chile	1.04	2.15	2.57	0.16	1.56
Philippines	0.73	2.15	2.57	0.1	1.59
Singapore	0.56	2.15	0	0.1	0.88
Argentina	0.51	0	0	0.1	0.65
Russian Federation	0.46	1.07	0	0.1	0.82

Source: Adapted from Dihel and Shepherd 2007.
Note: Scores range from 0 to 1; the more restrictive a regulation, the higher the score. Mode 1 = cross-border trade; Mode 2 = consumption abroad; Mode 3 = commercial presence; Mode 4 = presence of natural persons.

Table 2.6. Taxonomy for Classifying Regulations of Engineering Services

	Impact on entry/establishment	Impact on operations
Nondiscriminatory	• Form of establishment • Investment and ownership by nonprofessional investors • Licensing and accreditation of domestic professionals (scores additive)	• Activities reserved by law to the profession • Multidisciplinary practices • Advertising, marketing, and solicitation • Fee setting
Discriminatory	• Foreign partnership/association/joint venture • Investment and ownership by foreign professionals • Nationality/citizenship requirements • Residency and local presence • Quotas/economic tests on the number of foreign professionals and firms • Licensing and accreditation of foreign professionals • Movement of people (permanent)	• Licensing requirements on management • Other restrictions (scores additive) • Movement of people (temporary)

Source: Adapted from Nguyen-Hong 2000.

Table 2.7. Scores and Weights Used in Nguyen-Hong's Study of Regulation of Engineering Services

Restriction category	Score	Weight	Apply to domestic providers?
Barriers to establishment			
Form of establishment		0.08	Yes
Prohibition on incorporation	1.0		No
Some form of incorporation permitted	0.5		No
No restrictions	0		No
Foreign partnership/association/joint venture		0.08	No
Prohibition on partnership/association/joint venture with foreign professionals	1.0		No
Partnership/joint venture with foreign professionals required	0.5		No
No restrictions	0		No
Investment and ownership by foreign professionals		0.05	No
Investment and ownership by nonprofessional investors		0.05	Yes
Nationality/citizenship requirements		0.135	No
Nationality required to qualify, become member of professional body, or practice	1.0		No
Nationality required to obtain professional title, but practice is relatively free	0.25		No
No restrictions	0		No
Residency and local presence		0.135	No
Permanent or prior residency (more than 12 months) required	1.0		No
Less than 12 months prior residency	0.75		No
Prior residency required for local training	0.5		No
Domicile or representative office only	0.25		No
No restrictions	0		No
Quotas/economic tests on the number of foreign professionals and firms		0.1	No
Quotas/economic needs tests	1		No
Some restrictions apply	0.5		No
No restrictions	0		No
Licensing and accreditation of foreign professionals		0.1	No
Local retraining required for full license	1.0		No
Local examination required in all cases	0.75		No
Case-by-case assessment of foreign qualification/license	0.5		No
Aptitude tests	0.25		No
Foreign license/qualifications sufficient to practice	0		No
Licensing and accreditation of domestic professionals (scores additive)			Yes
Compulsory membership of domestic professionals (scores additive)			
Professional examination requirements	0.25		No

(continued on next page)

Table 2.7. Scores and Weights Used in Nguyen-Hong's Study of Regulation of Engineering Services *(continued)*

Restriction category	Score	Weight	Apply to domestic providers?
Practical experience requirements	0.25		No
Higher education requirements	0.25		No
Movement of people (permanent)		0.02	No
No entry of executives, senior managers, or specialists	1.0		No
Executives, specialists, or senior managers can stay a period of up to 1 year	0.8		No
Executives, specialists, or senior managers can stay a period of up to 2 years	0.6		No
Executives, specialists, or senior managers can stay a period of up to 3 years	0.4		No
Executives, specialists, or senior managers can stay a period of up to 4 years	0.2		No
Executives, specialists, or senior managers can stay a period of 5 or more years	0		No
			No
Barriers to ongoing operations			No
Activities reserved by law to the profession		0.05	Yes
4 core activities and over	1.0		No
3 core activities	0.75		No
2 core activities	0.5		No
1 core activity	0.25		No
None	0		No
Multidisciplinary practices		0.05	Yes
Prohibition on partnership with other professionals	1.0		No
Majority partnership required	0.5		No
No restrictions	0		No
Advertising, marketing, and solicitation		0.05	Yes
Advertising, marketing, and solicitation restricted	1.0		No
Some form of advertising, marketing, or solicitation allowed	0.5		No
No restrictions	0		No
Fee setting		0.05	Yes
Mandatory minimum or maximum fees	1.0		No
Restrictions for some groups or activities	0.5		No
No restrictions	0		No
Licensing requirements on management		0.02	No
All directors/managers or at least a majority of them must be nationals or residents	1.0		No
At least one director/manager must be a national or resident	0.75		No
Directors and managers must be locally licensed	0.5		No
Directors and managers must be domiciled	0.25		No
No restrictions	0		No
Other restrictions (scores additive)		0.02	No
Restrictions on hiring professionals	0.33		No
Restrictions on the use of firm's international names	0.33		No
Government procurement: restrictions toward foreigners	0.33		No
No restrictions	0		No
Movement of people (temporary)		0.01	No
No temporary entry of executives, senior managers, or specialists	1.0		No
Temporary entry of executives, senior managers, or specialists up to 30 days	0.75		No
Temporary entry of executives, senior managers, or specialists up to 60 days	0.5		No
Temporary entry of executives, senior managers, or specialists up to 90 days	0.25		No
Temporary entry of executives, senior managers, or specialists over 90 days	0		No

Source: Adapted from Nguyen-Hong 2000.

MODULE 2

For each category of regulations, the scores range from 0 to 1; the more stringent a regulation in a country, the higher the score. Score is inversely related to maximum equity participation permitted in a professional firm. For example, maximum ownership of 49 percent receives a score of 0.51. Both research teams compile the scores of individual regulations into regulatory indexes (figure 2.1). For each country, they construct a global indicator and subindicators based on the taxonomy chosen. The two studies employ different weighting methods. Nguyen-Hong uses a subjective set of weights, in which heavier weights are given to categories considered to have greater impact on services trade and activity. He assigns the heaviest weight to regulations on the nationality and residency of professionals. To avoid subjectivity in allocating weights to restrictions, Dihel and Shepherd (2007) apply principal component analysis (PCA). They construct indicators using the first factor of the PCA.

Step 3: Constructing Econometric Models

Both research teams collected accounting data on the price-cost margins of engineering firms to use as a dependent variable in their econometric model. They used information on industry- and firm-specific characteristics as control variables (that is, to isolate the effect of service regulations on firms' profits from other factors influencing firms' price-cost margins). Some of the control variables they used included the concentration of the engineering

services market (a proxy for market structure at the industry level) and some firm-level characteristics, such as size and market share.

Both teams conducted cross-sectional analysis in which they compare regulatory impact across countries but not over time. Both used a version of the following simplified model:

$$\ln(PCM_{ij}) = \beta_0 + \beta_1 RI_i + \sum_{k=1\ldots K} \alpha_k X_i$$

$$+ \sum_{f=1\ldots F} \delta_f X_{ij} + \mu_{ij} \qquad (2.1)$$

where the price-cost margin (PCM_{ij}) charged by engineering firm j in country i is explained by the country's Regulatory Index (RI_i) and a set of control variables (X), of which K variables are industry specific (X_i) and F are firm specific (X_{ij}). In both studies, the dependent variable (the price-cost margin) is calculated as a firm's earnings before interest and taxes plus accounting depreciation, all divided by revenues. Regarding the regulatory index, the authors include the subindicators as explanatory variables (hence, Dihel and Shepherd estimate the regulatory impacts by mode of supply, and Nguyen-Hong estimates the regulatory impacts using the two-way classification). In the model, μ_{ij} is an error term and β_0, β_1, α_k, and δ_f are the

MODULE 2

Figure 2.1. Regulatory Indexes for Engineering Services in Selected Economies

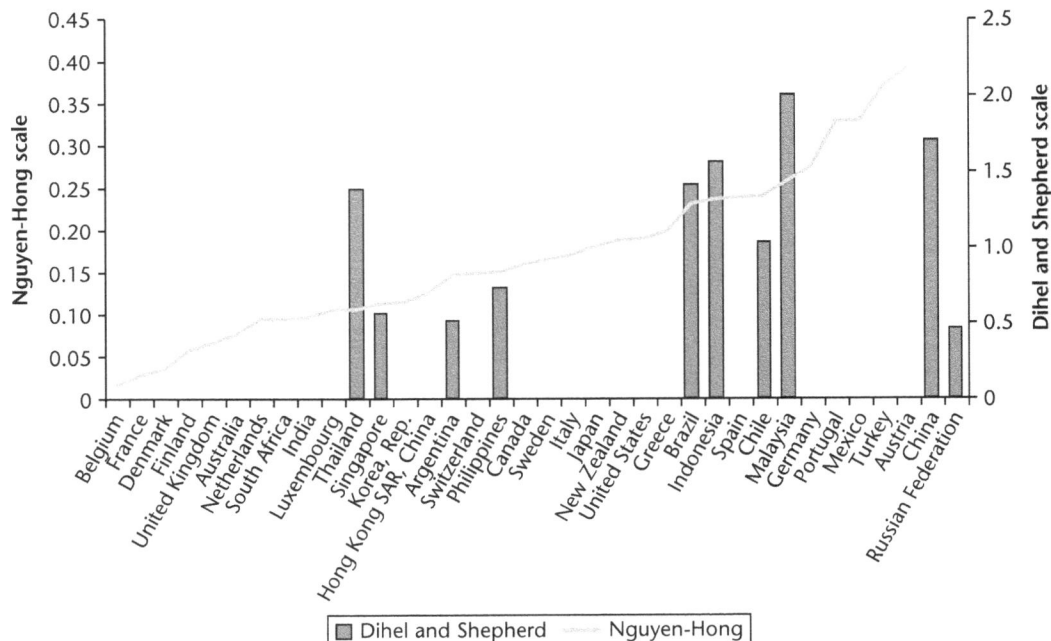

Sources: Nguyen-Hong 2000; Dihel and Shepherd 2007.

coefficients to be estimated. In step 4, the coefficient on the regulatory index (β_1) is used to estimate countries' tariff equivalents.

Step 4: Assessing Impact on Price, Cost, and Productivity
Using the estimation model in equation 2.1, the authors estimate tariff equivalents using the following equation:

$$Tariff\ equivalent_i \cong 100\left[\frac{PCM_{ij} - PCM_{0j}}{PCM_{0j}}\right]$$

$$\cong 100\left[e^{\beta_1 RI_i} - 1\right] \qquad (2.2)$$

In this equation, the tariff equivalent is calculated as the difference, in percentage terms, between what the price-cost margin of a firm would be in the absence of regulatory restrictions (PCM_{0j}) and what it actually is (PCM_{ij}), given the level of restrictions in the country where the firm operates. All other things held constant, the tariff equivalent can be estimated for each country by using the last terms in equation 2.2—that is, by using the coefficient on the regulatory index β_1 and the actual level of a country's regulatory index RI_i.

The tariff equivalent is proportional to a country's regulatory index (although the relationship is not linear): a country with a higher regulatory index has a higher tariff equivalent. Therefore, whenever regulatory indexes or tariff equivalents are used, countries' rankings must be the same, as in Dihel and Shepherd (2007). However, the magnitude is different. For instance, among the 10 countries in their analysis, Malaysia has the most restrictive regime, with a regulatory index of 2. Using this information and equation 2.2, Dihel and Shepherd estimate Malaysia's tariff equivalent to be 3.72 percent.

Although the principle is always the same, the formula for calculating the tariff equivalent depends on the form of equation 2.1. Nguyen-Hong (2000) does not include the dependent variable in its log form but instead uses the price-cost margin directly. In this case, the tariff equivalent will depend not only on β_1 but also on the price and cost of engineering services in each country. Countries' rankings from tariff equivalents and regulatory indexes may therefore differ.

Figure 2.2 compares the tariff equivalents and regulatory indexes obtained in Nguyen-Hong. In most cases, the two measures are similar. Austria, which has the most restrictive regime, has a regulatory index of 0.4 and an estimated tariff equivalent of 14.5 percent. At the other extreme, Belgium, which has the least restrictive regime, has a regulatory indicator of 0.02 and an estimated tariff equivalent of 0.5 percent. The tariff equivalents indicate that further liberalization of engineering services would reduce prices by 0.5 percent in Belgium and 14.5 percent in Austria.

Figure 2.2. Tariff Equivalents and Regulatory Indexes in Engineering Services in Selected Economies

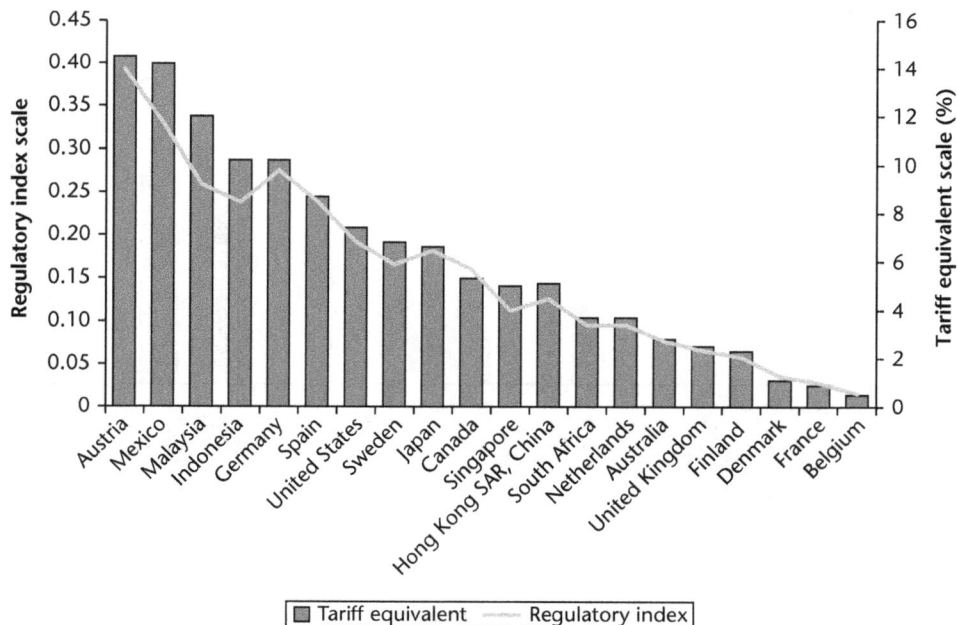

Source: Adapted from Nguyen-Hong 2000.

The results from the estimation model in Nguyen-Hong show that services regulation has a positive impact on engineering firms' profits (that is, price-cost margins). As there is no plausible explanation of why regulations would decrease firms' costs, the increase in profits is interpreted as the result of an increase in the price of engineering services. For this reason, the estimated tariff equivalents in Nguyen-Hong are referred to as the price impact of regulatory regimes.

Indirect Methods

Some studies employ indirect methods to estimate barriers to trade and investment in services. Researchers use these methods when they do not have information on restrictions. They estimate or infer the level of openness, restrictiveness, or contestability of a market by comparing countries with a benchmark. This approach is less suitable than direct measures as a guide to policy decisions, because the measures may capture more than trade barriers and because it is difficult to link indirect estimates to a specific policy measure. It is necessary, however, where direct information is unavailable.

The simplest indirect method is the price gap, which compares product prices in countries that are similar except for their level of restrictions. The price differences are assumed to reflect the countries' differences in trade barriers. The price gap method has been widely used to estimate ad valorem equivalents of nontariff measures in agriculture, where prices are associated with relatively homogeneous products (see, for instance, Cadot, Malouche, and Saez 2012). It has been deemed inappropriate for services because of sector characteristics such as the high level of product differentiation and the incidence of monopolistic behavior, which imply that price differences across countries may not reflect barriers to trade but rather monopolistic pricing or product differentiation such as service quality (see, for instance Dee 2005; Deardorff and Stern 2008; McGuire 2008; and Francois and Hoekman 2010).

Other indirect methods involve estimating trade costs through discrepancies between actual and predicted trade flows by means of gravity equations and comparing estimated markups across countries and sectors. Both methods are examined in the sections that follow.

Gravity Approach

Gravity equations estimate import flows between pairs of countries. After estimating them, analysts compare each country's actual and predicted import flows and then compare them with those of a benchmark economy. The result is indicative of trade barriers. In addition to allowing policy makers to compare trade barriers across countries and sectors, this approach allows them to estimate tariff equivalents that can be used as inputs in CGE models. (Annex table 2A.2 identifies some studies employing this approach.)

As shown in equation 2.3, the gravity equation is a log-linear specification, in which trade (M) between exporting country i and importing country j is positively influenced by the size of each country and negatively affected by the distance between countries:[14]

$$\ln M_{ij} = \beta_0 + \beta_1 \ln GDP_i + \beta_2 \ln GDP_j$$
$$- \beta_3 \ln Dist_{ij} + \sum_k \alpha_k X_{ij} + \varepsilon_{ij} \qquad (2.3)$$

Unlike in merchandise trade, distance in services does not reflect transport costs (except for transport services). In this sector, the distance variable reflects transaction costs between exporting and importing countries. Gravity equations also include an array of variables and dummy variables reflecting other determinants of transaction costs, such as trade policy, a common language, and past colonial ties.

Once equation 2.3 is estimated for a set of exporting and importing countries, a tariff equivalent can be estimated, as follows:

$$-\sigma \ln(\textit{tariff equivalent}_j) = \ln\left(\frac{\overline{M}_j^a}{\overline{M}_j^p}\right) - \ln\left(\frac{\overline{M}_{benchmark}^a}{\overline{M}_{benchmark}^p}\right)$$
$$= \overline{\hat{\varepsilon}}_j - \overline{\hat{\varepsilon}}_{benchmark} \qquad (2.4)$$

The tariff equivalent for importing country j is obtained by using the simple average of the actual (M^a_j) and predicted (M^p_j) import values and the simple average of the predicted and actual import values for a benchmark country obtained from the econometric estimation (equation 2.3). In equation 2.4, tariff equivalents are obtained by using the average of the residuals (ε) associated with the imports of country j and those of the benchmark country. Typically, the country with the largest difference between actual and predicted import values is selected as the benchmark.

To transform the measure of restriction (expressed as the difference in imports) to a price measure, it is necessary to make an additional assumption about the elasticity of substitution (σ). The elasticity of substitution describes the level of product differentiation in an industry.[15]

The gravity approach allows analysts to estimate trade barriers for a large number of countries and to avoid the demanding task of collecting information on services regulations. Fontagné, Guillin, and Mitaritonna (2011) use it to estimate tariff equivalents for 65 countries and 9 services sectors. However, the resulting tariff equivalents are sensitive to the elasticity of substitution and to the specification of the estimated gravity equation. Tariff equivalents may be artificially high because of omitted variables; they may reflect not only trade barriers but also some aspects of market structure (such as, for instance, a dominant player that limits new competitors).[16]

This method is hampered by the poor quality and limited availability of trade data on services. Estimating a **gravity model** requires data that are broken down by trading partners, which are scarce. There is no worldwide collection of data broken down geographically for any of the four modes of supply (coverage is better for Modes 1 and 2, for which data are collected in balance of payments statistics). Given this lack of data, some studies rely on reconstructed data and apply this approach only to cross-border trade in services (Mode 1).

Most studies find that some Asian economies (including Indonesia, the Philippines, and Taiwan, China) are relatively open for most sectors and that the level of protection of services trade is not systematically related to the level of development. These findings contrast with analyses based on direct methods, which usually find that developed economies have less-restrictive services markets than developing countries and that Asian economies do not rank among the most open economies. Borchert, Gootiiz, and Mattoo (2012), for example, find that some Asian countries have some of the most restrictive policies in the world.

Estimated Markups

Some studies assess market contestability by estimating and comparing markups across sectors and countries. They follow the seminal paper by Roeger (1995), which proposes estimating markups by comparing the residuals obtained from countries' sectoral production functions with those from their cost functions. In particular, he compares the primal with the dual Solow residuals. Solow's **primal residual** refers to the part of the increase in the volume of production that cannot be explained by increases in the factors of production such as capital, intermediate products, and labor. This unexplained growth, or residual, is normally associated with technological progress or total factor productivity (TFP) growth. All production functions have a **dual function,** as they can

be written not only in terms of products but also in terms of production costs and thus prices. Following an analogous explanation, Solow's **dual residual** can be defined as the increase in marginal cost unexplained by increases in factor prices (wages, the cost of capital, the cost of intermediate products).[17]

In a world with perfectly competitive markets, the primal and dual residuals should be highly correlated. In practice, they are not.

Roeger finds that the difference between residuals is explained when the assumption of perfect competition is relaxed and firms can charge prices that exceed unit costs. He shows that by subtracting Solow's dual residual (*SRP*) from Solow's primal residual (*SR*), the markups charged in sector *j* in the country *i* can be estimated as follows:

$$SR_t^{ij} - SRP_t^{ij} = \beta_0 + \beta_1 \left(y_t^{ij} - k_t^{ij} \right) + \varepsilon_t,$$

$$\text{where } \beta_1 = \frac{p^{ij} - c^{ij}}{p^{ij}} \qquad (2.5)$$

where y is nominal growth in production, k is growth in the cost of capital, ε is the error term, and the βs are the coefficients to be estimated. Of particular interest is β_1, which is the **Lerner index** ([price − cost]/price), from which the estimations of markups can be obtained. The dependent variable, $SR - SRP$, can be constructed by using information on the expenditure of individual factors of production.

To estimate markups, analysts use data from national accounts statistics for countries such as the United States and Austria; the STAN (Structural Analysis) database for OECD economies; the EU KLEMS database for members of the European Union; and firm-level financial data from the Amadeus database on a set of European countries. Annex table 2A.3 lists some studies employing this approach.

Results suggest that firms often charge markups and that they are higher in the services sector than in the manufacturing sector. Using data for 1981–2004 from the EU KLEMS database, Christopoulou and Vermeulen (2008) estimate markups (as the price to unit cost ratio) for a set of European countries. They find that for all sectors in all countries, markup ratios generally exceed 1, implying that prices are usually higher than marginal costs (table 2.8). For all countries in the sample, markups are higher in the services sector than in other sectors. The authors argue that the higher markups in services reflect the fact that services are difficult to trade internationally and are subject to regulations and entry barriers that may reduce competition and generate rents.

Table 2.8. Weighted Average Markups in Manufacturing and Services Sectors in Selected Economies, 1981–2004

Country	Manufacturing and construction	Services	All
Austria	1.20	1.45	1.31
Belgium	1.14	1.29	1.22
Euro Area	1.18	1.56	1.37
Finland	1.22	1.39	1.28
France	1.15	1.26	1.21
Germany	1.16	1.54	1.33
Italy	1.23	1.87	1.61
Netherlands	1.13	1.31	1.22
Spain	1.18	1.37	1.26
United States	1.28	1.36	1.32

Source: Adapted from Christopoulou and Vermeulen 2008.
Note: Country average markups are constructed from sectoral estimates using sectoral gross output in the year 2000 as sector weights.

Comparing markups across countries and sectors can yield information about the contestability of markets and therefore help identify which markets and sectors are relatively competitive. It cannot identify whether a higher level of competition in a market reflects policy or other factors, such as market structure, the level of technology, and private practices.

Høj and others (2007), Badinger and Breuss (2005), and Badinger (2007) try to identify the extent to which policy can explain estimated markups. Høj and others use the OECD–STAN database to estimate markups for 17 countries and 18 industries, including 6 services sectors. Using econometric estimations, they regress the markups on the indicators of OECD product market regulation. They find that countries with more restrictive product market regulations tend to have higher markups, especially for nonmanufacturing sectors.

Badinger and Breuss (2005) and Badinger (2007) carry out a similar analysis. They investigate the extent to which new member countries' accession to the European Union influenced the level of competition in their economies. Using information on 46 industries for the period 1978–2001, Badinger and Breuss investigate the effect of Austria's accession to the European Union (in 1995) on the country's estimated markups. Badinger focuses on the participation of 10 EU members in the EU Single Market program. He finds that countries' participation in the Single Market increased competition in the manufacturing sector, where markups declined. In contrast, in most services, markups increased, a trend that, according to the author, may reflect the slow progress in services liberalization under the framework of the EU Single Market program.

Prospective Analyses: CGE Models

Prospective analyses studies employ partial equilibrium and CGE models to estimate the impacts of future trade liberalization (see Francois and Hoekman 2010 for a review of CGE modeling and Dihel 2003 for CGE studies). They assess the impact of deregulation not only on the services category and country under study but also on other sectors of the economy and the rest of the world. Prospective analyses typically simulate the welfare gains and losses for consumers, producers, and the government, thus revealing the economy-wide impact of services trade liberalization.

Most research has focused on trade in goods rather than services, partly because of the lack of comprehensive data on both trade and barriers to trade in services. Estimates of services barriers in CGE modeling are based on tariff equivalents obtained from studies based on direct and indirect methods.

Unlike models of trade in goods, CGEs of services must account for different modes of supply; focusing only on cross-border trade in services would leave out important sources of gains. Konan and Maskus (2006) model both cross-border trade and foreign direct investment (FDI) in services in Tunisia. They find that the most important component of welfare gains comes from the removal of barriers to FDI in services sectors. Moreover, services are highly heterogeneous, and services categories play different roles in the economy. Decisions about their production functions and their link to other sectors in the economy may affect the final result. This finding is consistent with other studies that show that liberalization of trade services, in particular barriers that affect FDI, yields welfare gains that are several times larger than the gains from liberalizing goods trade (Tarr 2012).

By and large, the literature shows that liberalization of services trade can generate overall welfare gains, which tend to be higher for developing countries, partly because of the relatively high level of restrictions on services in these economies. However, the reliability of results from CGE modeling depends on whether different modes of supply are implicitly included, on the assumptions on the economic functions for the different service categories, and on the accuracy of estimated services barriers, which depends on the availability of tariff equivalent measures from direct and indirect methods. Improvement in the collection of data on services regulations and the sophistication of these methods is therefore crucial for obtaining accurate estimations of the economy-wide impact of services trade liberalization.

MODULE 2

Conclusion

This module describes several methods and provides practical guidance on how countries can quantify the impact of regulatory frameworks in the services sector. It focuses on the impact of regulations on the provision, price, and cost of services.

The module reviews direct methods and two indirect methods. It helps analysts identify which type of assessment they can carry out given their data and resource constraints.

Even countries with limited data and resources can undertake some parts of a quantitative assessment. All countries can estimate the impact of the regulatory framework based on the results of a previous study (that is, conduct an out-of-the-sample estimation). These efforts can provide policy makers with estimates of the impact of regulations on the provision, cost, and price of services. In addition, countries can use an out-of-the-sample approach to estimate tariff equivalents, which can then be used in CGE models to investigate the economy-wide impact of service regulations on welfare.

More detailed information on both the regulatory framework and sector performance allows countries to achieve more accurate quantitative assessments. By mapping regulation, governments can record changes in the regulatory framework over time, allowing them to investigate how the sequencing of regulations may affect outcomes. More detailed information can allow policy makers to investigate whether the effectiveness of individual regulations hinges on other regulations in place. Given these benefits, governments should try to establish mechanisms for systematically and periodically inventorying regulations and outcomes in the services sector.

Previous studies have confronted difficulties in identifying whether regulations have brought about the desired environmental, equity, and social outcomes. In addition, none of the studies reviewed in this module included the costs associated with enforcing regulations (compliance costs, such as administrative burdens and paperwork that firms incur to comply with regulations, and enforcement costs incurred by governments and regulatory agencies as part of inspections and audits). A well-conducted mapping of the regulatory framework can improve the quantitative analysis presented here. Measurable objectives of regulations and implementation and enforcement costs can be identified and included in the quantitative analysis. Coordination among governmental bodies, rather than strong technical skill, is crucial for this task.

Annex 2A

Table 2A.1. Selected Studies Estimating the Impact of Regulation on Services Trade Using Direct Methods

Sector	Study	Coverage	Dependent variable[a]	Data source
Professional services				
Legal services	Nguyen-Hong (2000)	Regulatory index for 29 economies		
Accounting services		Regulatory index for 34 economies		
Architectural services		Regulatory index for 34 economies		
Engineering services	Dihel and Shepherd (2007)	Regulatory index for 34 economies, econometric model for 84 companies in 20 economies	Price-cost margin	Disclosure's Worldscope Database (firms' accounting data)
		10 economies	Price-cost margin	Datastream
Telecommunications[b]				
Fixed telephone services	Borchert and others (2012)	About 100 countries	Market concentration (Herfindahl index), penetration rates	TeleGeography's GlobalComms database and International Telecommunication Union (ITU)
	Lee, Ure, and Lee (2011)	21 Asia-Pacific Economic Cooperation economies	Penetration rates	ITU

(continued on next page)

Table 2A.1. *(continued)*

Sector	Study	Coverage	Dependent variable[a]	Data source
	Bottini, Marouani, and Munro (2011)	Arab Republic of Egypt, Jordan, and Morocco	Price-cost margin	Datastream
	Fontagné and Mitaritonna (2009)	11 developing economies	Price-cost margin	Dihel and Shepherd (2007)
	Dihel and Shepherd (2007)	24 countries	Price-cost margin	Datastream
	Fink, Mattoo, and Rathindran (2003)	86 developing countries	Penetration rates, productivity (mainlines per employee)	ITU and World Bank
	Doove and others (2001)	47 countries	Price	ITU, OECD: Communications Outlook, and OECD: Telecommunications database
	Boylaud and Nicoletti (2001)	24 OECD members	Price, labor productivity, quality	OECD: Communications Outlook, and OECD: Telecommunications database
Mobile services	Borchert and others (2012)	About 100 countries	Market concentration (Herfindahl index), penetration rates	TeleGeography's GlobalComms database and ITU
	Lee, Ure, and Lee (2011)	21 APEC economies	Penetration rates	ITU
	Bottini, Marouani, and Munro (2011)	Egypt, Arab Rep., Jordan, and Morocco	Price-cost margin	Datastream
	Fontagné and Mitaritonna (2009)	11 developing economies	Price-cost margin	Dihel and Shepherd (2007)
	Dihel and Shepherd (2007)	24 countries	Price-cost margin	Datastream
	Doove and others (2001)	47 countries	Price	ITU, OECD: Communications Outlook, and OECD: Telecommunications database
	Boylaud and Nicoletti (2001)	24 OECD member economies	Price, productivity	OECD: Communications Outlook and OECD: Telecommunications database
Broadband	Lee, Ure, and Lee (2011)	21 APEC economies	Penetration rates	ITU
Distribution services				
	Fontagné and Mitaritonna (2009)	11 developing economies	Price-cost margin	Dihel and Shepherd (2007)
	Dihel and Shepherd (2007)	19 countries	Price-cost margin	Datastream
	Kalirajan (2000)	38 countries from the Asia-Pacific, European, and American regions	Price-cost margin	Disclosure's Worldscope Database
Financial services				
Banking[c]	Bottini, Marouani, and Munro (2011)	Egypt, Arab Rep., Jordan, Lebanon, and Morocco	Net interest margin	Datastream
	Dihel and Shepherd (2007)	29 countries	Net interest margin	Datastream and Banker's Almanac
	Barth, Caprio, and Levine (2004)	107 countries	Bank development, net interest margin, overhead costs, nonperforming loans, probability of banking crisis	Net interest margin and overhead cost variables from Beck and others (2001). For bank development data, they update Levine, Loayza, and Beck (2000); for data on crises, they use Caprio and Klingebiel (1999). Data on nonperforming loans come from their own survey.

(continued on next page)

Table 2A.1. Selected Studies Estimating the Impact of Regulation on Services Trade Using Direct Methods *(continued)*

Sector	Study	Coverage	Dependent variable[a]	Data source
Financial services (cont.)				
Insurance	Dihel and Shepherd (2007)	25 countries	Price-cost margin	Datastream
Transport				
Air	Borchert and others (2012)	About 100 countries	Number of international flights, total seat capacity, number of flights per airline versus number of airlines servicing a market (intensive versus extensive margin)	Air Transport Intelligence's (ATI) Flightglobal database
	Sourdin (2011)	APEC economies	Trading cost: (CIF – FOB)/ FOB of imported goods	Import data collected by customs agencies of four importing economies (Australia, Brazil, Chile, United States) at the six-digit level of aggregation of the Harmonized System
	Micco and Serebrisky (2006)	United States and its trading partners	Trading cost (cost of all freight, insurance, and other charges excluding U.S. import duties per unit of weight)	U.S. Imports of Merchandise Database from U.S. Department of Commerce
	Doove and others (2001)	35 countries	Price (business, economy, and discount airfare)	International Civil Aviation Organization (ICAO)
	Gönenç and Nicoletti (2001)	27 OECD countries, for a set of 102 air routes connecting 14 international airports	Efficiency: load factor and distance from production efficiency frontier Price: business, economy, and discount airfares	Online air ticket reservation systems and ICAO
Maritime	Sourdin (2011)	APEC economies	Trading cost: (CIF – FOB)/ FOB of imported goods	Import data collected by customs agencies of four importing economies (Australia, Brazil, Chile, United States) at the six-digit level of aggregation of the Harmonized System
	Clark, Dollar, and Micco (2004)	United States and its trading partners	Port efficiency (various measures), trading cost (cost of all freight, insurance, and other charges excluding U.S. import duties per unit of weight)	Waterborne Trade Database compiled by the U.S. Department of Transportation
	Fink, Mattoo, and Rathindran (2002)	United States and 59 U.S. trading partners	Trading cost (cost of all freight, insurance, and other charges excluding U.S. import duties per unit of weight)	Waterborne Trade Database compiled by the U.S. Department of Transportation
Energy				
Electricity	Dee (2011)	APEC economies	Price: industrial electricity prices Efficiency: utilization rate, calculated as gross production (GWh)/ net capacity (MWe), and deviation of reserve margin from optimal, calculated as abs[(capacity – peak)/ peak – 0.15]	Electricity information and energy prices and taxes from the International Energy Agency (IEA)

(continued on next page)

Table 2A.1. *(continued)*

Sector	Study	Coverage	Dependent variable[a]	Data source
	Doove and others (2001)	50 economies	Industrial electricity prices	Electricity information and energy prices and taxes from the IEA
	Steiner (2001)	19 OECD countries	Price: industrial electricity prices, ratio of industrial to residential electricity prices	Electricity information and energy prices and taxes from the IEA
			Efficiency: utilization rate, reserve plant margins	
Gas	Dee (2011)	APEC economies	Price: industrial gas prices	Electricity information and energy prices and taxes from the IEA
			Efficiency: utilization rate, calculated as gas consumption (million m3)/pipeline length (kms)	

Note: CIF = Cost, insurance, and freight; FOB = free on board.

a. The price-cost margin is typically measured using firms' accounting data and calculated as earnings before interest and taxes plus accounting depreciation all divided by revenues.

b. Depending on the telecommunications category, penetration rates are the number of telephone main lines, the number of mobile phone subscribers, or the number of fixed broadband subscribers, all of them expressed as per 100 inhabitants.

c. The net interest margin employed in the banking sector is typically measured as banks' interest income (interest earned minus interest paid on borrowed funds) divided by total interest-earning assets (any asset, such as a loan, that generates interest income).

Table 2A.2. Selected Studies Estimating Impact of Regulation on Services Trade Using the Gravity Approach

Study	Year(s) of data	Coverage	Sectors	Data source
Park (2002)	1997	52 economies	7 sectors: construction, transport, trade, communication, financial, business, and other services (including education, health, and administration)	Global Trade Analysis Project (GTAP) version 5 database, bilateral data
Francois, Meijl, and van Tongeren (2003, 2005)	1997	16 groups, including not only regions such as EU and South America but also such individual countries as France, Germany, India, and China	2 sectors: business services (including business, financial, and communication) and other private and public services	GTAP version 5 database, using importing country totals
Walsh (2006)	1999–2001	49 economies	All services	OECD statistics on international trade in services, bilateral data
Fontagné, Guillin, and Mitaritonna (2011)	2004	65 economies	9 sectors: construction; communication; trade; finance; other services (education, health, defense, and public administration); business; transport; water transport; and insurance	GTAP version 7.4 database, bilateral data
	2002–06	OECD countries and partners	Total services (aggregated), transport, communication, and construction	OECD statistics on international trade in services, bilateral data
Guillin (2013)	2005	63 economies	11 sectors: transportation; other business services; travel; communication; construction; insurance; financial services; royalties and license fees; computer and information services; personal, cultural, and recreational services; and government services	Eurostat international trade in services database, bilateral data

MODULE 2

Table 2A.3. Selected Studies Estimating Impact of Regulation on Services Trade Using the Markups Approach

Study	Years of data	Coverage	Sectors	Data source
Roeger (1995)	1953–84	United States	24 manufacturing sectors	U.S. National Income and Product Accounts (NIPA) and Bureau of Economic Analysis (BEA)
Badinger and Breuss (2005)	1978–2001	Austria	46 sectors (two-digit NACE Rev. 1.1), including 19 services sectors; markups were estimated for 7 industry groups	Statistics Austria
Badinger (2007)	1981–99	10 European Union (EU) member states (Austria, Belgium, Finland, France, Germany, Italy, the Netherlands, Spain, Sweden, and the United Kingdom)	18 sectors, including 6 services sectors; and 3 groups (manufacturing, construction, and services)	STAN (Structural Analysis) database of the OECD
Høj and others (2007)	1975–2002	17 countries	18 sectors, including 6 services sectors	STAN database of the OECD
Christopoulou and Vermeulen (2008)	1981–2004	8 Euro Area countries and the United States	50 sectors	EU KLEMS (2007 release)
Bottini and Molnár (2010)	1993–2006	20 European OECD countries	28 services sectors	Amadeus database
Molnár (2010)	1995–2005	Slovenia	37 sectors, including 17 services sectors	Amadeus database

Notes

1. The authors would like to thank Daniel Reyes and David Tarr for their valuable comments and suggestions on an early draft of this module.

2. The Australian Productivity Commission is the research and advisory body on economic, social, and environmental issues of the Australian government.

3. Part of this work can be found in Findlay and Warren (2000); the rest can be found on the website of the Productivity Commission (http://www.pc.gov.au/research/memorandum/servicesrestriction).

4. Hoekman (1996), Langhammer (2005), Eschenbach and Hoekman (2006), Gootiiz and Mattoo (2009), and Roy (2011) document GATS commitments and proposals.

5. GATS coverage of air transport excludes traffic rights and is limited to three ancillary services: aircraft repair and maintenance services, selling and marketing of air transport services, and computer reservation system services.

6. This limitation recently motivated the change of the weighting method in the construction of the Product Market Regulation (PMR) Indicators of the OECD (Wölfl et al. 2009).

7. For instance, Barth, Caprio, and Levine (2004) find that restrictions on entry are positively associated with overhead costs in the banking sector; they find no significant link between entry restrictions and net interest margins.

8. See Kalirajan (2000) for the logic behind using price-cost margins to distinguish between cost-creating and rent-creating restrictions.

9. When equal weights are assigned, the regulatory impacts are assumed to be the same across regulations. When researchers want to assess the impact of regulations on cost-price margins, they may use a regulatory index including both cost-creating and rent-creating restrictions.

10. Among the few studies using data with time variation are Boylaud and Nicoletti (2001); Steiner (2001); Fink, Mattoo, and Neagu (2002); and Micco and Serebrisky (2006).

11. Banks' involvement in real estate activities could lead them to extend mortgages to people with a high risk of defaulting.

12. Some studies that construct tariff equivalents are Nguyen-Hong (2000); Dee (2005); Bottini and Marouani (2009); Dihel and Shepherd (2007); and Fontagné and Mitaritonna (2009).

13. When the impact of service regulations is evaluated by quantity (that is, the number of services provided), price elasticity measures are needed to transform the quantity impact into a price impact.

14. Gross domestic product (GDP) is usually used as the proxy for size, and distance between countries' capital cities is used for distance. Increasingly, country fixed effects have been used to capture country-specific characteristics such as GDP, remoteness, and price indexes.

15. This elasticity refers to the elasticity of substitution between different varieties of products in a particular industry. Trade models with intraindustry trade and imperfect competition, such as new economic geography models, typically employ a constant elasticity of substitution.

16. Although the elasticity of substitution has an impact on the magnitude of the tariff equivalents, it does not affect countries' ranking.

17. In perfect competition, at equilibrium, changes in product prices equal changes in marginal costs. Solow's dual residual refers to the part of the change in product prices that cannot be explained by the changes in the price of production factors.

References

Amadeus (database), Bureau van Dijk, London, http://amadeus.bvdinfo.com.

Badinger, Harald. 2007. "Has the EU's Single Market Programme Fostered Competition? Testing for a Decrease in Mark-Up Ratios in EU Industries." *Oxford Bulletin of Economics and Statistics* 69 (4): 497–519.

Badinger, Harald, and Fritz Breuss. 2005. "Has Austria's Accession to the EU Triggered an Increase in Competition? A Sectoral Markup Study." *Empirica* 32: 145–80.

Balistreri, Edward J., Thomas F. Rutherford, and David G. Tarr. 2009. "Modeling Services Liberalization: The Case of Kenya." *Economic Modelling* 26 (3): 668–79.

Barth, James R., Gerard Caprio, Jr., and Ross Levine. 2004. "Bank Regulation and Supervision: What Works Best?" *Journal of Financial Intermediation* 13 (2): 205–48.

Beck, Thorsten, Asli Demirgüç-Kunt, and Ross Levine. 2001. "The Financial Structure Database." In *Financial Structure and Economic Growth: A Cross-Country Comparison of Banks, Markets, and Development*, ed. Asli Demirgüç-Kunt and Ross Levine, 17–80. Cambridge, MA: MIT Press.

Borchert, Ingo, Batshur Gootiiz, Arti Grover, and Aaditya Mattoo. 2012. *Landlocked or Policy Locked? How Services Trade Protection Deepens Economic Isolation*. Policy Research Working Paper WPS5942, World Bank, Washington, DC.

Borchert, Ingo, Batshur Gootiiz, and Aaditya Mattoo. 2012. *Policy Barriers to International Trade in Services: New Empirical Evidence*. Technical Report, World Bank, Washington, DC.

Bottini, Novella, and Mohamed A. Marouani. 2009. "An Estimation of Service Sectors Restrictiveness In the Mena Region." Working Paper, Economic Research Forum, Cairo.

———. 2011. "Service Sector Restrictiveness and Economic Performance: An Estimation for the MENA Region." *World Economy* 34 (9): 1652–78.

Bottini, Novella, Mohamed Ali Marouani, and Laura Munro. 2011. "Service Sector Restrictiveness and Economic Performance: An Estimation for the MENA Region." *The World Economy* 34(9): 1652–78.

Bottini, Novella, and Margit Molnár. 2010. "How Large Are Competitive Pressures in Services Markets? Estimation of Mark-Ups for Selected OECD Countries." *OECD Journal: Economic Studies* 1: 1–51.

Boylaud, Olivier, and Giuseppe Nicoletti. 2001. "Regulation, Market Structure and Performance in Telecommunications." *OECD Economic Studies* 1: 4.

Cadot, Olivier, Mariem Malouche, and Sebastián Sáez, eds. 2012. *Streamlining Non-Tariff Measures: A Toolkit for Policy Makers*. Washington, DC: World Bank.

Caprio, Gerhard, Jr., and Daniela Klingebiel. 1999. "Episodes of Systemic and Borderline Financial Crises." World Bank, Washington, DC.

Christopoulou, Rebekka, and Philip Vermeulen. 2008. "Markups in the Euro Area and the US over the Period 1981–2004: A Comparison of 50 Sectors." Working Paper, European Central Bank, Frankfurt.

Clark, Ximena, David Dollar, and Alejandro Micco. 2004. "Port Efficiency, Maritime Transport Costs, and Bilateral Trade." *Journal of Development Economics* 75 (2): 417–50.

Crozet, Matthieu, Emmanuel Milet, and Daniel Mirza. 2011. "The Discriminatory Effect of Domestic Regulations on International Services Trade: Evidence from Firm-Level Data." Document de travail, Université Panthéon-Sorbonne (Paris 1), Centre d'Economie de la Sorbonne, Paris.

Deardorff, Alan V., and Robert M. Stern. 2008. "Empirical Analysis of Barriers to International Services Transactions and the Consequences of Liberalization." In *A Handbook of International Trade in Services*, ed. Aaditya Mattoo, Robert M. Stern, and Gianni Zanini, 169–220. New York: Oxford University Press.

Dee, Philippa. 2005. *A Compendium of Barriers to Trade in Services*. Australian National University, Asia-Pacific School of Economics and Government, Canberra.

———. 2011. "Quantifying the Benefits from Structural Reforms in Electricity and Gas Markets in APEC Economies." In *The Impacts and Benefits of Structural Reforms in Transport, Energy and Telecommunications Sectors*, ed. Christopher Findlay, 124–44. Singapore: Asia-Pacific Economic Cooperation.

Dihel, Nora. 2003. "Quantifying Costs to National Welfare from Barriers to Services Trade: A Review of the Literature." In *Quantifying the Benefits of Liberalising Trade in Services*, 113–44. Paris: OECD Publishing.

Dihel, Nora, and Ben Shepherd. 2007. "Modal Estimates of Services Barriers." Trade Policy Working Paper, Organisation for Economic Co-operation and Development, Paris.

Doove, Samanatha, Owen Gabbitas, Duc Nguyen-Hong, and Joe Owen. 2001. "Price Effects of Regulation: Telecommunications, Air Passenger Transport and Electricity Supply." Productivity Commission, Canberra, Australia. http://128.118.178.162/eps/othr/papers/0110/0110004.pdf.

Eschenbach, Felix, and Bernard Hoekman. 2006. "Services Policies in Transition Economies: On the EU and WTO as Commitment Mechanisms." *World Trade Review* 5 (3): 415–43.

EU KLEMS Growth and Productivity Accounts (database). 2011. http://www.euklems.net/index.html.

Findlay, Christopher. 2011. *The Impacts and Benefits of Structural Reforms in Transport, Energy and Telecommunications Sectors in APEC Economies*. Technical Report, Asia-Pacific Economic Cooperation, Singapore.

Findlay, Christopher, and Tony Warren, eds. 2000. *Impediments to Trade in Services: Measurement and Policy Implications*. London: Routledge.

Fink, Carsten, Aaditya Mattoo, and Ileana C. Neagu. 2002. "Trade in International Maritime Services: How Much Does Policy Matter?" *World Bank Economic Review* 16 (1): 81–108.

Fink, Carsten, Aaditya Mattoo, and Randeep Rathindran. 2002. "An Assessment of Telecommunications Reform in Developing Countries. *Information Economics and Policy* 15 (4): 443–66.

Fontagné, Lionel, Amélie Guillin, and Cristina Mitaritonna. 2011. "Estimations of Tariff Equivalents for the Services Sectors." Working Paper, CEPII Research Center, Paris.

Fontagné, Lionel, and Cristina Mitaritonna. 2009. "Assessing Barriers to Trade in the Distribution and Telecom Sectors in Emerging Countries." Working Paper, CEPII Research Center, Paris.

Francois, Joseph, and Bernard Hoekman. 2010. "Services Trade and Policy." *Journal of Economic Literature* 48 (3): 642–92.

Francois, Joseph, Hans van Meijl, and Frank van Tongeren. 2003. *Trade Liberalization and Developing Countries under the Doha Round*. Discussion Paper, Tinbergen Institute, Amsterdam.

———. 2005. "Trade Liberalization in the Doha Development Round." *Economic Policy* 20 (42): 349–91.

Gönenç, Rauf, and Giuseppe Nicoletti. 2001. "Regulation, Market Structure and Performance in Air Passenger Transportation." *OECD Economic Studies* 1: 6.

Gootiiz, Batshur, and Aaditya Mattoo. 2009. "Services in Doha: What's on the Table?" Policy Research Working Paper, World Bank, Washington, DC.

Guillin, Amélie. 2013. "Assessment of Tariff Equivalents for Services Considering the Zero-Flows." *World Trade Review* 12 (3): 549–75.

GTAP (Global Trade Analysis Project) (database), Purdue University, Indiana, http://www.gtap.agecon.purdue.edu.

Hoekman, Bernard. 1996. "Assessing the General Agreement on Trade in Services." In *The Uruguay Round and the Developing Countries*, ed. Will Martin and L. Alan Winters, 88–124. Cambridge: Cambridge University Press.

Hoekman, Bernard, and Aaditya Mattoo. 2011. "Services Trade Liberalization and Regulatory Reform: Re-invigorating International Cooperation." Policy Research Working Paper, World Bank, Washington, DC.

Høj, Jens, Miguel Jimenez, Maria Maher, Guiseppe Nicoletti, and Mikael Wise. 2007. "Product Market Competition in the OECD Countries: Taking Stock and Moving Forward." Economics Department Working Paper, Organisation for Economic Co-operation and Development, Paris.

Jensen, Jesper, Thomas F. Rutherford, and David Tarr. 2004. "The Impact of Liberalizing Barriers to Foreign Direct Investment in Services: The Case of Russian Accession to the World Trade Organization." Policy Research Working Paper, World Bank, Washington, DC.

———. 2008. "Modeling Services Liberalization: The Case of Tanzania." Policy Research Working Paper, World Bank, Washington, DC.

Jensen, Jesper, and David Tarr. 2007. "The Impact of Kazakhstan Accession to the World Trade Organization: A Quantitative Assessment." Policy Research Working Paper, World Bank, Washington, DC.

MODULE 2

———. 2011. "Deep Trade Policy Options for Armenia: The Importance of Services, Trade Facilitation and Standards Liberalization." Policy Research Working Paper, World Bank, Washington, DC.

Kalirajan, Kaleeswaran. 2000. *Restrictions on Trade in Distribution Services.* Labor and Demography Series, Australian Government Productivity Commission, Adelaide.

Kalirajan, Kaleeswaran, Greg McGuire, Duc Nguyen-Hong, and Michael Schuele. 2000. "The Price Impact of Restrictions on Banking Services." In *Impediments to Trade in Services: Measurement and Policy Implications,* ed. Christopher Findlay and Tony Warren, 215–30. London: Routledge.

Kang, Jong-Soon. 2000. "Price Impact of Restrictions on Maritime Transport Services." In *Impediments to Trade in Services: Measurement and Policy Implications,* ed. Christopher Findlay and Tony Warren, 189–200. London: Routledge.

Kemp, Steven. 2000. "Trade in Education Services and the Impact of Barriers to Trade." In *Impediments to Trade in Services: Measurement and Policy Implications,* ed. Christopher Findlay and Tony Warren 247–61. London: Routledge.

Konan, Denise E., and Keith E. Maskus. 2006. "Quantifying the Impact of Services Liberalization in a Developing Country." *Journal of Development Economics* 81 (1): 142–62.

Langhammer, Rolf J. 2005. "The EU Offer of Service Trade Liberalization in the Doha Round: Evidence of a Not-Yet-Perfect Customs Union." *JCMS: Journal of Common Market Studies* 43 (2): 311–25.

Lee, Roy C., John Ure, and Hsin C. Lee. 2011. "Quantifying the Impacts of Structural Reforms in Telecommunications Markets in APEC Economies." In *The Impacts and Benefits of Structural Reforms in Transport, Energy and Telecommunications Sectors,* ed. Christopher Findlay, 179–208. Singapore: Asia-Pacific Economic Cooperation.

Levine, Ross, Norman Loayza, and Thorsten Beck. 2000. "Financial Intermediation and Growth: Causality and Causes." *Journal of Monetary Economics* 46: 31–77.

McGuire, Greg. 2003. "Methodologies for Measuring Restrictions on Trade in Services." In *Quantifying the Benefits of Liberalising Trade in Services,* 33–62. Paris: OECD Publishing.

———. 2008. "Measuring and Modelling Restrictions on Trade in Services: A Case of Asia-Pacific Economic Cooperation Economies." MARKHUB Working Paper 13, United Nations Economic and Social Commission for Asia and the Pacific, Bangkok.

McGuire, Greg, and Michael Schuele. 2000. "Restrictiveness of International Trade in Banking Services." In *Impediments to Trade in Services: Measurement and Policy Implications,* ed. Christopher Findlay and Tony Warren, 201–14. London: Routledge.

McGuire, Greg, Michael Schuele, and Tina Smith. 2000. "Restrictiveness of International Trade in Maritime Services." In *Impediments to Trade in Services: Measurement and Policy Implications,* ed. Christopher Findlay and Tony Warren, 184–200. London: Routledge.

Micco, Alejandro, and Tomas Serebrisky. 2006. "Competition Regimes and Air Transport Costs: The Effects of Open Skies Agreements." *Journal of International Economics* 70 (1): 25–51.

Molnár, Margit. 2010. "Measuring Competition in Slovenian Industries: Estimation of Mark-Ups." Economics Department Working Paper, Organisation for Economic Co-operation and Development, Paris.

Nguyen-Hong, Duc. 2000. *Restrictions on Trade in Professional Services.* Technical Report, Productivity Commission of the Australian Government, Canberra.

Nicoletti, Giuseppe, Stefano Scarpetta, and Olivier Boylaud. 2000. "Summary Indicators of Product Market Regulation with an Extension to Employment Protection Legislation." Economics Department Working Paper, Organisation for Economic Co-operation and Development, Paris.

OECD (Organisation for Economic Co-operation and Development). 1996. *Inventory of Measures Affecting Trade in Professional Services.* Paris: OECD.

Park, Soon-Chan. 2002. "Measuring Tariff Equivalents in Cross-Border Trade in Services." Institute for International Economic Policy, Seoul.

Roeger, Werner. 1995. "Can Imperfect Competition Explain the Difference Between Primal and Dual Productivity Measures? Estimates for U.S. Manufacturing." *Journal of Political Economy* 103 (2): 316–30.

Roy, Martin. 2011. "Services Commitments in Preferential Trade Agreements: An Expanded Dataset." WTO Staff Working Paper ERSD-2011-18, World Trade Organization, Geneva.

Services Trade Restrictions Database (database). World Bank, Washington, DC. http://iresearch.worldbank.org/servicestrade/.

Sourdin, Patricia. 2011. "Quantifying the Impacts of Structural Reforms on International Transport Margins." In *The Impacts and Benefits of Structural Reforms in Transport, Energy and Telecommunications Sectors,* ed. Christopher Findlay, 66–87. Singapore: Asia-Pacific Economic Cooperation.

STAN (database), OECD, Paris, http://www.oecd.org/industry/ind/stanstructuralanalysisdatabase.htm.

Steiner, Faye. 2001. "Regulation, Industry Structure and Performance in the Electricity Supply Industry." *OECD Economic Studies* 32: 143–82.

Tarr, David. 2012 "Putting Services and Foreign Direct Investment with Endogenous Productivity Effects in Computable General Equilibrium Models." Policy Research Working Paper, World Bank, Washington, DC.

Walsh, Keith. 2006. "Trade in Services: Does Gravity Hold? A Gravity Model Approach to Estimating Barriers to Services Trade." Discussion Paper, Institute for International Integration Studies, Dublin.

Warren, Tony. 2000. "The Impact on Output of Impediments to Trade and Investment in Telecommunications Services." In *Impediments to Trade in Services: Measurement and Policy Implications,* ed. Christopher Findlay and Tony Warren, 93–108. London: Routledge.

Whalley, John. 2004. "Assessing the Benefits to Developing Countries of Liberalisation in Services Trade." *World Economy* 27 (8): 1223–53.

Wölfl, A., I. Wanner, T. Kozluk, and G. Nicoletti. 2009. "Ten years of product market reform in OECD countries: Insights from a revised PMR indicator." OECD Economics Department Working Paper 695, OECD, Paris.

MODULE 2

IDENTIFYING ALTERNATIVES IN REGULATORY STRATEGIES AND MEASURES

Objectives

This module provides an overview of regulatory strategies and alternatives to regulation that can be adopted in the services sector. Upon completing it, readers will be able to:

- *Identify key strategies for regulating the services sector and evaluate the costs and benefits associated with each*
- *Identify the factors that favor some strategies over others*
- *Link regulatory strategies to the broader institutional framework needed to ensure efficient and effective regulation, and appreciate the limitations of this approach in developing countries*

Trade costs are high in services sectors—perhaps twice the level observed for goods trade (Miroudot, Sauvage, and Shepherd 2010). Costs are high partly because many countries have in place a raft of policies that restrict trade in services. Sometimes these measures are protectionist in intent, explicitly designed to reserve a market for domestic incumbents and insulate them from foreign competition. Often, however, measures that restrict services trade do so inadvertently, in the pursuit of other social objectives.

This module examines some common regulatory strategies that can restrict trade in services, analyzes their possible justification, and proposes alternative strategies that can achieve the same goals at lower economic cost. The perspective is one of regulatory cost-benefit analysis. The objective of economic analysis should be to identify social goals and find the most efficient way possible of achieving them. Of course, the first-best solution will not always be achievable in developing countries, particularly where governance institutions and regulatory oversight are weak. It is therefore important to keep alternative strategies as simple as possible.

The module is organized as follows. The next section discusses common restrictions on services trade, focusing on their identification and the classification of their economic impacts. The second section considers alternative regulatory strategies. A third section advises on how to take into account the political economy challenges in the assessment. The last section summarizes the main policy implications.

Regulating services sectors effectively in a way that distorts trade as little as possible is complex.[1] To do so, countries need a policy-making framework that allows them to consider the impact of regulatory measures on trade in services.

One principle that is critical to making regulation as unrestrictive of trade in services as possible is **proportionality**—the notion that the trade-restrictive effect of regulation should not be out of proportion to the desired policy objective. In addition, regulation should be targeted at addressing the specific risks and problems identified as requiring government action (World Bank 2010a). Ideally, a regulatory intervention should be based on an analysis showing that the benefits outweigh the costs and that the benefit-cost ratio is maximized by the instrument chosen.[2] To determine whether the proposed regulatory intervention maximizes achievement of a social goal and minimizes the costs to trade and investment in services, analysts need to conduct an economy-wide review (that is, a general rather than **partial equilibrium analysis**), because a regulation may be optimal from the point of view of a sector but not the economy as a whole.

Regulatory impact analysis (RIA) offers a mechanism for comparing the cost-benefit ratios of different regulatory measures (box 3.1).

RIAs require well-designed regulation-making procedures with fluid interagency coordination. They also require strong quantitative skills and ample reliable data. Although some developing countries have implemented some elements of RIAs (World Bank 2010b), most lack the institutional arrangements and resources to do so.

To overcome these challenges, low-income countries, with the assistance of donors and international

Box 3.1. Regulatory Impact Analysis

Regulatory impact analysis (RIA) is a key tool for improving the efficiency, transparency, and accountability of regulatory decision making (OECD 2008). The contribution of RIA to regulatory decision making rests on the systematic assessment of the impacts of a regulatory measure and adherence to the principles of accountability, transparency, and consistency. RIAs usually focus on the quality of the regulation-making process, assessing the likely impacts of new regulations in quantitative and qualitative terms.

organizations, can focus on adopting basic principles such as transparency and accountability (World Bank 2010a). They can develop in-country capacity in the area of regulatory reform, including through South-South knowledge exchange. They can use cost-benefit analyses undertaken in other countries as a basis for their own work. This approach is a second-best solution, because a general equilibrium cost-benefit analysis depends on country-specific factors. Nevertheless, some information on the costs and benefits of different regulatory options is better than none. International institutions can act as intermediaries in this process by collecting and disseminating national experiences. They can also learn from experience elsewhere. Even without the benefit of rigorous cost-benefit analysis of the type advocated here, many countries—including low-income ones—have reformed services sectors in ways that have dramatically improved performance. Their experience has given rise to rules of thumb that can guide low-income country policy makers in their regulatory reform efforts. The last section of this module offers some examples of these guidelines.

Regulatory Strategies

This section reviews the main strategies for regulation.[3] The next section examines alternatives to them.

Provision of Services by the State

The most interventionist regulatory strategy is direct intervention by the state. Under this strategy, it is the state itself that provides the services. This is always the case, for example, with services provided by security forces. Some states also provide some services related to some specific assets, such as distribution of energy or administration of ports and airports. In a less interventionist variant of this model, the government is responsible for initial investment in infrastructure like ports or airports, but operation of the facilities is then put out to competitive tender (see the later section on franchising). This approach ensures a particular level of investment in goods or services but avoids the inefficiencies of governments as service providers. It sets prices and ensures the supply of a particular quality and quantity of services.

One of the main disadvantages of the direct intervention strategy is that government failure can be just as much of a problem as market failure. As discussed in module 1, governments may be unduly influenced by private lobbies seeking to benefit from a new investment or may lack private incentives to reduce costs. In addition, direct intervention can lead to the stalling of technology at a particular level, as the private sector has no incentive to innovate once the state has intervened in the market in a decisive way. For these reasons, developed countries have tended to avoid direct intervention in recent decades. Instead, countries tend to opt for more market-based approaches, which generally yield a higher benefit-cost ratio. The remainder of this section discusses regulatory strategies that can be combined with a minimal degree of direct action to help achieve overarching social goals.

Command and Control Regulation

Regulation by command and control usually involves the imposition of binding standards by the state. These standards are enforced by legal sanctions: civil, criminal, or administrative penalties for noncompliance.

Command and control covers a wide range of regulatory stances, including rule-making and enforcement and licensing arrangements, under which operators must acquire a permit to be allowed to engage in a particular activity. Command and control regulation can extend beyond standards and rules designed to preserve the quality of a service or its manner of delivery to include the allocation of resources, prices charged to consumers, and profits earned by service providers.

Ogus (2004) provides a typology of standard-setting within the context of the command and control strategy, differentiating each type of regulatory measure by the degree of intervention involved (figure 3.1). At the low intervention end of the spectrum, information standards require firms to disclose certain types of information to the public so that consumers can make informed decisions (this approach overlaps with disclosure regulation, which is discussed later as a separate regulatory strategy). The midrange of intervention takes the form of behavioral control over market participants. The highest level of intervention is prior approval, or licensing,

MODULE 3

Figure 3.1. Degrees of Intervention of Mandatory Regulation

Source: Adapted from Ogus 2004.

which is usually subject to stringent training or capacity requirements.

Ogus (2004) distinguishes three types of behavioral control standards, based on their level of intervention in firm decision making:

- Target standards prescribe no specific conduct by the supplier but hold them liable for certain harmful consequences arising from their output. This type of regulation is advantageous for suppliers, because it allows them to choose how to avoid the harmful consequences. Target standards are generally appealing because they are not costly to formulate—the desired goal can be easily translated into a rule. They are effective, however, only when the damage can be easily associated to a specific actor. Target standards are most valuable where the damage that needs to be avoided is a collective damage—such as pollution—for which no individual is likely to demand compensation. Although these standards are frequently associated with production of goods and extractive industries, they also apply to services industries that may cause such risks.
- Performance standards require that certain conditions of quality be met at the point of supply but leave the supplier free to decide how to meet those conditions. They focus on controlling certain outputs, such as gas emissions and noise levels affecting transport services. They are more costly to formulate than target standards, because they require familiarity with the industry. They can be firm specific, but they are easily monitored.
- Specification standards compel suppliers to follow a certain process or production method—requiring the use of certain equipment, for instance, or prescribing certain specifications for infrastructure. These design standards

are the most technical rules issued by the regulator; they may set out a series of specifications providing detailed guidance for the industry to achieve an outcome for which a single performance standard may suffice. They are less costly than performance standards to formulate and easy to monitor and enforce. Specifications may point, for instance, to the type of tires or the number of airbags that should be put in a car. In the services sector, specification standards are most commonly found in construction (an example is the prohibition on using asbestos) and telecommunications (an example is the requirement that certain equipment be used).

Unlike developed countries, which have shifted toward market-based approaches in recent decades, developing countries rely heavily (sometimes exclusively) on command and control regulation. There are both advantages and disadvantages of command and control from a development point of view. Advantages include the ability to prohibit particular types of conduct with the force of law, which means that the effect is relatively certain and immediate. Command and control regulation is also politically popular, because it gives the appearance of taking a strong stand against a particular social ill and using the law to protect the public from undesired outcomes or unscrupulous operators.

There are also problems with command and control regulation. Because of its strong legal authority, regulatory failures are particularly severe when embodied in mandatory regulatory standards. For example, the fact that the regulator needs information from regulated firms to put properly designed standards in place means that it requires a close relationship with business, leaving it particularly susceptible to regulatory capture.

MODULE 3

A second potential problem with command and control regulation is that it may introduce rigidity into the system. Setting standards, especially specification or performance standards, necessarily limits the capacity of business to adapt to changes in demand and technology that may make different production methods desirable. The need to go through a lengthy, legalistic process to change the standards means there can be a significant lag between the identification of a potential innovation and its implementation in the form of new or different products.

Related to both problems is the potential for command and control standards to operate as barriers to entry. Adopting a standard based on the practices of incumbent operators can discourage entry by new competitors, which would have to adapt their business models to meet the standard.

Another difficulty with command and control as a regulatory strategy is that it can be difficult and costly to enforce. Operators need to be inspected to assess compliance. Enforcement of legal penalties for noncompliance—especially with target standards—may require recourse to the courts, which adds substantial costs and uncertainty.

Incentive-Based Regimes

The essence of regulation based on economic incentives is the use of taxes or subsidies to encourage service providers to act in accordance with the public interest. Rather than setting down "pass or fail" standards, incentive-based regulation uses charges and credits to bring private and social costs into line, helping create an outcome that preserves market outcomes but achieves important public interest goals. This approach has a long history in the economic analysis of regulation: **Pigovian taxes**—taxes applied to market activities that generate negative externalities, such as "polluter pays" policies—were proposed in the early 20th century.

Incentive-based regulation has certain advantages over command and control. First, the danger of regulatory capture is greatly reduced, because economic incentives operate in a mechanical and transparent way once they are created. Whereas command and control regulation requires an ongoing close relationship between the regulator and the regulated industry, economic incentives can operate effectively with greater distance between the two. Oversight of the regulated industry and verification of the base used to calculate tax liabilities or subsidies are still needed, however. Incentive-based regulation does not, therefore, completely eliminate the risk of

regulatory capture, although in most cases it substantially reduces it.

Second, incentive-based regulation encourages firms to limit harmful conduct as much as possible. By contrast, command and control regimes require only that the harmful conduct be limited to the point set out in the standard.

One of the main disadvantages of incentive-based regulation is that a great deal of information is still required to set the tax or subsidy at the correct level. It is first necessary to estimate the relationship between the cost and the production of the harmful consequence it is intended to limit. There is thus considerable scope for trial and error in setting the appropriate level of tax or subsidy. Such an approach has two negative consequences. The first is that it creates uncertainty for business, which may limit investment, including foreign direct investment. The second is that if the initial tax or subsidy rate is set at a level that still results in substantial production of harmful consequences, irreparable damage may be done. For example, if taxes for environmental purposes are too low, they do not act as an adequate disincentive to pollute, thus failing to prevent the environmental harm.

For developing countries, there are two main disadvantages to using taxes and subsidies as regulatory tools. In the case of subsidies, it is necessary for the government to mobilize the necessary funds through its general budget. Doing so may be impossible given the competing uses (including social necessities such as health and education spending) and the low level of government revenue. Regulatory taxes can be difficult to administer in countries with limited fiscal capacity. For these reasons, the economic incentives approach may be more applicable to middle-income countries—particularly upper-middle-income countries with relatively strong administrative capacities—than to low-income countries.

Market-Harnessing Controls

Other regulatory approaches rely on market mechanisms to encourage private operators to conform to social goals, rather than on mandatory regulation. They include **competition law,** franchising, regulation by contract, and establishing **tradable permits**.

Competition Law

One of the goals of market-oriented regulation is to promote competition and ensure that it is harnessed in the public interest. General provisions of competition law can be used as part of a more general regulatory framework or even in place of specific regulatory provisions. Competition law is often used in the telecommunications, energy, and water sectors to ensure that incumbent network operators, which enjoy monopolies, allow access to their networks on reasonable terms. These laws create competitive pressure at the level of the supply of services to individual consumers.

One advantage of using competition law as a regulatory strategy is that it can be applied across the board (to multiple sectors), thus creating economies of scale in regulation. The lack of industry specificity also reduces the likelihood of regulatory capture and the corresponding possibility that regulations become barriers to entry.

Flexibility is both an advantage and a disadvantage of competition law as a regulatory strategy. On the one hand, firms value flexibility, as it leaves them free to exploit their competitive advantages within the framework of a given set of rules. Unlike command and control strategies, competition law does not unduly intrude into firms' private decision-making processes. On the other hand, flexibility leads to uncertainty. The courts play a major role in developing and interpreting competition law, and businesses may be unclear as to whether a particular conduct is in violation or not.

Franchising

Some activities display natural monopoly attributes. Traditionally, command and control techniques regulate these kinds of monopolies. An alternative approach that gives greater scope to market-based mechanisms is **franchising**: the replacement of competition within the market with competition for the market. Under a franchising, or **concession**, scheme, firms bid for a license to be the exclusive service provider for a particular activity within a geographical region, usually for a limited time. An auction mechanism can be used to encourage firms to compete on quantity, quality, and price. If properly instituted, this system incentivizes firms to bid based on assumptions of efficient operation. If the successful bidder can subsequently be held to the terms of the bid, the net operator behaves in many ways as if it were in a competitive environment, even though it is granted a monopoly right. An additional advantage is that franchising often includes the payment of a license fee, or negotiation of a minimum subsidy, which can have fiscal benefits for the government.

The main disadvantage of franchising for developing countries is that it requires a high level of governance capacity, including a clear and strong legal framework. If high license fees are involved, the potential for corruption is significant and can result not only in a loss of government revenue but also in granting of licenses to service providers that do not offer the best combination of quantity, quality, and price. Franchising is perhaps most appropriate for middle-income countries, especially upper-middle-income countries, with relatively well-developed governance structures. Alternative approaches may need to be adopted in low-income countries.

Regulation by Contract

In addition to their role as regulators, governments are also substantial purchasers of goods and services from private suppliers. Government procurement therefore provides a lever to achieve regulatory objectives.

A government can agree to purchase services from a provider on condition that it conform to certain conditions, such as the quality and quantity of services, the payment of minimum wages, or the employment of a certain percentage of local workers. Contracts for the acquisition of goods or services can be used as an indirect way of achieving regulatory objectives, by including appropriate conditions in the procurement agreement. Although the regulatory aspect is generally secondary to the acquisition of goods or services, the fact that any agent dealing with the government is required to behave in certain ways means that these kinds of agreements can nonetheless count as regulatory tools, especially in sectors where the government is a significant purchaser.

Tradable Permits

Tradable permits have received considerable attention in environmental protection. Under this approach, providers whose activities produce a social nuisance—such as carbon dioxide emissions—must acquire a permit to continue those activities. By issuing a fixed number of permits, the government caps the total amount of harmful activity. Once they acquire these permits, firms are free to trade them. The market for permits gives firms an incentive to engage in abatement activities while limiting the overall harm inflicted.

Rights and Liabilities

A precursor to the idea of tradable permits is the granting of rights and liabilities to particular parties in order to encourage socially desirable behavior. Civil law generally allows neighbors the right to take action against polluting businesses, which in some circumstances can be liable for any harm caused to neighboring properties. In this case, the right to pollute is not tradable, but the right to a clean environment gives rise to a liability to compensate sufferers for harm caused.

The main disadvantage of this regulatory strategy is that rights and liabilities are subject to considerable

MODULE 3

uncertainty, because they must generally be enforced through the courts. Moreover, because the costs of winning damages are relatively high, there is an incentive for parties to agree to a negotiated settlement at less than the full value of the damage.

The rights and liabilities strategy also interacts in troubling ways with insurance. The ability for harm-causing businesses to insure themselves against subsequent lawsuits blunts the incentive to reduce the conduct in question, because insurance spreads the losses widely across the community rather than imposing them solely on the producer of the harmful activity.

Disclosure Regulation

Where information asymmetry is a significant problem in free markets, a relatively light-handed government strategy is to require firms to make public information regarding the quantity, quality, and price of their outputs and in some cases the processes followed during production. The idea is that once the information is publicly available, individual consumers can make an informed choice that conforms to their levels of risk perception and tolerance, which differ from one person to another.

One major disadvantage of **disclosure regulation** is that the costs of disclosing and processing the information may be significant. Moreover, in some cases, the risks associated with certain types of business conduct may be so great that information disclosure is inadequate. In these cases, command and control regulation—such as prohibition—may be required. In medical services, for example, it is generally regarded as insufficient to require practitioners to reveal their training to potential patients. Instead, states set minimal levels of qualifications so that unqualified practitioners cannot do irreparable harm to patients.

Because of these types of problems, information disclosure is often not a sufficient regulatory strategy on its own; it must usually be combined with additional measures, such as some level of command and control regulation, to be effective. Information disclosure requirements may be sufficient alone when the risks of substantial harm resulting from substandard conduct are low, the cost of processing the information is low, and consumers can accurately assess risks.

Design Solutions and "Nudging"

Another form of regulation is for the government to set up a framework for private transactions so that particular forms of harm simply cannot occur. For example, setting

up a market for the sale of particular types of securities and prohibiting sales outside an organized market limits the types of securities individuals can purchase. This approach can be seen as an extension of the kinds of prohibitions used in command and control regulation in which the intervention takes place at an earlier stage, by making certain types of transactions or behaviors impossible, rather than imposing sanctions after they do occur. This type of regulation can be used to ensure that a sufficient degree of competition and consumer satisfaction exists within particular markets.

Nudging is also designed to steer behavior while preserving freedom of choice for consumers, albeit in a curtailed way. Nudging involves creating an architecture for choice that favors a particular decision. (The requirement to tick a box in order not to become an organ donor is a typical example of regulatory nudging.) Although nudging represents a promising and relatively light regulatory strategy in some areas, it is unlikely to be applicable across the board, especially in areas where economic incentives are strong or decisions are made collectively.

Self-Regulation

Under self-regulation, a group of firms or individuals sets standards for membership and behavior. Self-regulation has been very important in the professions, such as law and medicine, although many countries have moved to a mixed approach involving command and control strategies as well.

One main advantage of self-regulation is that it involves the people with the most expertise—the regulatees—in the process of developing, promulgating, and enforcing standards of conduct. Of course, this advantage is also a potential disadvantage, because the regulator has an incentive to use standards of conduct or licensing requirements as barriers to entry, thereby choking off competition, increasing prices, and limiting variety in the market. These strategies also need a well-developed and sophisticated private sector with adequate competition to ensure regulatory quality and lack of anticompetitive arrangements. It is generally necessary to combine self-regulation with enforcement of competition law to ensure that incumbents do not use it to erect barriers to entry.

Comparison of Regulatory Strategies

Table 3.1 highlights the strengths and weaknesses of selected regulatory strategies.

Table 3.1. Regulatory Strategies: Trends and Weaknesses

Strategy	Strengths	Weaknesses	Example
1. Direct intervention	• Can separate infrastructure provision from operation • Ensures acceptable level of provision • Allows state to plan long-term investment	• Involves costly funding • Requires heavy public sector involvement • May hamper market-driven innovation	State-owned transport services
2. Command and control	• Has force of law; use of penalties indicates forceful stance of authorities • Sets minimum acceptable levels of behavior • Screens entry • Protects social interests	• Intrudes on management decisions • Prone to capture • Involves complex rules, which tend to multiply • Is inflexible • Imposes severe informational requirements • Is expensive to administer and enforce • Requires strong institutional capacity • Can disguise restrictions to trade and limitations to competition • Imposes high compliance costs for firms • May inhibit innovation	Safety regulation in transport sector
3. Incentives	• Limits regulator discretion • Costs little to apply • Involves limited intervention in management • Includes incentives to reduce harm to zero, not just to standard • Creates economic pressure to behave acceptably	• Requires rules • Provides inadequate response to problems arising from irrational or careless behavior • Requires predicting outcome from given incentive, which is difficult • Is mechanical, so inflexible • Involves regulatory lag • Fails to prohibit offenses • Costs state revenue	Tax breaks for research and development
4. Market-harnessing controls	• Response is driven by firms, not bureaucracy	• No regulatory body addresses technical or commercial problems in the industry	
Competition policy	• Can be applied across industries • Creates economies of scale in regulation • Involves low level of intervention • Grants firms flexibility	• Increases uncertainty and transaction costs • Requires strong competition authority • Depends on courts, which move slowly • Develops principles only as policy is put into practice	Retail distribution services
Concessions	• Enforcement is low cost to public • Involves low level of restriction • Respects managerial freedom • Allows competition for market as substitute for competition in market • Response is from firms rather than government bodies' preferences	• Applies only to specific services • Creates tension between specification and responsiveness/innovation • Uncertainties impose cost on consumers • Requires multiple bidders • Nontransparent bidding procedures leave room for corruption • Terms of franchise need to be enforced	Administration of ports and airports
Contracts	• Combines control with provision of services • Sanctions through economic incentive or nonrenewal • Easier to operate than licensing and concessions	• May confuse regulatory and service provision roles • Is limited to selected services • Lacks transparency and accountability	Street-cleaning services
5. Information disclosure	• Level of intervention is low • Leaves market decisions to consumers • Reduces danger of regulatory capture	• Requires high degree of understanding by consumers • Is appropriate only in low-risk sectors • Economic incentives (for example, low price) prevail over information (risk) • Involves potentially high costs of disclosure • Requires monitoring of information quality and fraud	Mandatory disclosure of terms in insurance

(continued on next page)

MODULE 3

Table 3.1. Regulatory Strategies: Trends and Weaknesses *(continued)*

Strategy	Strengths	Weaknesses	Example
6. Design and Nudge	• Imposes low cost • Combines influence with freedom of choice	• May not work where decision processes are complex or are influenced by other incentives (for example, prices) • Lacks transparency and accountability • Is suitable only in low-risk sectors	Consent to organ donation
7. Rights and liabilities	• Decision remains with agents • Low degree of state intervention • Imposes low cost on state	• May not prevent undesired effects • Enforcing individual rights may be too costly • Legal uncertainties reduce enforcement • Insurance may temper deterrent effects	Tort law, individual rights

Source: Baldwin, Cave, and Lodge 2012.

Making Regulation Less Burdensome

This section examines examples of alternatives to specific regulatory approaches that are particularly restrictive to services trade. The first part looks at ways in which regulations can be made less burdensome while retaining the same overall strategy. The second part looks at changes in strategy. It discusses the relative costs and benefits of different approaches in particular sectors. The presentation is general. A box at the end of the section makes the discussion concrete by applying the concepts to the retail distribution sector.

Decreasing the Burden of Command and Control Regulation

Regulatory reform does not always involve a change in regulatory strategy. In many cases, reform can take the form of changes to a strategy's structure and implementation (table 3.2).

Reducing the Scope of Entry Restrictions

Licensing regimes in some sectors are an example of command and control regulation. Although this kind of regulation sometimes comes with high costs, it is difficult to imagine successful regulation of sectors like professional services, telecommunications, or retail banking without some form of licensing in place. The rationale is different in each case and is sector specific.

In professional services, the main rationale for licensing is primarily consumer protection. From a trade policy standpoint, the key issue is whether foreign-licensed professionals should be authorized to practice domestically.

The most restrictive approach to licensing is to require foreign professionals to satisfy the same educational requirements as domestic professionals. Chile takes this approach with respect to lawyers, subject to reciprocity or mutual recognition agreements. Nationality requirements are also common. In Algeria, for example, only citizens can practice domestic law.[4] Some countries also restrict cross-border trade in professional services. Brazil prohibits the cross-border supply of accounting, auditing, and legal services, presumably because it is difficult to control the activities and competence of professionals not located within the national jurisdiction. The establishment of a commercial presence is also heavily restricted in professional services, with some countries, such as Argentina, prohibiting equity participation by nonnationals.

Regulators can reduce the burdens imposed on business by licensing by requiring domestic licensing only for activities for which there is a public interest in doing so. In legal services, for example, requiring domestic law practitioners to be citizens may make sense; extending the regulation to experts in international law may not. In accounting, it is possible to separate out activities that require tight regulation on public interest grounds, such as the provision of statutory audits, from those where the rationale for consumer protection is weaker, such as routine back-office services. Limiting licensing or **nationality requirements** to particular activities where the consumer protection rationale is strongest is preferable to a blanket prohibition on the provision of services by foreign accounting professionals. The case for licensing is substantially weaker for business-to-business services than it is for services that affect individual consumers directly, as businesses are presumed to be familiar with the commercial activities they perform.

In cases where domestic licensing of foreign professionals is desirable from an economic efficiency standpoint, policy makers need to set education and training requirements. One possibility is to require that foreign lawyers comply with the same education requirements as domestic lawyers—the practice in Chile. An alternative is to recognize some foreign educational qualifications on a unilateral basis but submit all professionals—foreign and domestic—to a knowledge-based examination process, as some states in the United States do.

Table 3.2. Modifications to Common Regulatory Measures to Decrease Their Restrictiveness

Regulatory measure	Rationale	Problems/considerations	Modification of approach
Granting of exclusive right	Natural monopoly exists or state wants to ensure a large strategic investment or meet specific socioeconomic political objectives, such as universal access to services.	Natural monopoly must be carefully defined. (In what part of the market does it exist? Is it durable or likely to be eliminated over time by technology or other changes?) Regulating monopoly is difficult. Is the cost of regulating greater than the hoped-for gain?	• Carefully allocate monopoly right by limiting its scope and duration, auctioning it, and repeating the auction periodically. • Break up monopoly and encourage competition in areas not characterized by natural monopoly (such as electricity generation and distribution); focus regulation on core natural monopoly (such as electricity transmission). • Consider more direct ways to help target groups, sectors, and regions.
Licensing and permitting	State seeks to address market failure or achieve other public interest objectives, such as equity or better use of environmental resources.	Licenses can be manipulated to restrict entry, following lobbying from incumbents; encourage corruption; and be difficult and costly to administer.	• Explore scope to decrease anticompetitive impacts. • Review licensing and permitting to ensure that benefits of regulation exceed costs. • Consider alternatives, such as reliance on other regulations, fiscal instruments, information campaigns, market-based instruments, product liability laws, or quasi-regulation (such as industry codes of conduct).
Limiting government procurement to services from domestic suppliers	State seeks to favor local or small businesses in order to promote domestic enterprise/import substitution.	Policies are generally protectionist and impose high cost on suppliers. Other means of favoring particular groups are likely to be more effective and transparent.	• Carefully consider policy merits of favoring particular groups. • If warranted, consider subsidies, vouchers, or targeted removal of unwarranted impediments (regulatory or otherwise) to participation.
Raising the cost of entry or exit	States seeks to protect consumers.	Entry costs rise as a result of increased product testing requirements, need for greater financial capacity (including insurance) requirements, and so on. Policies disadvantage new entrants, protecting incumbents and reducing innovation and dynamism in the market. Many provisions yield relatively limited consumer benefits.	• Assess extent of consumer problems/potential harms and size of benefits caused by interventions. • Keep requirements to a minimum. • Consider consumer education as an alternative.
Restricting flow of goods, services, capital, or labor across borders	Often a tool of regional policy, in which state attempts to enhance viability of regional economies, increase employment, and so on.	Artificially reduces size of market. Significant efficiency costs are often created by excluding potentially larger and more efficient groups of alternative suppliers. Invites retaliatory action from other governments, creating a negative-sum game.	• Consider other regional policy tools, including provision of subsidies, targeted investments by government, and enhanced infrastructure.
Controls on prices of goods or services	Maximum prices often a corollary of entry restrictions. Minimum prices sometimes a response to concerns over predatory pricing, where price competition has been fierce.	Defeats market disciplines, protecting inefficient producers. Consumers pay higher prices. Even maximum prices may tend to increase average prices by serving as a price signal.	• Use general competition law to deal with predatory pricing, which is in any case rare. • Where entry restrictions lead to monopoly power, remove the restrictions. • Seek alternatives, as there are virtually no cases in which regulation of prices is a first-best solution.
Restrictions on advertising	State seeks to prevent false/misleading advertising or discourage overconsumption where it can result in negative impacts on consumers.	Limits consumer information and makes markets less efficient. Usually ineffective in limiting consumption, choice, or entry.	• Rely on general competition law to prevent false and misleading advertising.

(continued on next page)

MODULE 3

Table 3.2. Modifications to Common Regulatory Measures to Decrease Their Restrictiveness *(continued)*

Regulatory measure	Rationale	Problems/considerations	Modification of approach
Setting product standards at high levels	State may set standards above levels informed consumers would choose to reduce political risks or provide a level of protection considered desirable at the political or broader community level.	Limits consumer choice, especially ability to choose low-price/low-quality options. Likely to be a problem for poorer consumers.	• Competition laws allow for cooperation in setting standards if not used to unduly limit competition; emphasis should be on performance versus technical standards.

Source: World Bank 2010b, adapted from OECD 2007.

Regulation could also be modified in the transport sector. Licensing of operators and imposition of load limits are probably justifiable on economic grounds—although load limits could at least partly be replaced with a load-based tax to cover the negative externalities imposed by large loads, such as road damage. Differences in licensing requirements and load limits across countries impose additional costs on cross-border transport, however, because of the need to unload and reload merchandise at the border and change drivers. Countries can reduce transport costs by harmonizing regulations or accepting each other's requirements (mutual recognition). Smaller countries, which may not be able to negotiate such deals, may consider unilaterally recognizing their neighbors' requirements, particularly when they are part of a regional hub.

Creating an Appropriate Licensing Regime

An economically efficient licensing regime should have the following characteristics (Ogus 2004):

1. *Be independent of the operators being licensed.* The fact that professionals have traditionally been responsible for their own licensing has often led to anticompetitive conduct through the erection of barriers to entry. The close relationship between financial regulators and regulated financial firms has been brought into question in light of the global financial crisis of 2008–09.
2. *Be transparent.* Licenses should be granted according to preestablished criteria. When discretion is used, the regulator should explain its decision. Licenses should not be granted or refused based on the license giver's perceptions.
3. *Discriminate between foreign and domestic operators and between incumbents and potential entrants as little as possible.* Nondiscrimination helps ensure that market disciplines, not institutional preferences, play a fundamental role in determining the success or failure of individual service providers. By ensuring as little discrimination as possible, the regulator can reduce

barriers to entry, thus moderating prices and increasing variety for consumers.

4. *Use recognition arrangements wherever possible.* Recognition can be either unilateral or mutual (reciprocal or plurilateral). In many cases, the bulk of the economic gains from recognition can be obtained through a unilateral process, which has the advantage of being politically and administratively more straightforward than engaging in the international negotiations necessary for mutual recognition. Recognition can take the form of either complete recognition of foreign licenses and standards or partial recognition (such as recognition of foreign educational achievements even if an additional domestic licensing requirement is imposed). Recognition may not be appropriate in all cases, but in sectors such as transport and some subsectors within professional services, it can facilitate international trade by reducing the cost burdens facing businesses.
5. *Keep administrative costs to a minimum.* Although administrative costs are necessary to ensure the functioning of the licensing regime, paperwork and evidentiary requirements should not intrude into other areas of the license seeker's business or practices. Reducing the cost burden facing potential licensees should be a priority for licensing regimes, as it encourages entry and thus decreases prices and provides greater variety for consumers.
6. *Strictly define the licensed activities, and limit them to activities for which there is a strong economic case for licensing.* Within a sector, it is increasingly possible to divide activities into activities that require licensing and activities that do not.

Shifting Regulatory Strategies

In many services sectors, there is scope to employ incentive-based regimes, such as taxes and subsidies, in place of command and control regulation. This section discusses some examples.

Shifting to Incentive-Based Regimes

Regulators can consider shifting to incentive-based regimes in a variety of areas. For example, one horizontal regulation encountered in some developing countries is a restriction on repatriation of profits by foreign-owned firms. In Malawi, for instance, central bank approval is required before earnings can be repatriated. The objectives of this measure are likely twofold: to ration scarce foreign exchange and to ensure that foreign firms pay all relevant taxes and charges within the jurisdiction. However, this command and control approach—in which the central bank has broad discretion—creates considerable uncertainty for foreign firms, which may discourage them from entering the market, thereby limiting competition. Such measures can also have the perverse effect of discouraging inflows of foreign direct investment (FDI) and thus exacerbating shortages of foreign exchange.

If regulation in this area is necessary on economic grounds, it may be preferable to use an incentive-based approach, such as taxation of repatriated earnings. Such taxation can be imposed on a withholding basis, to ensure that foreign companies pay the appropriate taxes and charges in the domestic jurisdiction and are thus not afforded a competitive advantage over local firms. The tax rate should not be prohibitive or it will have the same effect of discouraging FDI as a command and control approach. If properly implemented, a tax-based approach is preferable to administrative discretion on grounds of transparency and nondiscrimination. Although it still discriminates against foreign companies, it does so less than other approaches.

Another area in which it is possible to make the transition from command and control regulation to incentive-based regulation is local content requirements. In services, these regulations require foreign firms to employ a minimum proportion of locals. In some cases, these requirements are applied horizontally (that is, to all sectors). In others, they are applied on a sectoral basis. Bolivia, for instance, requires that 85 percent of the employees of foreign-owned banks be locals. The public policy objective of such measures is to promote local employment.

In many countries, employment is taxed through payroll deductions. It is therefore possible to encourage local employment by providing payroll tax credits. There is no economic justification for applying such measures only in the case of foreign-owned enterprises. It would make sense to apply them across the board if labor market conditions are such that some degree of intervention is warranted. Of course, such measures cannot deal with structural unemployment linked to macroeconomic conditions and policies; alternative measures would need to be adopted if

such conditions and policies are the source of the problem. But at least on a short-term basis and a relatively small scale, payroll tax credits—an incentive-based regulatory strategy—could replace command and control methods such as local content requirements. The advantage of the tax approach is that it is less distortionary with respect to firms' hiring decisions. It is also transparent and not subject to evasion or manipulation. Moreover, far from discouraging FDI, tax credits are likely to encourage it by reducing the effective cost of local labor.

In addition to horizontal measures, there are also sector-specific policies in which at least a partial transition from command and control to incentive-based regulation could be made. Road transport is one example. Most countries impose command and control standards governing maximum loads that can be carried by trucks. Such an approach is appropriate from a road safety point of view. But an alternative justification for this type of regulation is that heavier loads impose greater externalities in the form of more damage to roads. There is therefore a case to be made for retaining standards-based measures as an absolute maximum but imposing taxes corresponding to load weights as well. Such an approach would have the advantage of internalizing the externalities caused by heavy loads and thus promoting economic efficiency. This kind of tax measure is transparent and relatively straightforward to administer, at least in countries with well-developed networks of weigh stations or traders who demonstrate a high level of compliance in declarations. It is probably more applicable to middle-income than low-income countries, where regulation probably needs to remain primarily command and control based.

Shifting to Market-Harnessing Regulation

In some situations, market-harnessing controls, such as competition policy and franchising, can help ensure that market disciplines play the largest possible role in regulation. Where appropriate, changing regulatory strategies in this way can yield significant economic gains.

Telecommunications and energy were both traditionally regulated as natural monopolies under a command and control strategy. This approach may have been appropriate in the past; advances in technology have made it less so today. Technological change has highlighted the possibility of using competition as a regulatory tool in at least some parts of these sectors. In both cases, two crucial issues emerge: network access and the separation of natural monopoly activities from activities where competition is possible.

As technology has improved, it has become increasingly possible to identify particular activities in sectors such as telecommunications and energy that have natural monopoly characteristics, rather than assuming that entire sectors are natural monopolies. In telecommunications, for instance, network development is often considered a natural monopoly, at least for some parts of the fixed line network. In energy, generation is a (local) natural monopoly. In both cases, market-harnessing mechanisms can represent an effective transition from command and control regulation. One option is to adopt a franchising approach, in which firms compete for, rather than within, the market. By taking competitive bids for a time-limited monopoly, regulators can encourage firms to adopt pricing models that approach competitive levels.

Several considerations are relevant in assessing the relative costs and benefits of franchising versus command and control regulation (Baldwin, Cave, and Lodge 2012). On the positive side, franchising results in a relatively market-friendly regulatory stance. Enforcement involves low costs to the public, and managers are left free to respond to changes in market conditions, rather than being hamstrung by possibly outdated bureaucratic standards. On the negative side, it is important to be realistic about the possibility for effective competition for the market, particularly in developing countries. Franchising is most effective when it attracts a large number of sophisticated bidders. For developing countries, which often lack capacity and financial resources, it is necessary to relax foreign investment laws in a nondiscriminatory way before franchising out activities such as energy generation or telecommunications network construction, in order to ensure the maximum possible level of competition for the market.

Even this may not be sufficient in very small markets, however. In such cases, where franchises are unlikely to prove attractive to foreign or domestic investors, regulators may need to stick with a command and control strategy, perhaps backed up by the use of competition law (box 3.2). It is important to avoid a situation in which foreign investment is opened up in a highly selective way—perhaps with one developed country partner—effectively killing off competition for the franchise and resulting in a case where monopoly profits may be repatriated overseas with only limited efficiency gains. It is therefore important for developing country governments to get the sequencing of reforms right.

A second market-harnessing control that is important in sectors such as energy and telecommunications is competition law, particularly market access regimes. When generation or network creation is separated from distribution or use, only generation or network creation need to be regulated as natural monopolies; distribution and use can be regulated on a competitive basis, provided that all operators have nondiscriminatory access to the network.

Use of competition law can be problematic in developing countries. Some middle-income countries have adopted competition laws and are enforcing them with increasing vigor. In contrast, most low-income countries lack the human resources and financial capacity to do so. A further drawback of using competition law as a regulatory strategy is that the law usually lays down broad principles that need to be elaborated by the courts to produce detailed regulatory policies. This process can take

---

Box 3.2. Using "Yardstick" Competition in Monopolistic Markets

A form of competition that could help reduce the burden on regulators is yardstick competition. Under this approach, regulators assess the performance of an infrastructure service provider (for example, prices and coverage) by comparing it with a provider in another place (such as a neighboring country) and adjusting regulations. Although this approach does not create competition in the market, it can have similar effects on incentives for infrastructure providers.

Competition among "monopolists" can reduce the need for sectoral regulation in sectors such as petroleum and electricity distribution. For example, the transport of petroleum by pipeline between two points may well be a natural monopoly. Producers at a particular location, however, may not require regulatory protection if they have alternative customers to that pipeline (for example, local buyers or customers elsewhere who can be reached through other means of transport). Similarly, customers at a particular point on a pipeline that is a monopoly may not require regulatory protection if they have alternative sources of petroleum, such as local producers or shipment by water or a pipeline from another origin. Similar conditions hold for some natural gas pipelines. In Argentina, pipelines from two different gas-producing areas—Gas Atacama (a joint venture of Chile's Endesa and the U.S. firm CMS Energy) and Norandino (Belgium's Tractebel)—are just beginning to compete to bring natural gas across the Andes Mountains to northern Chile.

Similarly, even if the long-distance transmission of electricity between the generation facility and the consuming enterprise or municipality is a natural monopoly, generators at a particular location may not require regulatory protection if they are served by different long-distance transmission lines serving different sets of customers. Customers at a particular location may not require regulatory protection if they are served by different long-distance transmission lines carrying power from different generators. Municipal and large industrial users are currently enjoying such competition from different generation facilities in Argentina, Brazil, Chile, and Peru.

Source: World Bank 2002.

years and is subject to considerable uncertainty, particularly where judicial capacity is low.

The combination of franchising and competition law does not usually remove the need for a sectoral regulator. It is possible to outline criteria that such a regulator should have. According to the World Trade Organization's *Reference Paper on Telecommunications Services*, sectoral regulators should be independent of incumbent operators, promote competition and network access, be transparent, and ensure nondiscrimination between domestic and foreign firms and between incumbents and potential entrants.

Many developing countries—except the smallest and very poorest—could benefit from using franchising as a regulatory strategy in such sectors as telecommunications and energy; it is probably only relatively high-capacity middle-income countries that can effectively use competition law to promote network access. Small, low-income countries may therefore need to continue to rely on command and control strategies, at least to some extent, in regulating these sectors. Command and control is not a "one size fits all" strategy, however; it is subject to many interpretations and combinations of measures. Countries that retain a significant role for command and control regulation should ensure that it erects as few barriers to entry as possible and reduces to a minimum the cost burdens facing operators.

Another sector in which alternative regulatory strategy can be applied is transport. The construction and operation of some port and airport facilities display natural monopoly characteristics and could therefore be regulated in appropriate cases via a franchising strategy. Ancillary operations—such as cargo handling—do not display such characteristics; they can be regulated through a competitive model, using competition law as appropriate.

Shifting to Disclosure Regulation

The financial and professional services sectors could potentially benefit from increased use of disclosure regulation. As there are important consumer protection rationales for regulation in both sectors, the provision of information could enable consumers to choose services that fit their preferences and risk profiles.

In finance, a command and control approach to regulation prohibits certain types of instruments or transactions based on their perceived risks. For instance, retail banks and insurance companies were traditionally allowed to invest only in a certain range of tightly regulated instruments. Although there is clearly a case for retaining a command and control approach to issues such as capital adequacy, the broader use of command and control is not without problems. For instance, the effectiveness of

regulation depends on the courts' interpretations of statutory instruments, which may lead to circumvention by regulated firms.

Disclosure regulation presents an attractive alternative. It is already being implemented to varying degrees in financial markets around the world, where firms are required to disclose to investors a wide range of factors that may affect the choice to invest.

One area that does not appear to have been addressed is retail banking. Many countries prohibit or limit cross-border retail banking transactions (Mode 1 trade). Even countries that are liberal on Mode 1, such as the United States and the United Kingdom, prohibit advertising by foreign retail banks, thereby limiting the market to a small number of well-informed investors. A more liberal approach would be to allow transactions and advertising by foreign-licensed retail banks, subject to full disclosure that they do not hold a banking license in the domestic jurisdiction, that they are not subject to the same capital adequacy requirements or other supervisory measures as domestic banks, and that deposits are not guaranteed by domestic deposit insurance mechanisms. Although a detailed cost-benefit analysis of this approach is needed to ensure that it would not result in significant investment in unsafe products by ill-informed consumers, it could be a more liberal regulatory strategy for retail banking services that would help promote trade.

Greater use of disclosure regulation could also be beneficial in professional services. It is desirable to limit the scope of domestic licensing to a relatively narrow range of activities, such as advice on domestic law in the case of legal services or the signing of statutory accounts in the case of accounting and auditing. To ensure that consumers do not mistakenly use unlicensed professionals, disclosure regulation could require professionals with foreign licenses whose practice is limited to foreign and international law or back-office accounting functions to identify themselves as such. Requiring foreign professionals to use titles such as "foreign lawyer" or "foreign accountant" would highlight to the public that the professionals in question followed an alternative procedure to gain access to the domestic market and are different from domestically licensed professionals in the range of services they can legally offer. The combination of limiting command and control regulation and increasing disclosure regulation would result in an increase in trade in professional services, at the same time ensuring that consumers remain protected from unscrupulous operators.

Alternative regulatory strategies could also be applied in the retail distribution sector. Box 3.3 discusses some options.

MODULE 3

Box 3.3. Adopting Alternative Regulatory Strategies in the Retail Distribution Sector

Retail distribution is a regulated sector in many economies. Regulatory measures include entry restrictions and measures that affect the ongoing operations of incumbents. For 1998, 2003, and 2008, the OECD's Product Market Regulation Indicators (PMRs) provide a snapshot of the regulatory environment in up to 40 countries. Most of the data cover OECD member countries; the 2008 version also covers Brazil, China, India, Indonesia, the Russian Federation, and South Africa.

Command and control, embodied in mandatory regulations, is the dominant regulatory strategy in the sector, sometimes combined with self-regulation. For instance, some countries require retail outlets selling food to be licensed or listed in a commercial register. This requirement is a classic licensing requirement that is consistent with a command and control approach. Unfortunately, the PMRs do not disclose the criteria used for the licensing decision—such as whether it is automatic or discretionary—so it is difficult to assess the performance of different countries on this metric.

An example of (partial) self-regulation in the retail sector is the inclusion by some countries of retail associations in licensing decisions. This strategy comes with considerable potential costs, as established retailers can easily capture the licensing system and use it to erect barriers to entry. Although any licensing system needs to be based on professional knowledge of the characteristics of the sector, direct involvement of regulated entities in the licensing decision can lead to undesirable and uncompetitive outcomes. A more efficient approach would be to institute a licensing system that is independent and transparent.

Another example of command and control in the retail sector is the application by some countries of specific regulations for outlets that exceed a certain surface area. If surface area is a genuine economic or social issue—because, for example, a large store leaves a deeper environmental footprint—an appropriate and more efficient regulatory strategy would be to use economic incentives. For instance, a tax could be applied to retail outlets based on their surface area. To the extent that large outlets cause more environmental damage than small ones, the tax would internalize the externality. Of course, the question would then arise as to why retail outlets—rather than all commercial facilities—should be subject to an additional tax. The appropriate approach would therefore be to embed the sectoral issue in a broader approach to environmental regulation of commercial facilities—preferably through a system of economic incentives.

In addition to these measures affecting market entry, retail distribution also sometimes involves regulations that increase the cost of doing business for incumbents. Examples are the regulation of shop opening hours and price controls. In neither case is there an obvious economic rationale. The goals of possible rationales for price controls—limiting inflation and ensuring that basic goods are accessible to poor people—can be achieved in more efficient ways using alternative regulatory strategies. With regard to inflation, macroeconomic policy (particularly monetary policy) is a more targeted response and introduces fewer microeconomic distortions than do price controls. To ensure that poor people have access to basic goods, it is more efficient—and probably more effective—to adopt an economic incentives strategy. Consumption subsidies for people below a certain level of income can ensure that they have access to sufficient food and other basic resources without distorting the consumption choices of other members of the community.

Examination of the PMRs at the country level reveals a range of approaches to these regulatory problems. Some countries, such as China, employ a relatively restrictive regulatory stance. Others, such as Brazil, have a more liberal approach, comparable to that of such developed countries as Australia. This range of experience among developing countries forms the basis for significant South-South knowledge exchange.

Source: World Bank, based on OECD Product Market Regulation Database.

Meeting Political Economy Challenges

Reform of services trade and investment does not take place in a vacuum.[5] Because of the significant interests involved in services, establishing and implementing reform is complex (Hoekman and Kostecki 2009).

Reforms may not be politically feasible unless they take into account the political economy reality in a country and how it constrains economic choices. A Regulatory Assessment of Services Trade and Investment (RASTI) must therefore identify the factors that influence the regulatory framework for services and assess how influential they may be in preventing the implementation of technically sound policy options.

Assessment of the political economy context should help policy makers design a sustainable reform strategy. The focus should be on finding feasible approaches for reform and assessing whether the priorities identified in the regulatory assessment are realistic, what vulnerabilities may affect the implementation of the reforms, and how

governance should be reformed to strengthen the reforms' feasibility. The analysis allows policy makers to widen the space for reform by improving and targeting an information and communication strategy, working more intensively with stakeholders, and building and strengthening supporting coalitions.

A political economy assessment includes the following steps:

- *Identify the problem, issue, or vulnerability* (the services sectors and modes that will be reformed, how they will be reformed, and the winners and losers from those reforms).
- *Map existing institutional and governance arrangements,* in order to understand how supportive (or not) of development concerns they are. The analysis of institutions is concerned with the access stakeholders have to the institutional context, the rules of the game, the distribution of resources of power/influence, and the

importance of the institutional context in the results of the reforms, including how the existing configuration and interaction among them will be affected by the reform process.

- *Understand political economy drivers.* This step involves analyzing stakeholders' interests, leadership, priorities, motivation, resources, capacity to influence, and capacity to build alliances and incentives; the ways in which stakeholders interact (formally and informally) with existing institutions; and the ways these interactions have evolved over time at the country or sectoral level (World Bank 2008; Corduneanu-Huci, Hamilton, and Masses Ferrer 2013). More important, the analysis should determine how the proposed regulatory reforms will affect stakeholders.

In line with the desired scope of the RASTI, the political economy analysis may take place at the country, sector, or policy or project level. Country-level analysis is appropriate when the analysis of the political economy seeks to assess the overall governance situation in the country (Fritz, Kaiser, and Levy 2009). Box 3.4 provides a set of basic questions for country-level analysis.

Sector-level analysis of the political economy context complements the regulatory assessment at the sectoral level, by identifying factors that can influence the success or failure of the regulatory reform. Box 3.5 provides examples of appropriate questions to pose when assessing the political economy factors at the sectoral level.

Analysis at the policy or project level is narrower in scope. It aims to address a more specific issue identified during the regulatory assessment.

The political economy analysis should be based on evidence (that is, supported by data). Data from the Worldwide Governance Indicators and other sources may help assess a country's capabilities to adopt reforms. Sources that identify stakeholders and their interactions, as well as data that help assess stakeholders' economic and political importance and relevance beyond the economic and political dimension, such as their relative economic importance and population significance, should also be used. At the sectoral level, the data should assess the influence of stakeholders and, if possible, compare it with their influence at the country level.

Corduneanu-Huci, Hamilton, and Masses Ferrer (2013) provide guidance on what this analysis allows policy makers to do:

- A political economy context identifies stakeholders and the consequences that reform could have for them.
- It creates maps of stakeholders that can be classified under different groupings that might support or oppose reform.

Box 3.4. Political Economy Analysis at the Country Level

Key issues to consider in a political economy analysis at the country level include the following:

- How does the country compare with other countries with respect to the provision of good policies generally and in the priority areas identified?
- The credibility and legitimacy of government (in relation to both elites and the broader society) are integral aspects of governance. Lack of credibility and legitimacy reduces the ability of public and private actors to plan with a long-term horizon and makes it more difficult to construct a durable coalition that favors reform. Both credibility and legitimacy are underpinned by the allocation of resources and rents. Are agreements regarding rent extraction and distribution accepted by a critical mass of elite interests? Are they stable and credible—that is, are beneficiaries of rent-seeking arrangements (whether private investors, key political actors, or social groups) confident that these arrangements will continue? Is there similar confidence in the credibility of property rights? What is the basis of this confidence?
- One key aspect of governance relates to the incentives of politicians to pursue policies in the broad public interest. What aspects of the political environment augment or diminish the political incentives to pursue such policies?
- Another key aspect of governance is the ability of the administration to carry out policies in the broad public interest predictably and sustainably. What limitations does bureaucratic capacity impose on the ability of politicians to promise and deliver on promises regarding policy reforms? Alternatively, what is the potential of the bureaucracy to implement priority reforms technocratically and sustainably?
- What are the sources of fragility in the country? What arrangements—economic and noneconomic mechanisms—seem to be essential to ensuring stability (in mediating among deeply divided social groups, for example)? What impact would the proposed priorities have on these mechanisms or social equilibriums?
- Are the development priorities identified by the assessment the right ones given the context? What additional priorities are important to consider?

Source: Adapted from Fritz, Kaiser, and Levy 2009.

Box 3.5. Political Economy Analysis at the Sectoral Level

Key issues to consider in a political economy analysis at the sectoral level include the following:

- What is the ownership structure in the sector (public and private)?
- How are responsibilities distributed between the national and subnational levels? Is this distribution clear? Does it generate significant distortions?
- How is the sector regulated (what are the rules and institutional structures)? Does existing regulation—including informal/de facto rules—ensure integrity? Does it allow the sector to maintain or expand services in line with demand (and commitments to poverty alleviation)? What interests drive/maintain the current regulatory system (including its weaknesses or gaps)?
- How are the sector and its components funded (user fees, taxes/general budget, earmarked taxes such as gasoline excise taxes, informal revenue generation, petty corruption from consumers, and so on)?
- What is the pricing structure for consumers? Which groups benefit (from subsidies, for example)? Are benefiting groups politically salient/powerful? Which consumer groups have a voice?
- Is there significant petty or grand corruption in the sector? If so, why does it persist, and what are the main impacts?
- What opportunities for rent-seeking and patronage are related to the sector? Who appears to benefit from rents? How is patronage being used?
- What are the legacies of the sector? What reforms were attempted or undertaken in the past? What were the results? How does this experience appear to shape current expectations of stakeholders?
- What are the relevant policy processes linked to past or proposed reforms?
- Are there social or ethnic factors that are relevant for sector dynamics?
- What is public opinion on sector performance or proposed reforms? Does the public trust/expect that reform will bring improvements?
- What stakeholders are (officially and unofficially) involved in discussions concerning sector reforms, and what are their interests? What veto points exist in the decision-making and implementation processes?
- What, if any, stake do the government/top executive/key political factions have in the reform?
- How would proposed reforms affect the existing set of interests and incentives?
- What risks exist in failure or negative unintended consequences of proposed reforms?
- What would a politically and institutionally feasible reform look like?

Source: Adapted from Fritz, Kaiser, and Levy 2009.

- It assesses the factors that determine the strength of the stakeholders' preference and their ability to act collectively.
- It provides an analysis of the institutional context in which actors' interaction occurs, which allows policy makers to better understand how to navigate the institutional framework and overcome existing obstacles.
- It improves the understanding of and incorporates into analyses the constraints that reform faces. It helps define what is feasible and under what time frame.

Conclusion and Policy Implications

This module assesses the advantages and disadvantages of various forms of regulation in order to identify strategies that are effective (achieve their objective) and efficient (do so at minimum economic cost). The two criteria most useful in assessing the costs and benefits of regulatory strategies are whether the strategy creates entry barriers that discriminate against either all potential entrants or foreign entrants and whether the strategy unnecessarily increases ongoing costs for market participants. Many countries employ regulations that are justified by reference to important social or economic goals but impose high economic costs. Cross-country

experience suggests that it is possible to liberalize services trade and eliminate measures that create barriers to entry by foreign services providers while ensuring high levels of consumer protection and achieving other important policy objectives.

The perspective put forward in this module is one of regulatory proportionality. Recent decades have seen a shift away from strategies such as direct action and command and control toward competition policy and economic mechanisms. Independent review and analysis from an economy-wide perspective is needed to bring about this kind of change. Analysis has to take a general equilibrium perspective that includes the gains and losses to consumers. Partial equilibrium analysis, which focuses primarily on the needs of producers, is likely to produce regulations that are unduly restrictive and that therefore result in less competition, higher prices, and lower variety for consumers.

Developing country policy makers can take away five rules of thumb from this module:

1. *Trade restrictions should be the exception rather than the rule as a means of promoting economic and social objectives.* In most cases, trade policy is not an efficient way of promoting social goals such as consumer

protection or job creation—and it tends to harm consumers. Because consumers of services include manufacturing firms and other producers, restrictive trade policy in services can reduce productivity and exports in manufacturing.

2. *Policies that target market failures are likely to be more efficient than indirect interventions, such as trade policy.* From an economic efficiency point of view, trade policy is the best policy for dealing with market failures that are fundamentally trade related. However, the market failures considered here are only incidentally trade related. With labor market problems, the most efficient approach is to design appropriate interventions that apply across the board, rather than constraining the activities of a relatively small number of foreign-invested firms.

3. *It may not be technically or financially feasible to implement an optimal policy, particularly where it requires an economic mechanism that presupposes a high level of financial and institutional development.* Trade policy may appear attractive as a second-best way of achieving an economic or social objective. If this is the case, the regulation should distort trade as little as possible. In general, the most important objectives discussed here and those that require the most government intervention relate to consumer protection. The rationale for restricting trade as a second-best consumer protection measure applies more strongly to cross border (Mode 1) trade than to commercial presence (Mode 3). As Mode 3 requires a foreign services provider to establish itself commercially in the local market, it is much easier to subject the foreign firm to the same consumer protection requirements that domestic firms are subject to. That process is much more problematic for Mode 1 trade. To the extent that developing country policy makers find themselves constrained to use trade policy as a second-best policy alternative, national welfare would be best served by concentrating restrictive measures on Mode 1 and leaving Mode 3 as open as possible.

4. *Services sector regulations should be designed to make maximum use of market mechanisms whenever possible.* Even where social objectives require the use of subsidies, policy makers can make the process more efficient by using an economic mechanisms strategy like an auction to allocate them. Similarly, the priority for regulatory reform should be to introduce competition in markets where it is restrained. In most cases, doing so will mean dismantling entry barriers before addressing other measures that increase the costs of doing business. In markets that are already relatively competitive, it may be appropriate to focus on measures that increase the real

economic resources used to do business. There will obviously need to be a case-by-case approach to such questions.

Developing countries are experimenting widely with services policies. Some countries have chosen to adopt a liberal stance regarding trade via Modes 1 and 3, whereas others have chosen to be more restrictive. Experience will provide guidance on the best mix of policies to achieve sectoral regulation that is effective in achieving economic and social objectives and economically efficient.

5. *A regulatory strategy normally relies on a combination of approaches.* Services sectors will normally not be exempted from competition law but will be regulated by specific sectoral provisions. Finding the right combinations is context and country specific, adding complexity to the assessment process. The people responsible for conducting the assessment should be mindful of the context within which alternative regulatory options are recommended.

Notes

1. This section draws on Dee (2006).

2. When the regulation in question is largely economic in nature or deals with measurable phenomena such as externalities, quantifying costs and benefits can be relatively straightforward, provided that sufficient reliable data exist. In the case of noneconomic social goals, quantification is much more challenging.

3. The section draws heavily on Baldwin, Cave, and Lodge (2012) and Ogus (2004).

4. The rationale behind this regulation is presumably that it gives clients the right of recourse against the service provider in cases of negligence.

5. This section is based on Fritz, Kaiser, and Levy (2009) and Corduneanu-Huci, Hamilton, and Masses Ferrer (2013).

References

Baldwin, Robert, Martin Cave, and Martin Lodge. 2012. *Understanding Regulation: Theory, Strategy, and Practice.* Oxford: Oxford University Press.

Corduneanu-Huci, C., Alexander Hamilton, and Issel Masses Ferrer. 2013. *Understanding Policy Change: How to Apply Political Economy Concepts in Practice.* Washington, DC: World Bank.

Dee, Philippa. 2006. "Institutional Strategies within APEC for Improving the Microeconomic Policy Foundations of East Asia's Economic Performance." Working Paper, Australian National University, Canberra. http://crawford.anu.edu.au/pdf/staff/phillippa_dee/concept_paper.pdf.

Fritz, Verena, Kai Kaiser, and Brian Levy. 2009. *Problem-Driven Governance and Political Economy Analysis: Good Practice Framework.* Washington, DC: World Bank

Hoekman, Bernard M., and Michel M. Kostecki. 2009. *The Political Economy of the World Trading System.* New York: Oxford University Press.

Miroudot, Sébastien, Jehan Sauvage, and Ben Shepherd. 2010. *Measuring the Cost of International Trade in Services.* MPRA Paper 27655, University Library of Munich.

MODULE 3

OECD (Organisation for Economic Co-operation and Development). 2007. *Integrating Competition Assessment into Regulatory Impact Analysis*. Paris: OECD.

———. 2008. *Introductory Handbook for Undertaking Regulatory Impact Analysis (RIA)*. Paris: OECD.

OECD Product Market Regulation Database. http://www.oecd.org/eco /reform/indicatorsofregulatoryconditionsintheretaildistributionsector .htm.

1994. *Regulation: Legal Form and Economic Theory*. Oxford: Hart Publishing.

Ogus, Anthony I. 2004. *Regulation: Legal Form and Economic Theory*. Reprint, Portland, OR: Hart Publishing.

World Bank. 2002. *World Development Report 2002: Building Institutions for Markets*. Washington, DC: World Bank.

———. 2008. *The Political Economy of Policy Reform: Issues and Implications for Policy Dialogue and Development Operations*. Washington, DC: World Bank.

———. 2010a. *Making It Work: "RIA Light" for Developing Countries*. Washington, DC: World Bank.

———. 2010b. *Regulatory Quality and Competition Policy*. Washington, DC: World Bank.

Worldwide Governance Indicators (database). World Bank, Washington, DC. http://info.worldbank.org/governance/wgi/index.asp.

MODULE 3

APPENDIX A: PROFESSIONAL SERVICES

Objectives

This appendix provides background information and straightforward guidelines for mapping the professional services market and regulatory framework. Upon completing it, readers will be able to:

- *Distinguish between the conditions affecting the markets for professionals and professional services*
- *Assess the reasons for skills shortages and mismatches that affect the professional services market*
- *Recognize regulatory failures in the professional services market*
- *Classify the nature of regulatory restrictions to trade and investment*
- *Identify possible regulatory alternatives, in particular alternatives to formal restrictions to professional services*

This appendix presents the conceptual framework for the analysis of professional services sectors and trade in professional services.[1] The first two sections focus on the market for professionals and professional services. They present a methodological approach for identifying the main shortcomings affecting the market. The third section focuses on policies relevant to trade in professional services—namely, education, domestic regulation, trade barriers, and labor mobility—and discusses their main regulatory measures, including alternatives that are less trade restrictive of trade. Drawing on these elements, the fourth section considers policy implications, suggesting possible national and international actions to promote trade in professional services. The last section summarizes the main findings on regulatory barriers to professional services. A questionnaire on legal, accounting, and engineering services, available at http://www.worldbank.org /trade/RASTI, offers additional practical guidance for conducting a regulatory mapping. It draws attention to pertinent issues to raise in interviews with government officials and stakeholders when conducting a regulatory mapping.

Professional services play a critical role in the functioning of modern economies and are among the fastest-growing services sectors in many developed and developing economies. Accounting, for example, is a critical component in the infrastructure of a market economy. In addition to generating and processing information on the financial position and profitability of operations—essential for good financial management and accountability—accounting provides the foundation of a country's fiscal system and plays a key role in corporate governance (Trolliet and Hegarty 2003). Effective law and justice systems are key structural pillars of sustainable development and poverty reduction (Cattaneo and Walkenhorst 2010). The engineering sector plays a vital role in the development and maintenance of a country's physical infrastructure and is essential to the productivity and sustainability of other economic activities

The use of professional services is associated with higher labor productivity. In all six southern African countries documented in the *World Bank Survey of Users of Professional Services*, for instance, firms that used accounting, legal, and engineering services had higher average labor productivity than firms without professional services linkages (World Bank 2011b).

Shortages and Skills Mismatches in the Market for Professionals

A diagnostic of the market for professionals should determine whether there are sufficient numbers of them and whether they have the skills that are in demand. Such a diagnostic helps frame recommendations for more targeted skills formation and the reform of selected curriculums. It should answer the following questions:

- How many qualified professionals work in the country?
- Are there skill shortages in any professional services subsectors? If so, what is the magnitude of these shortages, and what are the projected skill gaps?
- Is there evidence of skills mismatches in professional services?

Understanding the causes of the identified outcomes requires data on the salaries and fees earned by professionals and comparable categories of workers in particular countries and their neighbors. As scarcity may manifest itself by higher wages paid to certain professional skills, the diagnostic needs to document potential labor market premiums for professional skills. Such wage premiums can be based on estimates of returns to tertiary education or returns to specific professional degrees.

Analysts also need information on the extent to which immigration and foreign professionals are filling the national skills gap, the capacity of higher education institutions to train professionals and the cost of obtaining qualifications, and the extent of skilled emigration. From this information, it is possible to determine whether there are incentives to acquire professional skills, whether students are able to acquire the desired degrees/skills, and whether there are incentives for graduates to work as professionals. Figure A.1 outlines the steps in this analysis and identifies the underlying explanatory factors for the potential outcomes.

One possible outcome is the absence of wage premiums despite skill shortages (outcome 1 in figure A.1). In such cases, it is necessary to identify why the market is not creating institutions for skills acquisition. Possible explanations include the following:

- Foreign professionals are to some extent bridging the skills gap
- Labor market regulations or the **monopsony** power of employers maintain wages at low levels
- Skills are perceived as an undersupplied public good

Shortages of professionals can reflect a lack of incentives to acquire skills (outcome 2 in figure A.1). Such an outcome could be explained by

- Lower wage premiums in professional services than in other sectors that require tertiary education
- Insufficient information about the benefits of acquiring professional skills (as a result of weak or nonexistent links between the labor markets and professional associations)
- Liquidity constraints

Skill shortages and mismatches can persist despite incentives to acquire professional degrees (outcome 3 in figure A.1) because many potential students are not able to acquire the desired skills, for a variety of reasons, including:

- Liquidity constraints and limited access to financing
- Poor quality of secondary education, which prevents students from being admitted to institutions of higher learning
- The absence or insufficient capacity of educational institutions

Other explanations for this outcome include inappropriate or absent regulations and standards that prevent the emergence of certain professionals (such as midlevel professionals).

Despite incentives and ability to acquire skills, professionals may find limited incentives to practice domestically or over a longer period of time (outcome 4 in figure A.1). Higher returns abroad could motivate professionals to emigrate, or higher returns in other activities (such as management tasks for professional accountants) could create shortages of senior-level professionals.

Sector-specific skill mismatches (outcome 5 in figure A.1) could arise because of the following factors:

- The lack of domestic specialization courses or practical training
- The lack of links between professional institutions and the private sector
- The inability of professionals to access courses abroad (possibly because of financial credit constraints)

Distortions in the Market for Professional Services

A complementary diagnostic examines the professional services market to determine whether, even if sufficient professionals do exist, regulatory obstacles are distorting the market, leading to an inefficient allocation of professional services. Key questions to ask as part of this analysis include the following:

- Who are the main providers of professional services, and what is their market share?
- What is the degree of concentration and the level of fragmentation in the sector?
- What is the ownership structure of the main providers?
- How much foreign direct investment is there in the sector, and what is the potential for more?
- How transparent are the fees and tariff structures of professional service firms?
- How important are imports of professional services?
- Which tasks within the selected professional services are traded cross-border, both within and outside the region?

Figure A.1. Determining Whether Education and Migration Policies Contribute to Skill Shortages and Mismatches in Professional Services

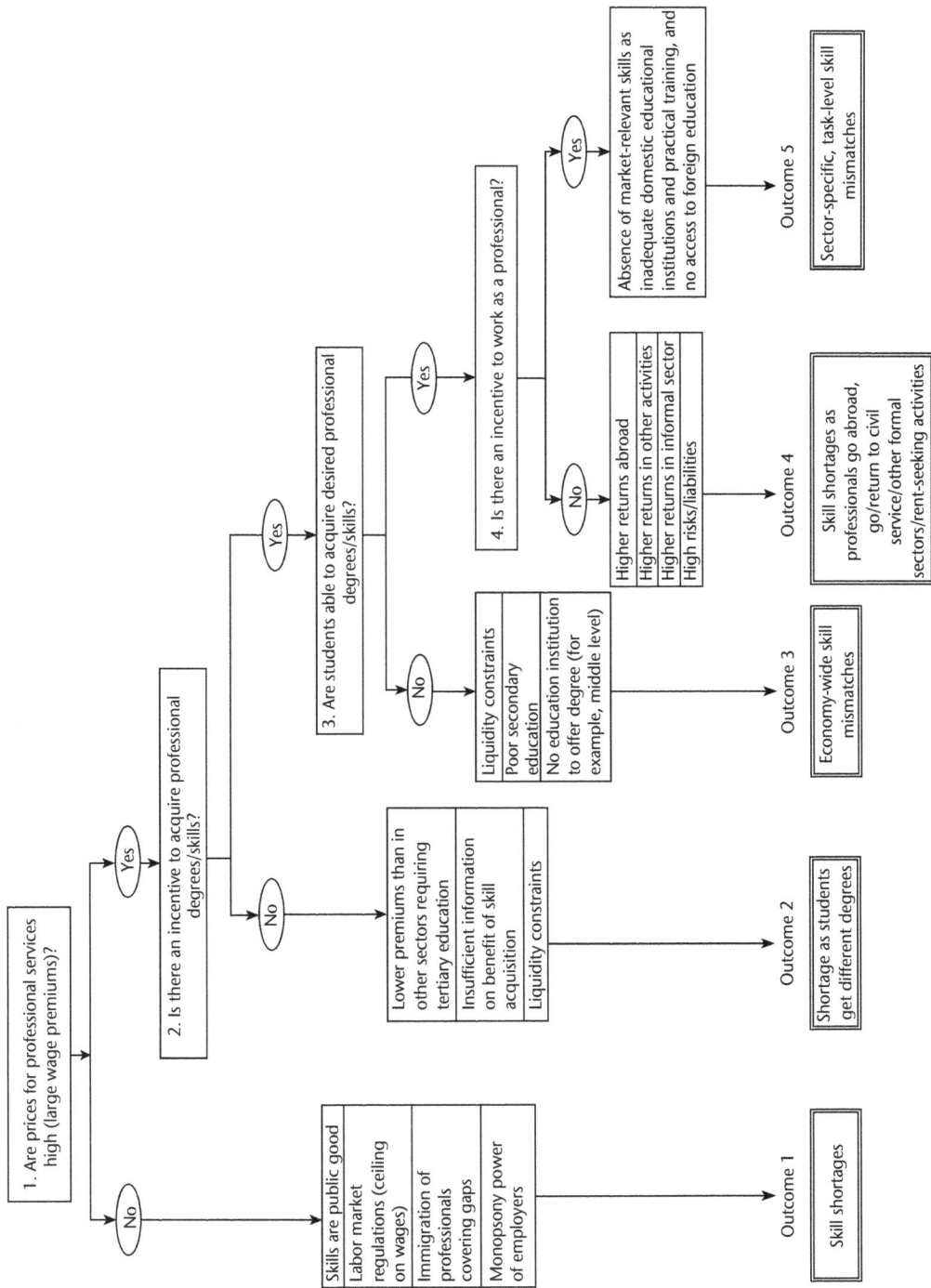

Information on the use of professional services by size and sectors is needed to determine the demand for—and accessibility and quality of—professional services. Figure A.2 details the steps of this analysis.

One possible outcome is limited demand for professional services (outcome 1 in figure A.2). The prevalence of informal arrangements—such as handshake deals, oral agreements, and other customs and practices—may limit demand for certain legal services. Limited monitoring of compliance with financial reporting or safety standards may curb demand for accounting and consulting engineering services.

Other possible outcomes are unsatisfied demand for professional services given skills shortages or mismatches or trade barriers and inadequate regulation of domestic and foreign professionals and firms (outcomes 2–4 in figure A.2). Examples of regulations that limit the incentives or abilities of potential providers to enter the markets include the following:

- Quantitative entry regulations, such as limits on the number of professionals in relation to the population
- Qualitative entry regulations, such as professional examinations
- Minimum required periods of professional experience
- Compulsory membership in a professional body
- Activities reserved to specific licensed professionals
- Exclusive or shared exclusive rights to provide certain services
- Entry restrictions on foreign providers

Professional services could remain unaffordable or be of inadequate quality because of inappropriate regulation, such as limitations on prices or business structure, multidisciplinary practices, and advertising restrictions (outcomes 5 and 6 in figure A.2). The export potential of professional services also needs to be considered. The assessment needs to examine the following factors:

- Fundamentals, such as the country's factor endowment, especially of human capital, and institutional quality, especially the regulatory environment
- Policies affecting trade, investment, and labor mobility
- Proactive policies, such as export promotion activities (Goswami and others 2012)

Policy Challenges

A variety of factors affect the markets for professionals and professional services. Each of them needs to be examined.

Education Policies

Professional services require a skilled workforce. The quality of education is thus critical. Possible education-related barriers include financial constraints, which may prevent individuals from acquiring professional education, and limitations in the capacity and quality of educational institutions, which may prevent students from acquiring market-relevant skills.

Domestic Regulation

Professional services have traditionally been subject to heavy regulation. Measures, which range from qualitative and quantitative entry regulation to conduct regulation, are a result of both direct governmental regulation and rules by self-regulatory bodies. Entry regulation includes educational and professional qualification requirements, exclusive or shared exclusive rights to provide services, ownership restrictions, and restrictions on the numbers of providers. Conduct regulation includes regulations governing business structure and multidisciplinary practices, pricing, and advertising. It can be applied to domestic and foreign providers.

Public interest theories claim that many of these regulatory measures are justified to address such market failures as information asymmetries, externalities, lack of economies of scale, and equity concerns. **Private interest theories** have been critical of many aspects of professional regulation, especially self-regulation, focusing on the private sector's ability to **capture** the regulatory process.

Public interest theories argue that qualitative regulatory measures are necessary to guarantee high-quality services and avoid **adverse selection**. Qualitative entry restrictions may thus be necessary. Private interest theories warn that qualitative regulations may be disproportionate because of excessive entry requirements set by rent-seeking professionals and professional associations. In addition, if the profession gains a monopoly over the training organization, the education of professionals may be limited.

It is difficult to determine whether qualitative requirements are disproportionate. Examples of qualitative requirements are restrictions on access to the profession, which reflect the monopoly of professional associations over training institutions, and multiple certification requirements. For instance, a country's banking and insurance laws may require that all companies use auditors approved by the banks or insurance institutions—generally auditors affiliated with one of the "Big Four" or

Figure A.2. Determining Whether Trade Barriers, Domestic Regulation, and Migration Policies Contribute to Skill Shortages and Mismatches in Professional Services

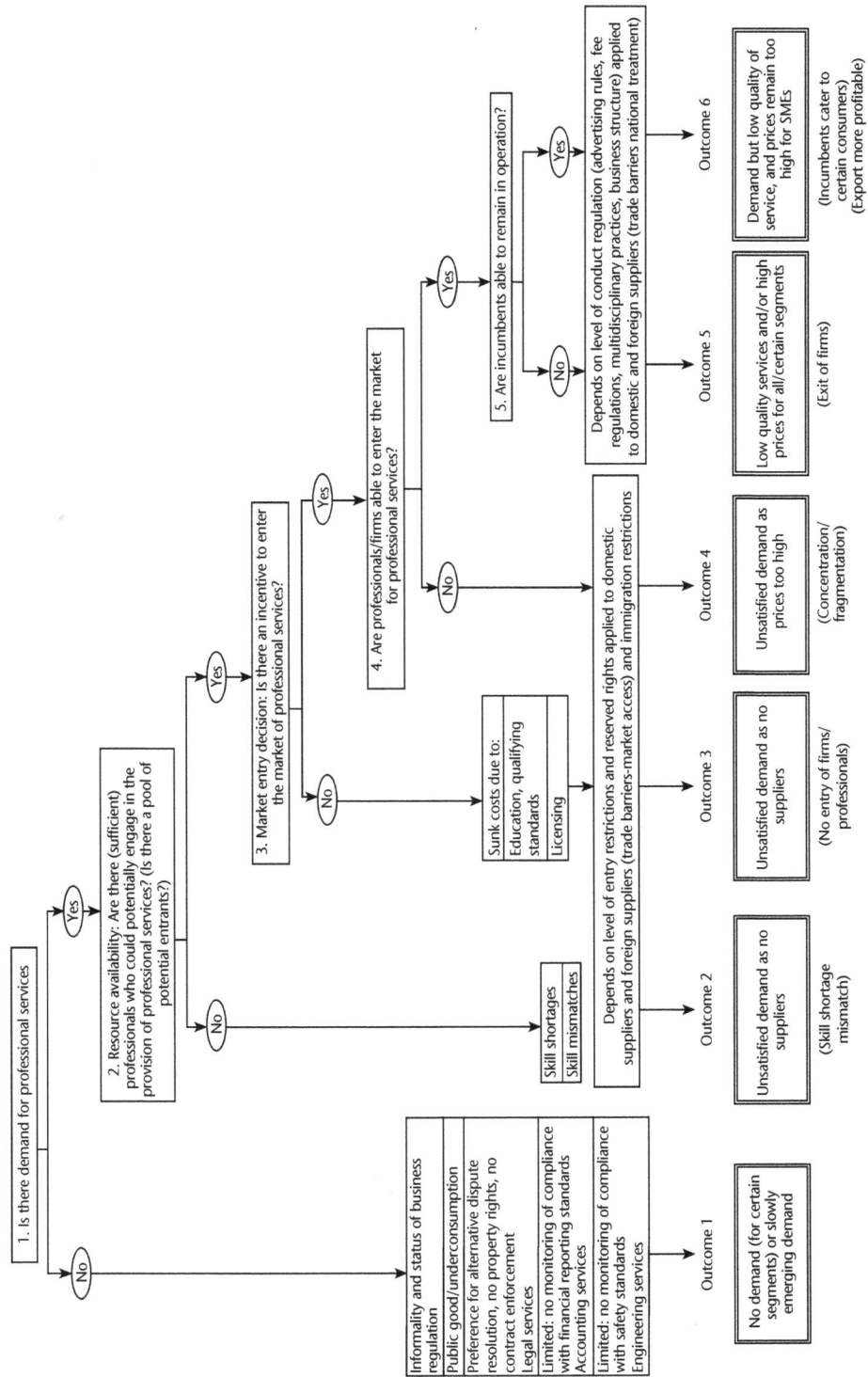

other large companies—to prepare financial statements for outside investors or other external parties to obtain a credit. These requirements may limit the access of smaller suppliers to the market. Box A.1 provides examples of the key regulatory developments in the accounting sector in recent years.

Highly skilled professionals in all sectors have exclusive rights to perform certain activities, such as auditing,

---

Box A.1. Key Developments Affecting the Regulatory Environment for the Accounting Sector

Reliable accounting services are essential to the implementation and enforcement of prudential requirements and other financial regulatory measures, which support stability in financial markets. For this reason, many developed countries and international organizations have passed regulations or established standards to promote sound and transparent accounting practices.

Reports on the Observance of Standards and Codes Initiative
In 1999, the World Bank and the International Monetary Fund initiated the Reports on the Observance of Standards and Codes (ROSC) initiative, covering data dissemination; fiscal transparency; transparency in monetary and financial policies; banking supervision; securities market regulation; insurance supervision, payments, and settlements; anti–money laundering and the combating of financing of terrorism; corporate governance; accounting and auditing; and insolvency and creditor rights. Objectives of the ROSC program include analyzing the comparability of national accounting and auditing standards with international standards, determining the degree to which applicable accounting and auditing standards are followed, and assessing the strengths and weaknesses of the institutional framework in supporting high-quality financial reporting. The ROSC initiative also assists countries in developing and implementing action plans for improving institutional capacity, with the aim of strengthening the corporate financial reporting regime.

Sarbanes-Oxley Act
The Sarbanes-Oxley Act (SOX), enacted in the United States in July 2002, significantly revised the oversight and regulation of the U.S. accounting profession, most notably by strengthening corporate governance requirements and improving transparency and accountability. SOX required the U.S. Securities and Exchange Commission to implement new rules, including rules on independence, to address areas such as prohibited nonaudit services, audit partner rotation, and conflicts of interest. SOX also established the Public Company Accounting Oversight Board (PCAOB) to oversee the audit of public companies. Although SOX rules are considered necessary and important, they may limit the number of accounting firms able to audit large companies.

With respect to multidisciplinary practices, SOX limits possibilities for conflicts of interest, as did the 2006 Directive on Statutory Audits of the European Union. Some countries prohibit multidisciplinary practices, such as accounting and legal services. Among the potential conflicts of interests could be the obligation of lawyers to protect client interests, which may conflict with the transparency requirements for accounting.

Group of 20
The G-20, in its declaration of April 2009, stated that accounting standard-setters should take action by the end of 2009 to reduce the complexity of accounting standards for financial instruments; strengthen accounting recognition of loan-loss provisions by incorporating a broader range of credit information; improve accounting standards for provisioning, off-balance sheet exposures, and valuation uncertainty; achieve clarity and consistency internationally in the application of valuation standards, working with supervisors; make significant progress toward a single set of high-quality global accounting standards; and, within the framework of the independent accounting standard-setting process, improve the involvement of stakeholders, including prudential regulators and emerging markets, through the constitutional review of the International Accounting Standards Board.

International Financial Reporting Standards
Since 2001, almost 120 countries have required or permitted the use of International Financial Reporting Standards (IFRS). They are firmly established in Australasia and Europe, Canada, South Africa, the Republic of Korea, the Russian Federation, and Turkey and are set to be adopted in other jurisdictions. The United States is reducing the differences between its Generally Accepted Accounting Principles (GAAP) and the IFRS, with the expectation of reaching convergence in the near future. The economic and financial crisis brought additional issues to the already wide-ranging debates on the implementation of the IFRS, especially the debates related to financial reporting in a distressed economic situation. They include such challenges as measurement in illiquid markets, the procyclicality of the IFRS, provisioning aspects, and risk management and related disclosures and audit considerations. One of the most important new issues is how to ensure that the financial reporting system not only provides a fair and objective reflection of companies' financial status and performance but also provides early warning signals that may help avert major financial disasters. The new issues are particularly challenging for countries with less developed financial markets and accounting infrastructure.

International Standards on Auditing
More than 100 countries are using the International Standards on Auditing (ISA), are in the process of adopting or incorporating them into national auditing standards, or are using them as a basis for preparing national auditing standards. ISA are intended for use in all audits, including audits of publicly traded companies, private businesses of all sizes, and government entities at all levels. They are issued by the International Auditing and Assurance Standards Board (IAASB), a standard-setting body operating independently under the auspices of the International Federation of Accountants (IFAC). The goals of the IAASB include setting high-quality auditing, assurance, quality control, and related services standards and facilitating the convergence of international and national standards, which should enhance the quality and uniformity of practice throughout the world and strengthen public confidence in the global auditing and assurance profession.

Source: WTO 2012.

representing clients before courts, providing advice on legal matters, conducting feasibility studies, and designing and planning of infrastructure. The argument in favor of exclusive rights is that they can lead to increased specialization of professionals and guarantee higher-quality service. The price and allocation effects of exclusive rights, which act as monopolies, can be substantial, however, especially if they are granted for standardized services that can be provided at a lower cost by less regulated or unregulated providers. Figure A.3 describes three models for regulating legal services based largely on the extent of the exclusive rights granted to legal professionals.

Price regulations are often introduced and supported by national professional associations. But most of the economic literature concurs that these regulatory instruments can seriously harm competition by eliminating or reducing the benefits that competitive markets provide. Most agree that less-restrictive mechanisms, such as better information on the services provided, should be used instead.

Public interest theories justify advertising restrictions by the need to protect consumers. Private interest theories maintain that there is no justification for prohibiting advertising that is relevant, truthful, and not misleading. Advertising fosters competition by informing consumers about different products and allowing them to make better-informed buying decisions. Advertising, especially comparative advertising, can be a crucial competitive tool for new firms entering a market.

Professional associations justify restrictions on business structure on the grounds that professionals are more likely to give independent advice if certain forms of intraprofessional partnerships are prohibited and that restrictions on multidisciplinary activities prevent potential conflicts of interest that are detrimental to consumers. Private interest theories stress that these regulations are clearly anticompetitive and may prevent providers from developing new services or cost-efficient business models. For example, these regulations might prevent lawyers and accountants from providing integrated legal and accounting advice for tax issues. In general, restrictions on collaboration among members

Figure A.3. Regulatory Models for Legal Services

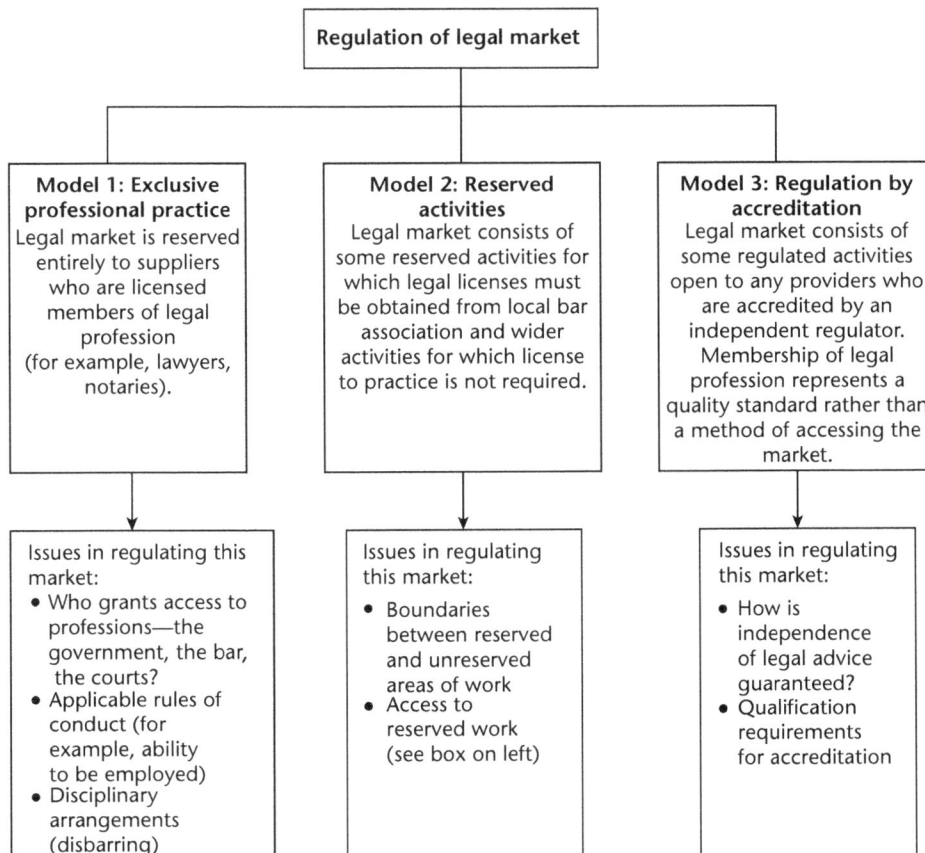

Source: Delimatsis 2010.

of the same profession seem to be less justifiable than restrictions on collaboration among members of different professions where there is a strong need to protect the independence and liability of professionals.

Like all regulation, regulation of professional services seeks to prevent or correct market failures or achieve noneconomic public interest goals. Market failures common in the professional services market relate to **asymmetric information**, the presence of positive and negative externalities, and anticompetitive practices by dominant services providers. Regulation for noneconomic goals is usually based on distributional justice considerations. Limited market size often hampers the development of some professions, which can be spurred through regulatory measures.

Asymmetric Information

Professional services require that practitioners have a high level of technical knowledge. Many knowledge-intensive professional services are **credence goods**—goods whose quality clients may not have the knowledge to judge.

A possible market-based correction mechanism for this problem is the **reputation premium,** which allows professionals with good reputations to charge higher prices. However, in many professional services, reputation (and high prices) is not enough to provide adequate information about quality to consumers. Public interest theories assert that consumers need to be protected through professional standards such as education and qualification requirements; by other qualitative entry requirements, such as limiting certain tasks to professionals; and by advertising regulations.

Public interest theories claim that regulatory intervention is needed to address supplier-induced demand. In some cases, the services provider has an incentive to oversupply quality in order to charge higher prices even if the consumer would be better off with a lower-quality service at a more reasonable price. Such **adverse selection** issues are often addressed by (minimum) standards or price regulation.

Externalities

The use of professional services may bring benefits not only to users but also to third parties. For example, an accurate audit can help companies obtain credit while also helping creditors and investors make informed lending and investment decisions.

However, some providers and potential users, particularly small enterprises, may be unaware of the private and social benefits that the use of professional services offers. Intervention in many professional services markets tries to ensure that positive social externalities occur and negative externalities are avoided.

Negative externalities can be addressed through liability regulations, but this approach operates ex post and has limited success, because of the high costs of enforcement. Ex ante quality requirements, such as standards related to education and training, seem preferable. Positive externalities include the creation of public goods. Many professional services benefit parties not involved in the transaction. Lawyers, for example, define and enforce property rights, which support innovation.

Market Power

In certain professional services, such as accounting, leading firms (which are often foreign owned) control a significant share of the market, and a large gap exists between the leading firm and other firms. This type of market structure may reflect regulatory failure, such as uniform standards or licensing controls at multiple levels. In such cases, interventions may be needed to address inadequate direct or indirect regulation.

Distributional Justice

Markets sometimes exclude certain actors from access to education or services. Therefore, governments or professional associations justify regulatory measures, such as price regulation, to ensure access to services for low-income consumers.

Market Size

The small size of the domestic market may prevent the development of a large professional services sector, including the skills base necessary to support it. Local business services providers often lack the expertise to support manufacturing exporters. Professional services may lack investment from foreign firms. In such cases, it is essential to identify unnecessary measures and trade barriers that prevent local companies from exploiting economies of scale and examine how regional or multilateral liberalization (along with mutual recognition agreements) can help compensate for underdeveloped local services markets.

Explicit Trade Barriers

Most international trade in professional services takes place through commercial presence and the temporary presence of natural persons. Restrictions on professional services exporters thus relate to Mode 3, in General Agreement on Trade in Services (GATS) terminology, including limitations on the foreign ownership of **juridical persons**, **joint venture requirements**, and numerical quotas on the number of operating licenses available to providers of professional services.

The supply of professional services through Mode 3 is often accompanied by Mode 4 supply to provide skilled and professional services directly to projects and to maintain local offices. Professional services firms employ a variety of professionals, such as auditors, lawyers, engineers, and specialized technicians. Restrictions on Mode 4 may also arise from a country's overall immigration policy or specific labor market conditions, including visa requirements, labor market tests, and **residency requirements**.

The deployment of professionals for temporary assignments in export markets, separately or as a complement to foreign direct investment, is common in these sectors. The movement of natural persons is a sensitive issue in many countries because of illegal immigration and security concerns.

Trade in selected professional services, such as engineering consultancy services, can be provided via Mode 1 by using mass communications (mail, fax, telephone, Internet). The principal restrictions on the cross-border supply of professional services are the need to certify services by locally registered service providers and the need for cross-border service providers to have a commercial presence in the importing country.

Migration

The trade-migration linkage is an important part of the debate on migration reform. Trade policy officials should not neglect the immigration and labor market perspectives when considering temporary entry or Mode 4 issues. Policies related to visas, work permits, and treatment of foreign workers must be considered.

Implications for Policy Action

Policy measures in education, trade, domestic regulation, and migration must be coordinated to address skills shortages and mismatches and failures in the markets for professional services. Many policy measures can be implemented at the national level or by unilateral domestic liberalization. Regional and international engagement can help countries mobilize resources for and lend credibility to domestic reform.

Policy Action at the National Level

Reforms at the national level need to create conditions that address skills shortages and mismatches and attempt to facilitate the growth of professional services. Regulatory reforms need to focus on incremental, qualitative improvements in domestic regulation.

Education reforms need to focus on the following issues:

- If financial constraints prevent individuals from acquiring a professional education, then developing new and expanded means of financing higher education (such as student loans schemes) must be a priority.
- If weaknesses in educational systems mean that students are poorly equipped to acquire professional skills, then enhancing the quality and capacity of schools (especially in mathematics, sciences, and technical studies) needs to be a priority.
- If professional education institutions suffer from capacity constraints and poor quality, improving existing institutions and encouraging the creation of new ones should be priorities.

Entry requirements can be relaxed by narrowing the scope of tasks reserved to licensed professionals. Exclusive rights can lead to increased specialization of professionals and guarantee a higher quality of service. If they create monopolies, however, they can have adverse price and allocation effects, especially when granted for services for which adequate quality can be provided at a lower cost by less regulated midlevel professionals.

Policy Action at the International Level

Policy action is called for in two main areas. The first is relaxing the explicit trade barriers applied to the movement of natural persons and commercial presence of professional services. Examples of possible reforms include the following:

- Articulating the economic and social motivations for nationality and residency requirements
- Developing transparent criteria and procedures for applying any quantitative restrictions on the movement of professionals, such as **economic needs tests**
- Minimizing restrictions on the forms of establishment allowed
- Developing a transparent and consistent framework for accepting professionals with foreign qualifications

The reduction of explicit trade barriers needs to be complemented with the reform of immigration laws.

The second area is the coordination of trade liberalization with regulatory reform and cooperation at the regional level. Ideally, trade barriers should be liberalized on a most-favored-nation or nonpreferential basis, because it would generate the largest welfare gains. Such liberalization may not be technically feasible or politically acceptable, however, especially when impediments arise from differences in regulatory requirements. Deeper regional integration through regulatory cooperation with neighboring partners that have similar regulatory preferences can usefully complement nonpreferential trade liberalization. Regional integration would also enhance competition among services providers, enable those providers to exploit economies of scale in professional education, and produce a wider variety of services. A larger regional market can attract greater domestic and foreign investment. Regionalization may also help regulators take advantage of scale economies in regulation, particularly where national agencies face technical skills or capacity constraints.

Regulatory cooperation to overcome regulatory heterogeneity can be particularly useful in the following areas:

- *Mutual recognition of professional qualifications and licensing requirements.* A full-fledged mutual recognition agreement of professional qualifications needs to cover areas such as education, examinations, experience, conduct and ethics, professional development and recertification, scope of practice, and local knowledge.
- *Development of appropriate standards.* The development of appropriate standards may be desirable at the regional rather than the national level to exploit economies of scale in regulatory expertise, prevent fragmentation of the market, and limit the scope for regulatory capture. Inappropriate standards can stifle demand for services. Although uniformity of standards may improve the quality, completeness, and comparability of the reported information, and international standards remain appropriate in specific cases, applying common international standards to large firms and small and medium-size

enterprises can prevent smaller firms from using auditing and accounting services. A single standard may be appropriate if there is little demand for service variety and no anticompetitive risk from having a single standard. However, if the market requires variety to satisfy different types of users, a single standard may not be appropriate.

- *Removal of restrictions to the free movement of labor.* Regional cooperation in removing restrictions on the free movement of labor (including visa and immigration laws) is crucial to the provision of professional services. The mobility of businesspeople is a key factor in the promotion of free and open trade.
- *Improvement of professional education.* The absence of institutions that offer specialized (postgraduate) courses (in law and engineering, for example) or the absence of institutions offering academic and professional training courses for midlevel professionals can be addressed at the regional level. Where the market in a country is too small to justify the creation of institutions or courses, policies to facilitate access to foreign training are needed, including policies on the portability of course credits and scholarships. Specialized courses for which a concrete need is identified can be designed and implemented at the regional level. Regional institutions can exploit economies of scale and recoup the large fixed costs of establishing training programs to produce students with the necessary specializations.

These objectives, and more broadly the integration of markets for professional services, can be supported through the adoption of regional programs for the sector. One such effort is being developed by the World Bank in Africa (box A.2).

Box A.2. The World Bank's Professional Services Knowledge Platform for Eastern and Southern Africa

The Professional Services Knowledge Platform for Eastern and Southern Africa will provide the following:

- Information and analysis on the performance of a particular sector and its impact on other sectors and the wider economy, possibly obtained through surveys of users and service providers
- Assessment of barriers to trade and foreign investment and current regulatory policies, in the form of a trade and regulatory audit in addition to an assessment of their impact on entry and conduct in the market
- Review of the necessary steps to remove explicit barriers to trade and the regulatory options for an integrated services market, including measures that can be pursued at the national level and measures that are likely to be more effective in collaboration with partner countries at the regional level. This review will be informed by analysis of the experience of other countries that have implemented reform programs in the specific sector, drawing on inputs and interactions with officials and experts from these countries.
- Assessment of capacity building that will be necessary for effective implementation and monitoring of outcomes in the sector and the impact of current regulation

In pursuing these outputs, the platform aims to support a process that ensures regular consultation between private and public stakeholders; effective communication between regulators, sector specialists, and relevant government ministries; and extensive dissemination of information and analysis at the national and then regional levels to increase awareness and deepen understanding of the policy issues affecting each sector.

Conclusion

Entry restrictions are pervasive in the professional services sector. Although some can be justified on the grounds that consumers have limited information about the quality of services providers, restrictions often reflect regulatory capture by domestic constituencies. This risk is higher where regulation of professional services is handled by professional associations, as is common.

Regulations governing the movement, stay, and employment of foreigners are among the horizontal measures most relevant to professional services. In addition to horizontal restrictions on establishment, entry restrictions include the following:

- Qualitative restrictions, in particular examination and education requirements
- Exclusive and shared rights
- Restrictions on ownership of professional services firms or the use of foreign name brands for domestic establishments
- Limitations on the form of establishment: professional services cannot usually take the form of incorporated companies; enterprises can usually be established only in the form of associations or limited liability companies.
- Limitations on the numbers of professionals or their geographical distribution

Note

1. This appendix draws heavily on World Bank (2010) and World Bank (2011a), under the guidance of Nora Dihel.

References

Cattaneo, Oliver, and Peter Walkenhorst. 2010. "Does More Trade Rhyme with Better Justice?" In *International Trade in Services: New Trends and Opportunities for Developing Countries*, ed. Olivier Cattaneo, Michael Engman, Sebastián Sáez, and Robert Stern, 67–98. Washington, DC: World Bank.

Delimatsis, Pangiotis. 2010. "Transnational Private Regulation in Professional Services." Tilburg Law and Economics Center (TILEC), Tilburg Law School, Tilburg, the Netherlands. http://ssrn.com/abstract=2140927.

Goswami, Arti Grover, Poonam Gupta, Aaditya Mattoo, and Sebastián Sáez. 2012. "Service Exports: Are the Drivers Different for Developing Countries?" In *Exporting Services: A Developing Country Perspective*, ed. Arti Grover Goswami, Aaditya Mattoo, and Sebastián Sáez, 25–80. Washington, DC: World Bank.

Trolliet, Claude, and John Hegarty. 2003. "Regulatory Reform and Trade Liberalization in Accountancy Services." In *Domestic Regulation and Services Trade Liberalization*, ed. Aaditya Mattoo and Pierre Sauvé, 147–66. Washington, DC: World Bank.

World Bank. 2010. *Reform and Regional Integration of Professional Services in East Africa: Time for Action*. Washington, DC: World Bank. http://siteresources.worldbank.org/INTAFRREGTOPTRADE/Resources/NEWReformProfessionaServicesEACReport.pdf.

———. 2011a. *Harnessing Regional Integration for Trade and Growth in Southern Africa*. Washington, DC: World Bank. http://siteresources.worldbank.org/INTAFRREGTOPTRADE/Resources/Harnessing_Regional_Integration_Trade_Growth_SouthernAfrica.pdf.

———. 2011b. "Towards a Regional Integration of Professional Services in Southern Africa." Trade Policy Note 10, World Bank, Washington, DC. http://siteresources.worldbank.org/INTAFRREGTOPTRADE/Resources/10SouthernAfricaProfessionalServicesREDESIGN.pdf.

WTO (World Trade Organization). 2012. "Regulatory Issues in Sectors and Modes of Supply." Note by the Secretariat S/WPDR/W/48, Geneva.

APPENDIX B: INFORMATION TECHNOLOGY–ENABLED SERVICES

Objectives

This appendix reviews the main determinants of trade in **information technology–enabled services** *(ITES) and provides guidance on the main regulatory barriers that affect the sector. Upon completing it, readers will be able to:*

* *List the main ITES*
* *Identify conditions for success of exports of ITES*
* *Assess the services sectors that support the ITES sector by providing infrastructure or inputs*
* *Evaluate regulatory measures that indirectly affect the development of ITES*
* *Propose regulatory changes that promote the ITES sector*

This appendix describes the regulatory issues governments must address to help developing countries increase their participation in information technology (IT) services trade. The first section describes the growth of IT-enabled services. The second section examines factors that can spur the growth of the sector. The third section identifies barriers to entry. The fourth section discusses the regulatory framework for telecommunications services, the main infrastructure supporting ITES. A concluding section summarizes the main findings.

A questionnaire, available at http://www.worldbank.org/trade/RASTI, complements this appendix. It offers practical guidance on identifying the common formal regulatory barriers to trade and investment and the existence of an enabling governance framework. The International Telecommunication Union (ITU) (2006) examines how countries can implement these principles.

Technological Change and the Growth of the Sector

Changes in technology have increased the tradability of services in recent years. Information technology (IT) allows the digitalization of services, facilitating storability and transmission across borders and reducing the need for producers to be near consumers.[1] World exports of services related to IT grew at an average annual rate of 16 percent between 2000 and 2012 to reach 6 percent of total cross-border services exports (figure B.1).

Information technology–enabled services (ITES) include services directly related to information technology, including software development, system integration, and web page design. They also include business services that use IT to, for example, process insurance claims, perform desktop publishing, conduct audits, complete tax returns, and transcribe medical records. Table B.1 lists ITES that are commonly traded internationally.

Trade in ITES still represents a small share of total exports of most developing countries. Although several countries are enjoying the gains from trade in ITES, only a handful have developed sizable, export-oriented IT and ITES sectors. These countries include Brazil, China, Costa Rica, India, the Philippines, and Uruguay. Increasingly, companies based in developing countries have been successfully competing in international markets for these services, for a variety of reasons (Engman 2010):

* Essential supply-side requirements in the IT sector match factor endowments in many developing countries.
* Widespread connectivity to international telecommunication networks enables ITES entrepreneurs to compete for business independent of location.
* Companies with the necessary talent can tap into international markets and grow on the back of foreign demand; although a dynamic domestic market may help, it is not a prerequisite for success.

The rapidly growing ITES market consists of numerous subsectors and niche markets.

Figure B.1. World Production of Information Technology (IT) Services, 2000–12

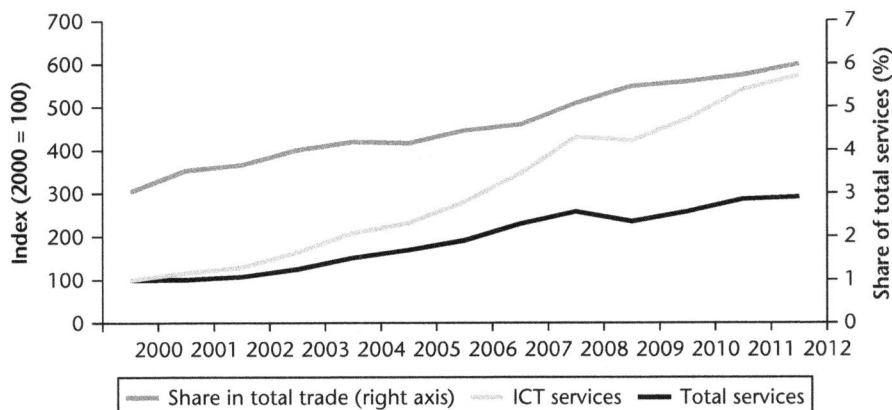

Source: UNCTAD Statistics (http://unctadstat.unctad.org).

Table B.1. Internationally Traded Information Technology–Enabled Services

IT services		Business services
Application services	**Engineering services**	**Business services**
Application development and maintenance	***Manufacturing engineering***	***Business processing outsourcing (BPO) services***
• Application development	• Upstream product engineering	***Vertical processes***
• Application development integration and testing	o Concept design	• Banking
• Application maintenance	o Simulation	• Insurance
	o Design engineering	• Travel
System integration	• Downstream product engineering	• Manufacturing
• Analysis	o Computer-aided design, manufacture, and engineering	• Telecommunications
• Design	o Embedded software	• Pharmaceuticals
• Development	o Localization plant and process engineering	• Other
• Integration and testing		
• Package implementation	***Software product development***	***Horizontal processes***
	• Product development	• Customer interaction and support (such as call centers)
IT infrastructure services	• System testing	• Human resource management
• Help desks	• Porting/variants	• Finance and administration
• Desktop support	• Localization	• Supply chain (procurement logistics management)
• Data center services	• Maintenance and support	
• Mainframe support	• Gaming	***Knowledge processing outsourcing (KPO) services***
• Network operations		• Business and financial research
		• Animation
Consulting		• Data analytics
• IT consulting		• Legal process and patent research
• Network consulting		• Other high-end processes

Source: Sudan and others 2010.

Determinants of Success

Successful provision of ITES depends critically on the availability and quality of human resources. Appendix A, on professional services, can be used to assess the pool of available skills to support the development of this sector. In addition, policy makers should ask the following questions regarding the availability of human resources (Engman 2010):

• Are new engineering and computer science graduates adequately trained? If not, where is education failing? Are curriculums up to date and in line with what the IT services sector demands? What can be done to raise educational standards in these fields and the relevance of training? Does the government have the capacity to enforce regulations for quality assurance?

- Is the local education system producing enough computer science engineers to meet demand? If not, are there barriers to private provision of training services in the IT field? If there are barriers, do they fulfill a clear policy objective? Are the barriers discriminating against foreign providers of training and technical education? If so, to what purpose? Is there scope to reform these rules?

- Are new graduates trained in foreign languages? Are there rules that prohibit or discourage teaching in foreign languages? If so, what are the objectives of such prohibitions, and can the same goals be reached with increased flexibility?

- Are postgraduate courses offered in computer science and related engineering fields? If not, is there scope to initiate collaboration with the private sector to finance and design such programs and help sponsor students?

- Are there specific barriers affecting female students of computer science and engineering or issues that reduce their desire to work in the industry? If so, what are they and how can they be removed?

Governments that wish to take advantage of global opportunities in ITES can benefit from a structured assessment of the strengths and weaknesses of their location. Consulting firms have developed benchmarking frameworks, locational indexes, and rating criteria for determining the e-readiness and attractiveness of different locations for ITES industries (Sudan and others 2010) (table B.2). Among these studies, there is broad agreement that several key factors determine locational competitiveness: the availability of skills (including IT skills), competitive costs, the quality of public infrastructure relevant to the ITES industries, and the overall business environment.

The existence of competitive telecommunication markets, especially for broadband services, and the availability of employee skills are the most important factors, according to Sudan and others (2010). The rapid growth of the industry has created a situation in which skills scarcity creates opportunities for countries new to the industry to offer and develop strong local talent pools.

The main cost components of concern to potential market entrants are labor; infrastructure; facilities; and selling, general, and administrative expenses. The most important costs are wages, infrastructure, and training (table B.3).

Costs affecting the establishment of services suppliers in the ITES sector can be reduced through targeted policies that seek to attract investment, through reductions in tariff or trade restrictions on imports and exports;

lower corporate tax rates; investment-friendly regulations on profit remittances and repatriation of capital, capital gains on assets, and other property transfers; and special incentives and tax holidays (Sudan and others 2010).

In countries with weak infrastructure and poor business environments, a common approach is to let private real estate developers build software and high-tech parks near population centers with engineering colleges (Goswami, Mattoo, and Sáez 2012). These policies usually aim to create an enabling business environment in which the private sector, national or foreign, has access to better infrastructure, often benefits from incentives, and enjoys a more streamlined regulatory environment (Engman 2010). These parks provide modern office facilities with a guaranteed power supply and Internet broadband connectivity. These nurturing clusters allow ITES companies to enjoy economies of scale in procuring input services and overcome infrastructure bottlenecks. The key focus in the parks is services provision. A streamlined interface to public authorities and ready-to-use facilities are the main attractions. Some high-tech parks offer their export-oriented investors fiscal incentives, such as time-limited income tax holidays, duty-free importation of capital goods, and grants for training new employees. Fiscal incentives are seldom necessary to attract investment in the IT sector. Essential incentives include full equity ownership for foreign investors and facilitated employment of foreign nationals in supervisory and technical positions.

Inadequate Internet connectivity is one of the key supply constraints to trade in ITES (Sudan and others 2010). Many countries, in particular in Africa, are restricted from the international ITES market because of expensive, unreliable, and low-capacity Internet connectivity. Policy makers in such countries should investigate local market conditions and assess whether low capacity and high prices may be a result of the regulatory environment or anticompetitive behavior of local providers. If necessary, they should take action to improve competition or modify the rules and regulations that cover telecommunications and Internet broadband providers and by extension stimulate private investment. Policy makers should also reassess local labor market policy and telecommunication policy with regard to restrictions to voice communications over the Internet (Voice over Internet Protocol [VoIP]) and night shifts to ensure that these policies are conducive to IT services trade.

The assessment should obtain answers to the following key questions (Engman 2010):

- How do local broadband connectivity, reliability, and prices compare with those in other countries in the region and the world? Are there any local rules and regulations that hold back investment in network capacity?

Table B.2. Frameworks for Assessing Locations for Information Technology–Enabled Services (ITES)

A. T. Kearney's Global Services Location Index	Gartner's 10 criteria	Hewitt's international benchmarking model	McKinsey's Location Readiness Index
Availability of people and skills • Remote services sector experience and quality ratings • Labor force availability • Education and language • Attrition risk *Financial attractiveness* • Compensation costs • Infrastructure costs • Tax and regulatory costs *Business environment* • Country environment • Infrastructure • Cultural exposure • Security of intellectual property	*Infrastructure* • Power • Telecommunications • Transport *Labor pool* • Quality • Quantity • Scalability • Work conditions *Educational system* • Quality • Number of institutions • New grads in IT *Cost* • Labor • Real estate, infrastructure • Telecommunications *Political and economic environment* • Stability of government • Corruption • Geopolitical risks • Financial stability *Language* *Government support* • Promotional support • Institutional support • Education *Cultural compatibility* • Cultural attributes • Adaptability • Proximity • Ease of travel *Global and legal maturity* *Data and intellectual property security and privacy*	*Infrastructure* • Real estate • Telecommunications power *Connectivity* *Talent* • Availability • Quality • Cost *General demographics* *Environment* • Macroeconomic • Business environment • Geopolitical environment *Clusters* *Incumbent ITES subsector*	*Infrastructure* • Telecommunications and network • Real estate • Transportation • Power *Talent* • Availability • Suitability • Willingness • Accessibility • Trainability *Cost* • Labor • Infrastructure • Taxes *Market maturity* • ITES employees as percentage of total services sector employment • ITES as percentage of gross domestic product (GDP) from services • Presence of subsector association *Risk profile* • Regulatory environment • Country investment • Data protection *Other incentives* *Environment* • Government support • Business and living environment • Accessibility • Living environment

Source: Sudan and others 2010.

• Are high prices a result of lack of competition? If so, what action can the government take to liberalize the market and increase investment?

• Are there barriers to market access for foreign providers of Internet/telecommunications services? If so, what purpose do they serve? Can foreign providers provide the necessary investment and source of competition to improve connectivity and capacity?

• Are tariffs imposed on the importation of the physical equipment for Internet connectivity? If so, to what extent are they likely to raise prices and reduce investment in broadband infrastructure?

• Is the country's connectivity dependent on a single-source cable? If so, would more points of connection increase reliability and network capacity? Could negotiations with neighboring countries help address some of the capacity issues?

• Are consumers prohibited from using VoIP services? If so, does the prohibition serve a useful purpose? Who benefits from the restriction? Can negotiations reform the current framework?

Infrastructure considerations include the availability, quality, and reliability of services such as telecommunications

Table B.3. Illustrative Cost Structure for Information Technology (IT) and Business Processing Outsourcing (BPO) Services
Percent of total costs

Cost component	IT services firms	BPO services firms
Wages	46	42
Physical infrastructure and support	18	17
Training and productivity	9	11
Transition and governance	7	8
Communications	3	5
Disaster recovery and business continuity	3	5
Resource redeployment	4	3
Travel	3	3
Advisory services	3	2
Exchange rate changes	3	2
Resource redundancy	1	2

Source: Sudan and others 2010.

(including broadband), power, and transportation and the availability of suitable real estate. A competitive broadband telecommunications market is also a critical factor for the growth of trade in ITES: policy makers can promote competition by ensuring that there is more than one international service provider, more than one international gateway, and multiple international cables linking the location to competitive global communication networks.

Regarding market access issues, policy makers need to ask the following questions (Engman 2010):

- Are there legal restrictions to market entry through commercial presence by foreign companies? If so, what types of restrictions exist and what purpose do they serve? What is their impact on foreign direct investment? Can the policy rationale of restrictions be addressed through less-trade-restrictive means? Can full ownership of local subsidiaries be allowed in high-tech parks for export-oriented activities?
- Are foreign suppliers required to establish themselves locally through a particular legal form? If so, which ones? Are restrictions to commercial presence compliant with the country's prospective World Trade Organization (WTO) commitments?
- Is the local IT services sector controlled by the public sector? Do these links give rise to market distortions at home and hold back expansions abroad? If so, what is the strategic value of government retaining stakes in the sector?

The empirical literature confirms that the general business and living environment of a country are important determinants of the success of the IT services sector.

When assessing markets for investment, providers consider the quality of the judicial system, the legal framework for contract enforcement, opportunities to arbitrate locally, the legal framework for intellectual property protection, and antitrust laws, among other factors (Sudan and others 2010; Goswami, Mattoo, and Sáez 2012). A country becomes an attractive ITES investment destination when it combines a deep and well-qualified talent pool, a cost advantage, good availability and quality of infrastructure, and other factors that facilitate the smooth and predictable day-to-day running of a business (Sudan and others 2010). Country risk, transparency of the law, macroeconomic stability, treatment of foreign capital, and protection of data and intellectual property are also important determinants of investment.

Business Parks

In countries with unreliable infrastructure, service providers can overcome this hurdle by developing **IT parks** that provide modern office space, high-speed broadband links, reliable power supply (including backup supply), security services, and other infrastructure, such as banks and travel agents. These parks also address land requirements and may be subject to special regulatory regimes that provide for simplified procedures for, for example, applying for permits and licenses. The availability of international airports with good flight connections near ITES locations is also an important factor (Sudan and others 2010).

Goswami, Mattoo, and Sáez (2012) review the empirical literature on service exports and estimate a **gravity model** to assess the importance of electronic infrastructure. According to their results, firms exporting services need access to high-quality electronic infrastructure that does not necessarily need to cover the general population of the exporter country. Internet penetration among the general population in the exporter country may not significantly affect service exports. Exporting firms in developing countries can own the equipment for better-quality telecommunications or the government can create special technology parks (as it has in the Arab Republic of Egypt, India, and the Philippines) to overcome the handicap of low technology penetration.

In Egypt, targeted policies have played a crucial role in services exports. Although Egypt is not a top-ranked developing country with regard to the quality of its educated labor force, it has nevertheless been able to promote ITES exports, especially within the Arab world. The government established the Information Technology Industry Development Agency (ITIDA) in 2004 with a mission to develop the IT sector and boost exports. It also created special technology parks for promoting ITES exports.

Expansion of India's services exports in the last decades was driven by the large pool of skilled IT professionals and the availability of personnel with management and entrepreneurial skills. Establishment of software technology parks that aimed to create an enabling business environment to overcome the bottlenecks in infrastructure and institutions facilitated India's services exports. By allowing duty-free/license-free imports of computer hardware, these parks promoted software development. Firms in technology parks were granted tax exemptions; guaranteed access to high-speed satellite links; and provided with reliable electric power (including core computer facilities), fully stocked office space, and communication facilities. Full foreign ownership was permitted in exchange for an export obligation. Firms were allowed to repatriate capital investment, royalties, and dividends free once they paid the taxes due.

In the Philippines, active private sector participation led to the establishment of the Philippine Economic Zone Authority (PEZA). In 2000, the government identified IT as one of the investment priorities sectors to be included under the PEZA incentives. Firms registered with PEZA and located in designated IT parks and IT buildings have been eligible for an income tax holiday of up to eight years, with a 5 percent gross income tax rate thereafter (in lieu of all national and local taxes) and duty-free importation of capital equipment, spare parts, and supplies. In addition, PEZA–registered **business processing outsourcing (BPO)** investors receive value added tax (VAT) exemptions on locally purchased goods and services (for example, telecom, electricity, and water) and a deduction of up to 150 percent of training expenses after the end of the income tax holiday. PEZA also supports BPO by expediting permits for key personnel and offering one-stop-shop services for starting a business.

Labor Mobility

The global delivery model that increasingly brings IT services to foreign markets is based on cross-border supply and the temporary movement of natural persons. Difficulties securing business visas and work permits for project managers in foreign markets has become a major impediment to trade in some countries. To facilitate trade, policy makers should address such concerns as quantitative restrictions and prohibitions; restrictive regulation of work permit holders; and slow, opaque, and burdensome consular and visa-processing services. Policy makers can also help by supporting industry associations that disseminate information, promote the industry at home and abroad, and raise operational standards. The awarding of professional certificates and international

quality standards are other areas in which policy makers can facilitate mobility.

Policy makers should ask the following questions when assessing labor mobility (Engman 2010):

- What types of restrictions affect labor migration in client countries? Do major export markets impose quotas, economic needs tests, or other impediments to the movement of project staff?
- Do local consulates of foreign countries provide expeditious, fair, and streamlined application procedures for business visas and work permits? If not, what is the scope for local policy makers to approach these consulates to build trust and seek facilitated procedures?
- What concerns do foreign consulates have, and what can policy makers and local IT services companies do to address them? Do the country's IT professionals have a poor record in respecting work permit rules in client countries? If so, what can policy makers do to make the sector improve its record?
- Is the business visa and work permit application process administered in an expeditious and cost-effective way? How can administrative efficiency in the local application process be improved?
- Are there restrictions or issues related to nonrecognition of qualifications for IT workers at home or in major export markets?
- Can temporary movement be facilitated through bilateral, regional, or multilateral negotiations?

Barriers to Trade

Trade in ITES such as back-office services, IT maintenance, and software development generally benefits from open regulatory regimes. Cross-border trade in ITES relies on telecommunications platforms, which make it difficult for regulators to monitor and therefore regulate. The most important barriers in this sector are thus found in supply-side constraints and limitations that affect the telecom infrastructure and other services sectors that serve as input for ITES, such as accounting, legal, and financial services (Engman 2010).

Some constraints reflect the inherent difficulty of supplying services remotely; others are linked to the enabling infrastructure for ITES, shortages of human capital, or regulatory and institutional conditions. Strategies for relieving these constraints are likely to include initiatives that help attract private investment from local and foreign investors, reward entrepreneurship by improving the business environment, and raise educational standards.

The most common barriers to the growth of ITES are indirect measures that restrict other services activities. Typically, limitations on cross-border provisions of professional services affect ITES that relate to that professional activity. For example, regulation of professional services may affect the scope of the development of business processing outsourcing BPO services related to legal, auditing, and accounting services. Other examples are regulations that seek to protect confidential information, which may affect the free flow of the data to be processed. These regulations may relate to insurance, health, or finance.

Provision of ITES depends on countries' electronic infrastructure. Countries in which competition in the telecommunications market is not allowed and basic regulatory principles are not in place or enforced generally have low-quality electronic infrastructure (often with high costs) and low broadband penetration that impairs the delivery of ITES or limits the sector's competitiveness.

Assessment of Telecommunications Regulations

The telecommunications sector requires regulations to ensure entry and competition among providers. Regulations must enable access and use of the telecommunication infrastructure by users and providers of other services that depend on this infrastructure.

Regulations affecting telecommunication services are extremely complex, affecting entry, operations, and the equipment necessary to access the infrastructure by such users as BPO industries. Regulatory frameworks differ across countries, but common elements necessary to regulate the sector have been agreed upon internationally. Topics include the function of regulatory authority, the decision-making process, accountability, consumer protection, dispute resolution, and enforcement powers (ITU 2012).

According to the International Telecommunication Union (ITU 2012), regulatory reform should aim to create a functional regulator, prepare the incumbent to face competition, allocate and manage scarce resources on a nondiscriminatory basis, expand and enhance access to telecommunications and IT networks and services, and promote and protect consumer interests, including universal access and privacy. Adopting such reforms should obviate the need for some regulation.

The regulatory assessment should focus on the basic issues identified at the international level as minimum regulatory requirements of any country. The six principles of the WTO telecommunications reference paper negotiated in 1997 (ITU 2006)—competitive safeguards, interconnection agreements, universal service obligations, public availability of licensing criteria, the independence of regulators, and the allocation of scarce resources—should serve as a "checklist of success" of reforms. The principles seek to address the following issues:

- *Competitive safeguards.* Competitive safeguards require members to adopt measures for preventing suppliers that alone or together represent a major supplier from engaging in or continuing anticompetitive practices. Such practices include engaging in anticompetitive cross-subsidization, using information obtained from competitors with anticompetitive results, and not making available to other services suppliers on a timely basis technical information about essential facilities and commercially relevant information necessary that allow them to provide services.

- *Interconnection agreements.* Interconnection with a major supplier must be ensured at any technically feasible point in the network and be provided on nondiscriminatory terms (including technical standards and specifications). Rates and the quality of interconnection should be no less favorable than provided for its own like services, for like services of nonaffiliated service suppliers, or for its subsidiaries or other affiliates. In relation to transparency, the reference paper requires that the procedures applicable for interconnection to a major supplier be publicly available and that a major supplier make publicly available either its interconnection agreements or a reference interconnection offer. Regarding possible dispute settlement, a service supplier requesting interconnection with a major supplier should have recourse at any time (or after a reasonable period of time that has been made publicly known) to an independent domestic body to resolve disputes regarding appropriate terms, conditions, and rates for interconnection within a reasonable period of time.

- *Universal service obligations.* The reference paper ensures the right to define the universal service obligations a member wishes to maintain and provides that such obligations will not be regarded as anticompetitive per se, insofar as they are administered in a transparent, nondiscriminatory, and competitively neutral manner and are not more burdensome than necessary for the kind of universal service defined by the member.

- *Public availability of licensing criteria.* Where a license is required, all criteria and the period of time normally required to reach a decision concerning an application for a license and the terms and conditions of individual licenses must be public. The reasons for the denial of a license must be made known to the applicant upon request.

- *Independence of regulators.* To ensure an impartial role of the regulatory authority, the regulatory body must be separate from, and not accountable to, any supplier of basic telecommunications services. Moreover, decisions and procedures of regulators must be impartial with respect to all market participants. An effective regulator must ensure credible market access, compliance, and enforcement of regulations. Structural and financial independence, accountability, transparency, and predictability are critical attributes of an effective regulator, which should have well-defined functions and responsibilities.
- *Allocation of scarce resources.* The procedures for allocating and using scarce resources, including frequencies, numbers, and rights of way should be carried out in an objective, timely, transparent, and nondiscriminatory manner.

Conclusion

ITES is not a regulation-intensive sector. IT and business services are not usually affected by specific licensing requirements but rather depend on the general regulatory framework. Mapping ITES hence requires a comprehensive scan of the general regulatory framework for services.

Because exports of ITES are usually associated with foreign investment, the mapping should pay attention to the conditions for establishing foreign companies. Typical restrictions affecting commercial presence in professional services include the following:

- Limitations on foreign equity ownership
- Economic needs test for approval of foreign investment
- Quotas on the number of operating licenses
- **Joint venture requirements**
- Regulation of contracts by value and number through an annual licensing system
- Nationality or residency requirements for establishment of foreign companies
- Requirements that foreign businesses hire specific ratios of domestic staff to foreign staff
- Reservation of some services sectors or activities for nationals or residents

The supply of ITES through Mode 3 (commercial presence) is often accompanied by the movement of personnel to provide specific expertise in projects or to direct local offices. Restrictions on labor movement arise from a country's overall immigration policy or specific labor market conditions and include visa requirements, labor market tests, and residency requirements. The following are examples of conditions for approving the entry of service suppliers:

- Visa requirements
- **Labor market needs test** for foreign employees
- **Residency requirements** for intracorporate transferees and a requirement that the foreign company employ specific numbers of local staff
- Authorization subject to nonavailability of locals
- Authorization subject to **performance requirements** (employment creation, transfer of technology, level of investment).

Although the IT and business services are not heavily regulated, the telecommunications platform that enables them is. A regulatory mapping for the ITES sector should thus pay particular attention to the regulatory framework for telecommunications. Specific areas that should be considered include the following:

- Allocation of resources and licensing procedures
- Operational conditions, including the "packages" of telecom services that operators are allowed to own or operate
- Regulation of anticompetitive conduct and interconnection requirements
- Universal access

Note

1. This appendix draws on Engman (2010), Sudan and others (2010), and World Bank (2011). The authors acknowledge the contributions of Michael Engman and Randeep Sudan.

References

Engman, Michael. 2010. "Exporting Information Technology Services: In the Footsteps of India." In *International Trade in Services: New Trends and Opportunities for Developing Countries,* ed. Olivier Cattaneo, Michael Engman, Sebastián Sáez, and Robert M. Stern, 177–218. Washington, DC: World Bank.

Goswami, Arti Grover, Aaditya Mattoo, and Sebastián Sáez. 2012. *Service Exports: Are the Drivers Different for Developing Countries?* Washington, DC: World Bank.

ITU (International Telecommunication Union). 2012. "Legal and Institutional Aspects of Regulation." ICT Regulation Toolkit, Module 6, Geneva. http://www.ictregulationtoolkit.org.

Sudan, Randeep, Seth Ayers, Philippe Dongier, Arturo Muente-Kunigami, and Christine Zhen-Wei Qiang. 2010. *The Global Opportunity in IT–Based Services: Assessing and Enhancing Country Competitiveness.* Washington, DC: World Bank.

World Bank. 2011. *Telecommunications Regulation Handbook,* 10th anniv. ed. Washington, DC: World Bank.

APPENDIX C: FINANCIAL SERVICES

Objectives

This appendix provides a methodology for conducting a regulatory assessment of financial services. It emphasizes the relationship between market-opening and domestic regulation, including the readiness of supervisory authorities for liberalization. Upon completing this appendix, readers will be able to:

- *Recognize the regulation that governs financial services*
- *Determine whether regulations fall within or outside the scope of a trade-related regulatory assessment*
- *Identify nonprudential measures that affect trade in financial services*

Financial services play a significant role at the macroeconomic and microeconomic level. The management of macroeconomic policies affects the performance of the financial sector and is affected by the strength of financial institutions. At the microeconomic level, well-functioning financial markets are necessary for the efficient allocation of financial resources (World Bank 2013).

Cross-border exports of financial services have grown more rapidly than exports of both goods and other services exports in recent years (figure C.1). This growth explains the importance of financial services in international negotiations and developed countries' interest in liberalizing financial services markets.

Financial services markets are complex and highly regulated. The economic literature offers various explanations of why regulation may be necessary; there is less consensus on what regulations should aim to protect—the payment system, systemic stability, bank solvency, depositors—and how far regulation should go (Dewatripont and Tirole 1994; Barth, Caprio, and Levine 2006).

Broadly speaking, regulations in this sector are justified by the existence of asymmetries of information across agents and the need to protect depositors and investors. Providers of financial resources have incomplete information about the level of solvency and integrity of borrowers, partly because it is costly to assess their financial standing. A market solution is to improve the availability of information to the public.

This sector has a unique characteristic among services sectors. When an institution faces a solvency or liquidity problem, or is perceived by other economic agents to be fragile, it can create a crisis of confidence that affects all institutions. This crisis is known in the literature as **systemic risk** or **contagion**. Regulations are need to prevent contagion and ensure the integrity and stability of the financial sector as a whole while addressing the specific problems of individual organizations.

The first section of this appendix discusses who regulates, why financial services are regulated, and categorizes financial services. The second section describes how financial services are regulated and highlights those measures relevant to a trade-related regulatory assessment. The third section examines the main components of a regulatory assessment. A questionnaire to facilitate the regulatory mapping is available at http://www.worldbank.org/trade/RASTI.

Who Regulates Financial Services?

Regulations that affect financial services are broad and affect many parties. Among other things, regulations prescribe which institutions are allowed to provide financial services, what services they are allowed to provide, how and to whom they can provide services, and how and what kind of information should be provided to the public and regulators.

There is no single approach to regulating the financial sector, and regulations are constantly evolving. Financial services policies are usually defined by finance ministries and central bank authorities, which are normally independent of the executive branch, and approved by the legislative branch. In some countries, a single authority regulates the three broad financial services subsectors (banking, insurance, and securities). (In the United Kingdom, for example, until recently, when responsibilities were transferred to the

Bank of England, these subsectors fell under the purview of the Financial Services Authority.) Other countries maintain a structural separation of these activities, using two or three regulators. In other cases, regulation and supervision of the banking sector fall under the mandate of the central bank, and securities and insurance are under the purview of finance ministries or dedicated regulators. This separation creates coordination problems among regulators, who have to exchange information to regulate financial conglomerates that provide a wide range of services (consolidated supervision) and to assess risk exposures of financial institutions. In addition, if these financial conglomerates have international operations, cooperation with regulators responsible for their supervision in foreign countries is also required. For certain

activities, self-regulation has also been encouraged as an alternative to government regulation.

Regulators may also be responsible for issuing regulations for large numbers of participants in the financial market. In addition to regulating banking, insurance, and securities activities, regulators also have to issue regulations for financial intermediaries such as insurance brokerage, auditing, and rating agencies.

Financial services are characterized by constant innovation of new and more complex products and services that require regulations. Financial innovation strengthens the need for regulations to protect consumers.

How Is the Financial Sector Regulated?

The World Trade Organization (WTO 1997) delineates four areas of public sector intervention in trade in financial services. Understanding these areas of regulatory intervention helps determine the scope of a Regulatory Assessment of Services Trade and Investment (RASTI). Regulations pertaining to monetary policies and exchange rate, as well as **prudential regulations**, normally fall beyond the scope of a RASTI. In contrast, **nonprudential regulation**, which covers other nondiscriminatory regulations as well as measures governing trade in financial services, are at the center of the RASTI (table C.1).

Regulations for Monetary and Exchange Rate Policies

The first area is monetary and exchange rate policies that may affect financial services. These measures include

Figure C.1. Exports of Total Services and Financial Services, 1986–2011

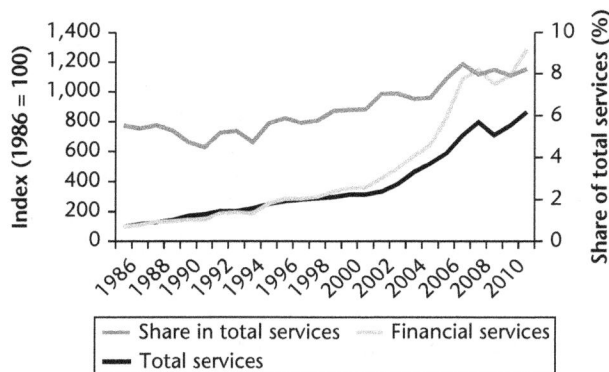

Source: World Development Indicators Database.

Table C.1. Trade-Related Regulatory Assessment of Financial Services

Type of regulation	Cover in a trade-related regulatory assessment?	
	Yes	No
Regulations aimed at setting monetary and exchange rate policies		Covers open market operations, required reserve ratios, discount rates, and so forth
Prudential regulations		Protects investors, depositors, policyholders, and persons to whom a fiduciary duty is owed by a financial service supplier; ensures integrity and stability of financial system (examples of regulators include the Basel Committee on Banking Supervision, the International Organization of Securities Commissions, and the International Association of Insurance Supervisors)
Nonprudential regulation		
Nondiscriminatory regulations	Regulates authorizations, auditing standards, scope of activities, services, and financial products	
Trade-related regulations	Restricts foreign investment in acquiring assets, stipulates specific forms for providing services, and restricts national treatment	

Source: Based on WTO 1997.

open market operations and those measures necessary for the conduct of monetary and exchange rates policies (for example, regulations affecting foreign exchange transactions). Although these regulations can affect trade in financial services, they fall outside the scope of this regulatory assessment.

Prudential Regulations

A second group of public policies that affect trade in financial services are prudential regulations. What matters for the financial sector is whether a country has in place the necessary regulations to protect depositors and ensure the stability and integrity of the financial sector. In international trade agreements such as the General Agreement on Trade in Services (GATS), the North American Free Trade Agreement (NAFTA), and others, prudential regulations are "carved out"—that is, these provisions are generally excluded from the main liberalization obligations of the agreement. Therefore, prudential measures need not be eliminated or listed in countries' commitments as nonconforming measures but can be challenged under the dispute settlement system. The exclusion covers a wide range of measures, including measures to protect investors, depositors, policyholders, or persons to whom a fiduciary duty is owed by a financial service supplier or ones to ensure the integrity and stability of the financial system.

Assessment of prudential regulations determines whether these regulations are in place and whether and how they are enforced by the regulatory authority. It assesses the enforcement capacity of institutions responsible for regulations of human and other resources.

In general, trade agreements do not define prudential regulations, although they typically include **minimum capital requirements**, appropriate capital adequacy requirements for banks that reflect the risks undertaken, risk management policies, concentration risk and large exposure limits, and transactions with related parties. The Basel Committee on Banking Supervision of the Bank for International Settlements has proposed a framework of minimum standards for sound supervisory practices that are considered universally applicable. These Basel Core Principles for Effective Banking Supervision (BCP), adopted by a large number of countries despite their nonbinding nature, cover access to the banking sector, banking sector supervision, and prudential regulations. Box C.1 explains how compliance with individual core principles is assessed.

Other financial services, such as insurance and securities, have adopted similar regulatory principles, recommended by their international organizations. In the insurance sector, the International Association of Insurance Supervisors (IAIS) adopted 26 core principles

---

Box C.1. Assessment of Compliance with Individual Core Principles

The primary objective of an assessment should be to identify the nature and extent of any weaknesses in the banking supervisory system and compliance with individual core principles. Although the process of implementing the core principles starts with the assessment of compliance, assessment is a means to an end, not an objective in itself. It allows the supervisory authority (and in some instances the government) to initiate a strategy to improve the banking supervisory system, as necessary.

For assessments of the core principles by external parties, the following four-grade scale is used:

- *Compliant.* A country is considered compliant with a principle when all essential applicable criteria are met without any significant deficiencies. There may be instances where a country can demonstrate that a principle has been achieved by other means. Conversely, the essential criteria may not always be sufficient to achieve the objective of the principle; other measures may be needed for the aspect of banking supervision addressed by the principle to be effective.
- *Largely compliant.* A country is considered largely compliant with a principle when only minor shortcomings are observed that do not raise concerns about the authority's ability and clear intent to achieve full compliance with the principle within a prescribed period of time. The assessment "largely compliant" can be used when the system does not meet all essential criteria but the overall effectiveness is sufficient and no material risks are left unaddressed.
- *Materially noncompliant.* A country is considered materially noncompliant with a principle when there are severe shortcomings, despite the existence of formal rules, regulations, and procedures, and there is evidence that supervision has clearly not been effective, practical implementation is weak, or the shortcomings are sufficient to raise doubts about the authority's ability to achieve compliance. The "gap" between "largely compliant" and "materially noncompliant" is wide, and the choice between the two ratings may be difficult.
- *Noncompliant.* A country is considered noncompliant with a principle when there has been no substantive implementation of the principle, several essential criteria are not complied with, or supervision is manifestly ineffective.

A principle is considered "not applicable" when, in the view of the assessor, it does not apply given the structural, legal, and institutional features of a country.

Source: Adapted from BIS 2012.

that cover all aspects of the supervisory framework (see IAIS 2011). These principles are similar to the ones proposed for the banking sector by the Basel Committee. A methodology for assessing compliance with them has been developed.

The International Organization of Securities Commissions (IOSCO) has issued its Objectives and Principles of Securities Regulation. These principles aim at guiding regulators and serving as a benchmark against which to measure progress toward effective regulation (see IOSCO 2011). They cover various securities activities, such as issuers, auditors, collective investment schemes, market intermediaries, secondary markets, clearing and settlements, and supervisors. IOSCO also provides a methodology on how to assess compliance.

On the basis of these principles, the International Monetary Fund and the World Bank conduct the Financial Sector Assessment Program (FSAP). This program, established in 1999, is a comprehensive, in-depth analysis of a country's financial sector that includes two main components: a financial stability assessment, which examines the soundness of the banking and other financial sectors, including financial market supervision against accepted international standards, and a financial development assessment, which examines the quality of the legal framework and the financial infrastructure (IMF 2013).

The assessment proposed in this toolkit focuses on the trade-related aspects of financial regulations, which are the core of trade agreement negotiations.

Nondiscriminatory Regulations

A third group of measures refers to regulations that are not prudential in scope or necessary to conduct monetary and exchange rate policies but may restrict market access or national treatment. They include such measures as authorizations for opening a branch. These measures are part of the regulatory assessment proposed to the extent that they may affect trade in financial services. They aim to assess the extent to which regulatory measures are necessary, whether less restrictive measures are available, and whether these measures are de facto applied to discriminate against foreign providers or restrict access.

Trade-Related Regulations

A fourth category of regulations is intended to restrict the participation of foreign suppliers in the local market. Regulations often restrict foreign investment from acquiring assets, stipulate specific forms for providing services, and restrict national treatment. Measures that restrict market access and national treatment are the primary concern of this regulatory assessment.

For simplicity, these two last categories of regulations are referred to as *nonprudential regulations*. When conducting a trade-related regulatory assessment, policy makers should ask the following key questions regarding nonprudential regulations (Sauvé 2010):

- Are there policy restrictions on new entry? If so, do such restrictions affect all new entrants or only entry by foreign suppliers? Is there a limit on the number of firms (or foreign firms) allowed in the market?
- If entry is restricted, what are the reasons the government provides? Where and how clearly are such limits spelled out?
- Are there services that locally established foreign suppliers are not allowed to supply?
- Can foreign firms or service suppliers serve the market on a cross-border basis (that is, without an established presence)?
- Are there restrictions on cross-border purchases of certain categories of services by consumers (firms or individuals) in the importing country?
- Can nonestablished foreign providers solicit business from foreign customers on a cross-border basis?
- Are foreign suppliers required to establish a local presence as a precondition for serving the importing market?
- Does the state or designated providers hold exclusive rights in particular market segments?
- Are there geographical limitations to serving the market?
- Are there limitations on the number of branches financial institutions can open?

In some cases, prudential and nonprudential regulations may overlap. There is overlap of regulations that determine market access conditions such as licensing criteria, transfer of significant ownership authorization, and terms and conditions imposed on major acquisition by financial institutions, as well as regulations regarding the scope and definitions of activities that can be performed by banking institutions (permissible activities). A regulatory assessment must examine regulations that affect market access and operations to determine whether they go beyond prudential considerations. In these cases, the assessor should consider the opinions and advice of relevant international organizations in order to provide an adequate assessment of the trade-related impact.

Key questions that have to be addressed in the regulatory assessment related to licensing that are of particular importance in trade negotiations include the following:

- If the number of providers is not restricted by policy, what are the main types of licenses that providers must obtain to operate in the market?
- What regulatory agencies are responsible for issuing licenses? What are the conditions governing the granting of licenses?
- Are licenses required for domestic companies, foreign companies, or both?
- Are foreign suppliers subject to different licensing conditions from domestic suppliers? Are additional requirements imposed on them?
- Is the validity of a license and the right to supply the market restricted temporally or geographically? Do licenses grant exclusivity periods or market segments?
- Where markets are regulated at both the national and subnational levels, are separate licenses required to supply services in each jurisdiction? Is a local presence required in each jurisdiction for licensing purposes?
- In sectors where policy limits the number of providers, through what mechanisms and according to what criteria are licenses allocated?
- Once licenses have been allocated, are there restrictions on the ability of foreign suppliers to sell or dispose of their licenses?

What is the impact of nonprudential regulations on financial markets? When assessing the trade-related regulatory environment in the financial sector, analysts can use indicators to compare a country's performance with the results of the assessment. Recently, the World Bank made publicly available the Global Financial Development Database, an extensive dataset of financial system characteristics for 203 economies. It includes the following measures:

- The size of financial institutions and markets (financial depth)
- The degree to which individuals can and do use financial services (access)
- The efficiency of financial intermediaries and markets in intermediating resources and facilitating financial transactions (efficiency)
- The stability of financial institutions and markets (stability) (Čihák and others 2012)

How restrictive are nonprudential regulations? Figure C.2 depicts the regulatory landscape in different regions. The World Bank Services Trade Restrictions Database collects information on regulatory measures affecting banking and insurance providers and services. This database allows users to compare regulations affecting services sectors across countries. When a country maintains a monopoly in a market, for example, the restrictiveness index is 100, meaning that the market is closed. The index covers a wide range of policies, including licensing criteria, foreign ownership restrictions, and other restrictions that apply to foreigners, for both the insurance and banking sectors. It also distinguishes among modes of supply, in particular Modes 1 (cross-border trade) and 3 (commercial presence) for financial services.

Developing regions regulate financial services more heavily than do countries in the Organisation for Economic Co-operation and Development (OECD) (figure C.2). The relatively high level of regulation provides scope for adopting more cost-effective regulations while preserving the stability of the financial market.

Preconditions for effective banking supervision include the following:

- Sound and sustainable macroeconomic policies
- A well-established framework for the formulation of financial stability policy
- Good public infrastructure
- A clear framework for crisis management, recovery, and resolution
- An appropriate level of systemic protection (or public safety net)
- Effective market discipline

Although these preconditions do not fall within their sphere of competency, policy makers should be aware of their effects on the efficiency or effectiveness of regulation and supervision.

Regarding public infrastructure, various services are needed to maintain a strong financial services sector. Regulators have identified the following as critical (BIS 2012; IAIS 2011):

- A system of business laws (including corporate, bankruptcy, contract, consumer protection, and private property laws) that is consistently enforced and provides a mechanism for the fair resolution of disputes
- An efficient and independent judiciary
- Comprehensive and well-defined accounting principles and rules that are widely accepted internationally

Figure C.2 World Bank Services Trade Restrictiveness Index, by Region, 2008

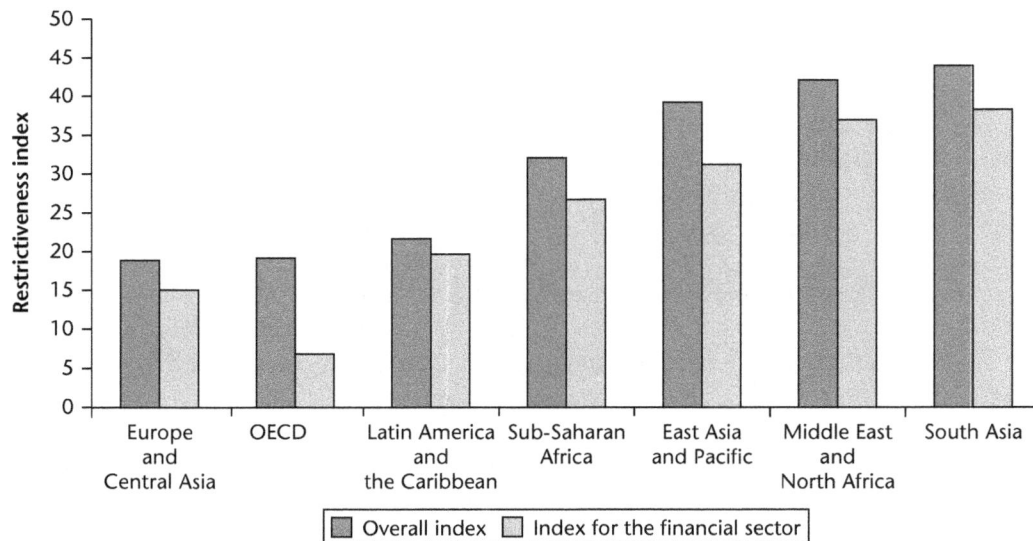

Source: Services Trade Restrictions database.
Note: OECD = Organisation for Economic Co-operation and Development.

- A system of independent external audits to ensure that users of financial statements, including banks, have independent assurance that the accounts provide a true and fair view of the financial position of the company and are prepared according to established accounting principles, with auditors held accountable for their work
- The availability of competent, independent, and experienced professionals (such as accountants, auditors, actuaries, and lawyers) whose work complies with transparent technical and ethical standards and is enforced by official or professional bodies consistent with international standards and who are subject to appropriate oversight
- Well-defined rules governing, and adequate supervision of, other financial markets and, where appropriate, their participants
- Secure, efficient, and well-regulated payment and clearing systems (including central counterparties) for the settlement of financial transactions where counterparty risks are effectively controlled and managed
- Efficient and effective credit bureaus that make available credit information on borrowers or databases that assist in the assessment of risks
- Public availability of basic economic, financial, and social statistics.

A RASTI will not address these infrastructure issues. In conducting one, however, it is necessary to fully understand the context in which financial services are operating.

Any reforms, in particular, liberalization reforms, should consider the state of the supporting public infrastructure.

Conclusion

Mapping of the financial services sector should include an analysis of the main laws and regulations that affect the market access, commercial presence, and operation of financial institutions (Sauvé 2010). The assessor should also consult additional sources, such as reports, studies, and the relevant academic literature. International organizations, such as the World Bank, International Monetary Fund, the Bank for international Settlements, the International Organization of Securities Commissions, and the International Association of Insurance Supervisors, provide a wealth of resources. Within the World Bank, the Bank Regulation and Supervision Survey (World Bank 2013) provides information on a wide range of issues related to banking regulation and supervision, including market entry and ownership conditions, ownership, capital, activities, external auditing requirements, banking sector characteristics, and governance settings.

References

Barth, James R., Gerard Caprio, Jr., and Ross Levine. 2006. *Rethinking Bank Regulations: Till Angels Govern.* Cambridge: Cambridge University Press.
BIS (Bank for International Settlements). 2012. *Core Principles for Effective Banking Supervision.* Basel: BIS.

Čihák, Martin, Asli Demirgüç-Kunt, Erik Feyen, and Ross Levine. 2012. "Benchmarking Financial Systems around the World." Policy Research Working Paper 6175, World Bank, Washington, DC.

Dewatripont, Mathias, and Jean Tirole. 1994. *The Prudential Regulation of Banks*. Cambridge, MA: MIT Press.

Global Financial Development (database). World Bank, Washington, DC. http://data.worldbank.org/data-catalog/global-financial-development.

IAIS (International Association of Insurance Supervisors). 2011. *Insurance Core Principles, Standards, Guidance and Assessment Methodology*. Basel: IAIS. http://www.iaisweb.org/ICP-on-line-tool-689.

IMF (International Monetary Fund). 2013. "Factsheet: The Financial Sector Assessment Program (FSAP)." http://www.imf.org/external /np/exr/facts/fsap.htm.

IOSCO (International Organization of Securities Commissions). 2011. *Methodology for Assessing Implementation of the IOSCO Objectives and Principles of Securities Regulation*. Madrid: IOSCO. https://www.iosco .org/library/pubdocs/pdf/IOSCOPD359.pdf.

Sauvé, Pierre. 2010. "Conducting a Trade-Related Regulatory Audit in Financial Services." In *Financial Services and Preferential Trade Agreements: Lessons from Latin America*, ed. Mona Haddad and Constantinos Stephanou, 101–20. Washington, DC: World Bank.

Services Trade Restrictions (database). World Bank, Washington, DC. http://iresearch.worldbank.org/servicetrade/home.htm.

van Empel, Martin, and Anna Morner. 2000. "Financial Services and Regional Integration." In *The Internationalization of Financial Services: Issues and Lessons for Developing Countries*, ed. Stijn Claessens and Marion Jansen-Jacobs, 37–61. London: Kluwer Law International.

World Bank. 2013. *Global Financial Services Report: Rethinking the Role of the State in Finance*. Washington, DC: World Bank. http:// go.worldbank.org/WFIEF81AP0.

World Development Indicators (database). World Bank, Washington, DC. http://data.worldbank.org/data-catalog/world-development-indicators.

WTO (World Trade Organization). 1997. *Opening Markets in Financial Services and the Role of the GATS*. WTO Special Studies, Geneva.

GLOSSARY

Ad valorem equivalent. See *tariff equivalent*.

Adverse selection. Phenomenon in which agents select an action based on private (asymmetric) information about themselves or the good or service being transacted, with undesirable consequences for the other party to the transaction. In insurance, for example, individuals who know that they represent higher risks tend to purchase more comprehensive coverage, thereby reducing the profitability of the insurance company.

Asymmetric information. Situation in which one party to a transaction has better information than another, allowing it to exploit the other party's incomplete knowledge.

Behind-the-border measures. Internal laws and regulations not necessarily related to foreign trade.

Business processing outsourcing (bpo). Subset of outsourcing that involves the contracting of the operations and responsibilities of specific business functions (or processes) to a third-party provider.

Capture. See *regulatory capture*.

Collusion. Agreement between rival companies or individuals to cooperate for their mutual benefit in a way that limits competition. Firms or individuals collude when they divide a market, set prices, limit production, or limit opportunities.

Competition law. Competition law (often used in the telecommunications, energy, and water sectors) ensures that incumbent network operators, who enjoy monopolies, allow access to their networks on reasonable terms.

Concession. The granting of rights, land, or property by a government, local authority, corporation, individual, or other legal entity.

Contagion. Scenario in which small shocks, which initially affect only a few financial institutions or a particular region of an economy, spread to other financial institutions and countries whose economies were previously healthy, in a manner similar to the transmission of a medical disease.

Credence good. Good whose value is difficult or impossible for a consumer to ascertain. Examples include car repairs and vitamins.

Cross-subsidization. Practice of charging higher prices to one group of consumers in order to subsidize prices for another.

Disclosure regulation. The requirement that firms make public any information regarding The quantity, quality, and price of their outputs and, in some cases, the processes followed during production.

Distributional justice. Redistributing wealth and income usually through fiscal policies, direct payments Or social benefits, compulsory social security systems, or national health and pension schemes. In services regulation, governments strive toward distributional justice by ensuring consumer rights and setting minimum conditions for services that, left unregulated, would not be accessible to consumers with little bargaining power.

Dual residual. The increase in marginal cost unexplained by increases in factor prices (wages, the cost of capital, or the cost of intermediate products).

Economic needs tests. A way for an institution to ascertain whether one qualifies for support services.

Externality. Consequence of an activity that affects other parties but is not reflected in the cost of the good or service produced. An externality is negative when the effect is harmful. Examples of negative externalities include pollution and traffic congestion. An externality is positive when the effect is beneficial. Examples of positive externalities include the effect of one person's education on others.

Factor analysis. A statistical technique to derive weights based on data characteristics.

Factor. See *latent variable*.

Franchising. Replacing competition within the market with competition for the market. Under a franchising scheme, firms bid for a license to be the exclusive service provider for a particular activity within a geographical region, usually for a limited time.

Free-rider problem. Situation in which some individuals or firms either consume more than their fair share or pay less than their fair share of the cost of a common resource. Free riding can lead to the underproduction of a public good or excessive use of a common property resource.

Gravity equation. The gravity equation is a log-linear specification, in which trade between an exporting country and an importing country is positively influenced by the size of each country and negatively affected by the distance between them.

Gravity model. This model allows analysts to estimate trade barriers for a large number of countries and to avoid the demanding task of collecting information on services regulations. However, estimating a gravity model requires data that are broken down by trading partners, which are scarce.

Horizontal measure. These measures affect a wide range of sectors—not just the laws and regulations governing a particular sector; for example, regulations on tourism affect services providers in the tourism sector, but also affect regulations on buying and selling foreign currency, laws on entry and stay of foreigners, etc.

Information technology–enabled service (ITES). Industry that provides services through the use of information technology. Examples include claims processing; medical transcription; and back-office operations such as accounting, data processing, and data mining.

IT park. Area of land in which office buildings that house information technology companies are grouped together.

Joint venture requirement. Requirement that a foreign firm form a joint venture with a domestic firm before it can operate in a country.

Juridical person. A legal entity that is not a natural person (such as a corporation created under state statutes) but having a distinct identity and legal rights and obligations under the law.

Latent variable. A statistical term, **latent variables** are inferred (through a mathematical model) from a much larger set of variables.

Lerner index. Index named after economist abba lerner that describes a firm's market power. It is defined by

$$L = \frac{P - MC}{P},$$

Where p is the market price set by the firm and mc is the firm's marginal cost.

Licensing. Certification which may include holding a degree from certain Schools or institutions, demonstrating certain technical skills, having experience, or passing an examination.

Market failure. Situation in which the allocation of goods and services by a free market is not economically efficient, as the result of information asymmetries, uncompetitive markets, externalities, public goods, or other problems.

Minimum capital requirement. The amount of capital a bank has to hold as required by its financial regulator; these requirements are put in place to ensure that institutions do not become insolvent.

Monopoly. Situation in which a single person or enterprise is the only supplier of a good or service.

Monopsony. Market in which a single buyer faces many sellers.

Multicollinearity. Statistical phenomenon in which two or more predictor variables in a multiple regression model are highly correlated, meaning that one can be linearly predicted from the others with a nontrivial degree of accuracy. In the presence of multicollinearity, the coefficient estimates of the multiple regression may change erratically in response to small changes in the model or the data.

Nationality requirement. Requirement that a provider of a good or service be a citizen of the country in which it is sold.

Natural monopoly. Situation in which the long-run average cost for production is lowest when a single firm produces a good or service, making participation by more than one firm unviable. Natural monopolies exist where capital costs are very high, creating huge economies of scale and high barriers to entry. Examples include public utilities.

Nonprudential regulations. Regulations governing the ways in which financial institutions conduct of business that do not address the financial soundness of individual financial institutions. Examples include reporting and disclosure requirements and restrictions on interest or deposit rates.

Nudging. Use of positive reinforcement and indirect suggestions to try to influence the motives, incentives, and decision making of groups or individuals.

Oligopoly. Market controlled by a small number of sellers.

Pareto efficiency. Allocation of resources in which it is impossible to make any one individual better off without making at least one individual worse off.

Performance requirements. Category of host country operational measures imposed on foreign affiliates to induce them to act in ways considered beneficial for the

host economy. Most common requirements relate to local content, export performance, domestic equity, joint ventures, technology transfer, and employment of nationals. Requirements can be mandatory (a precondition for entry or access) or voluntary (a condition for obtaining an incentive).

Pigovian tax. Tax applied to a market activity that generates negative externalities in order to improve an inefficient market outcome.

Predatory pricing. Practice of selling a good or service at a very low price in an attempt to drive competitors out of the market or create barriers to entry for potential new competitors.

Price fixing. Agreement among firms or individuals to buy or sell a good or service at an agreed upon price.

Primal residual. An increase in a firm's production volume that cannot be explained by increases in the factors of production such as capital, intermediate products, and labor.

Principal component analysis. A mathematical procedure that uses orthogonal transformation to convert a set of observations of possibly correlated variables into a set of values of linearly uncorrelated variables.

Private interest theory. A theory that regulators are motivated by a narrow concept of self-interest and that given a conflict between the public's interest and their own private interests, the public's interest will lose.

Proportionality. Principle that the means used to achieve an end must be as limited as possible.

Prudential regulations. Regulations governing the financial soundness of licensed financial institutions imposed in order to prevent financial system instability and avoid losses of deposits held by unsophisticated investors. Examples include capital adequacy requirements, liquidity requirements, and loan loss provisioning mandates.

Public good. Good that is both nonexcludable and nonrivalrous, in that individuals cannot be effectively excluded from use and use by one individual does not reduce the availability of the good to others. Examples include national defense and lighthouses.

Public interest theory. Theory first developed by arthur pigou that holds that regulation is supplied in response to the public's demand for the correction of inefficient or inequitable market practices.

Regulatory capture. Situation in which a regulatory agency, created to act in the public interest, instead advances the concerns of interest groups that dominate the industry it is charged with regulating.

Regulatory competition. Practice in which law makers use regulation to compete to attract businesses or other actors to operate in their jurisdiction.

Regulatory failure. Situation in which intervention by a regulatory agency fails to improve the allocation of goods and resources. One cause of regulatory failure is regulatory capture.

Rent. Any payment in excess of the normal level that takes place in a competitive market.

Reputation premium. A professional can charge a higher rate if he/she has established a good reputation in the field.

Residency requirement. Requirement that a provider of a good or service live in the country in which it is sold.

Systemic risk. Risk of collapse of an entire financial system or market.

Tariff equivalent. Nontariff barrier that has the same effect as a tariff. Examples include import quotas and licensing restrictions.

Tradable permit. Part of a market-driven approach to reducing greenhouse gas emissions in which a government first sets a total quantity of emissions and then divides it among firms, giving each a tradable emissions entitlement. Polluters that can reduce their emissions relatively cheaply may find it profitable to do so and to sell their emissions permits to other firms. Firms that find it expensive to cut emissions may purchase extra permits, which allow them to pollute more.

Universal access. The push for "universal access" is a movement to ensure that services are offered in all levels of society, not just in profitable areas.

Universal service. Practice of providing a baseline level of services to every resident of a country.

Yardstick competiton. Under this approach, regulators assess the performance of an infrastructure service provider by comparing it with a provider in another location (such as in a neighboring country), and they adjust the regulations accordingly.